Also available at all good book stores

9781801500081

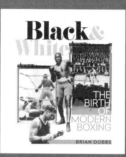

9781785318900

9781785316425

9781785316272

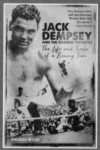

9781785316371

9781785315374

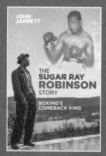

9781785315350

9781785314551

MUHAMMAD ALI

Fifteen
Rounds
in the
Wilderness

MUHAMMAD ALI

Dave Hannigan

First published by Pitch Publishing, 2022

Pitch Publishing
9 Donnington Park,
85 Birdham Road,
Chichester,
West Sussex,
PO20 7AJ
www.pitchpublishing.co.uk
info@pitchpublishing.co.uk

A CIP catalogue record is available for this book
from the British Library.

ISBN 978 1 80150 122 4

Typesetting and origination by Pitch Publishing
Printed and bound in India by Replika Press Pvt. Ltd.

CONTENTS

This book is dedicated to

George and Clare Frost

PROLOGUE

IN A makeshift ring erected on the baseball diamond of a community sports field in Nassau on 11 December 1981, after a contest in which the rounds were marked by the tolling of a cowbell borrowed from a nearby farm, Matt Helreich took centre stage. 'Ladies and gentlemen, we have a unanimous decision,' he announced. 'Judge Alonzo Butler votes it 97-94, judge Clyde Gray votes 99-94, judge Jay Edson, 99-94, a unanimous decision for Trevor Berbick.'

As Berbick celebrated, Muhammad Ali looked sombre and confused when a microphone was thrust under his chin and a question asked about whether he should retire now. 'I'm sure that this is enough to convince me,' said the 39-year-old. 'I didn't get hurt. I saw the shots but couldn't take them. Father Time just caught me. In my young days, I wouldn't have had much trouble, but I think time caught me. This is it. I'm sure I'll wake up next week saying I'm coming back but as of now I'm retiring. I don't think I'll change my mind.'

And he didn't. This time, finally, belatedly, he retired. For good. What followed was 15 of the strangest years in his life, an interlude where Ali embarked on something of an odyssey, one minute brilliant, the next bizarre, often appearing to be a man traversing the globe in search of a higher purpose.

Sometimes, he found one. Other times, he didn't. No matter. With Ali, always, the journey was as important as the destination.

ROUND ONE

1982

Take it slow, Muhammad Ali. Read a book now and then. Go to the supermarket once in a while. That's right, you just put the food in the basket as you wheel the thing around the aisles. Cut the lawn. Take out the trash. Ride a bus. There isn't a lot of stuff out here that you've been doing in the last 20 years but that's all right. You'll survive. We all do. Just don't watch a lot of television. That'll rot your mind faster than any combination Trevor Berbick ever imagined

Leigh Montville, The *Boston Globe*, 1 January 1982

ON NEW Year's Day, *Body and Soul* opened in select movie theatres across America. A blaxploitation flick crossed with a Rocky film, it starred Leon Isaac Kennedy as Leon Johnson, a wannabe doctor forced into the boxing ring to pay the medical bills of his ailing sister. Playing himself, Muhammad Ali is on screen for less than five minutes and one snarky review said of his performance, 'Laurence Olivier need not worry.'

Still, Ali's presence in the cast was enough to warrant a 'With Muhammad Ali' sticker on the posters advertising *Body and Soul*.

His most notable scene is in a gym where he briefly pummels the speed bag before Johnson begs him to become his trainer.

'Look, my friend, people come to me all the time for help, business deals,' says Ali. 'Buy this, invest in this, invest in that, train this man, train that man. Everybody knows I'm the greatest, right? But I'm not obligated and I don't have time to make you the greatest.'

* * *

An invited guest at the inauguration of Harvey Sloane for his second term as Mayor of Louisville on 4 January, Muhammad Ali wrote a poem for the occasion, poking fun at his long-time friend, a politician he affectionately used to call 'a hippie'.

> *'You're the finest of men, we all agree*
> *But why don't you ever call Muhammad Ali?*
> *Two times mayor makes you rate*
> *Three times champion make me great!'*

During the official ceremony at the Macauley Theatre, Ali sat just behind the city's first family on stage, causing a bit of a stir when he got up in the middle of proceedings and walked out. Later, he explained he had left to go perform Salat, one of the five times per day when every Muslim must kneel and pray towards Mecca.

* * *

On 13 January, a federal grand jury found Harold Smith, founder and CEO of Muhammad Ali Sports Promotions, guilty on 29 out of 31 charges related to embezzling more than $21m from the Beverley Hills branch of the Wells Fargo Bank. In 1977, Ali had granted Smith permission to use his name in return for a fee, but was not involved in the day-to-day operations of the company. 'I'm shocked,' said Ali. 'I'm just now hearing it. I'm surprised he was found guilty. I still don't believe it. I just don't think one man can embezzle a bank [out] of so much money and not be caught while committing the crime.'

* * *

A former Hudson County investigator and Verona police offer named Ron Lipton was on trial in the Superior Court of Newton, New Jersey. Following an incident in which he hit Alex Klein, 20, with a baseball bat, he faced a litany of charges. His defence was that he used the bat to disarm Klein, who was wielding a knife in a dispute outside Lipton's home. The victim had been one of several men who had, for some time, been terrorising the family and menacing the neighbourhood.

A one-time amateur middleweight prospect in the 1960s, Lipton spent more than a decade as a sparring partner of Muhammad Ali's. It was Lipton who first told Ali the story of the injustice done to the incarcerated boxer Rubin 'Hurricane' Carter and the pair travelled to Rahway State Prison together to visit him. Their relationship remained so strong that Ali flew 3,000 miles to testify to Lipton's good character in his hour of need. That he would do so seemed such a long shot when first mooted that one prosecutor had a bet with a journalist covering the trial that the celebrity witness would surely never show up.

Arriving at the Sussex County Courthouse in a chauffeur-driven yellow Cadillac on 21 January, Ali wore a brown pin-striped suit and caused an inevitable stir in the building even before he was brought to testify in front of Judge Frederic G. Weber. Asked by first assistant-prosecutor Vincent J. Connor Jr if he knew what Lipton was charged with, Ali said 'not exactly', then offered a resounding character reference. 'I love Ron and we have been through everything together,' said Ali. 'I am here today because there is no one I would do this for, not for $100,000, except for Ron. I will always be there for him. I wouldn't be here all the way from California for nobody if I didn't believe he was honest. I'm here because he's a good man and I wouldn't come up here and risk my reputation for somebody that I didn't know that well. He's a good man, a God-fearing man. He did all he could for Rubin even though he was white and Rubin was black. He put himself on the line, his family, his job. It's people like this man that's going to change the world and make it better for all races.'

When Connor questioned him about dates and times of events involving Lipton, Ali responded, 'If I knew I were going to be in court, I would have kept a diary.'

Not the last laugh he got from the gallery. 'People said I was hit on the head too many times,' said Ali. 'Who had the nerve to tell you that?' asked Connor.

After pausing a moment, Ali answered, 'My mother.'

And the whole court guffawed.

At the conclusion of his evidence, Ali left the witness box and shook hands with every member of the jury. An unorthodox move, the prosecutor told reporters afterwards he didn't think Ali's magnanimous gesture/breach of legal etiquette would affect the outcome of the case. If anything, he said, it was proof the defence had very little else to offer.

The jury acquitted Lipton of all charges except possession of a weapon. At a second trial, he was acquitted of that too.

* * *

Two weeks later, Muhammad Ali was at the New Frontier Hotel in Las Vegas, Nevada for a magic convention and an audience with the celebrated Siegfried and Roy duo. While a photograph of the double act with Ali and a plethora of white rabbits made newspapers all over the country, he immersed himself in the event.

At one point, he came across a blind man wearing a fedora and sunglasses, tapping his way down the corridor with a white cane. 'Are you a magician?' asked Ali. 'I am the amazing Haundini!' replied Gary Haun. He improvised the name on the spot but, after being rendered blind by an accident while serving in the US Marines, he had taught himself to do magic. With Ali rapt, he did a card trick and followed that up by making a coin disappear. 'Wow!' said Ali, 'You really are amazing!'

Everybody at the convention knew Ali had a voracious appetite for seeing magic up close. Bill Gardner, a young up-and-comer from Wichita, Kansas, was one of many invited to visit the only hotel room with a security guard standing sentry outside. For half an hour, even as Ali wolfed down some matzo ball soup, Gardner ran through a panoply of his go-to tricks, including the classic multiplying rabbits routine. When he pressed one of the yellow foam rabbits into Ali's hand as part of the act, he couldn't get over the size of the palm and the position in which he found himself. 'OK, I'm actually handling the hand that's just pummeled the crap out of a lot of people,' said Gardner. 'But he was incredibly gentle.'

* * *

In the first week of April, Muhammad Ali walked into a television studio in New York City wearing a business suit and carrying a briefcase, like a man getting ready to negotiate a deal. He had come to tape an episode of HBO's *Grudge Match* alongside Joe Frazier, their legends forever intertwined because of their three epic encounters in the ring.

'I'm going to introduce Joe and Muhammad,' said the host Barry Tompkins as the cameras prepared to roll.

'Two retired, washed-up bums,' muttered Ali.

Eight days before Ali lost to Berbick the previous December, Frazier, a tell-tale paunch where his washboard stomach used to be, fought a journeyman named Floyd 'Jumbo' Cummings to a mediocre draw in a half-empty amphitheatre hard by the stockyards on the southside of Chicago. At HBO, the icons had come not to discuss the ignominious way their careers had ended – Frazier actually insisted he might still fight again – but to revisit the glory days. Contests that defined an era in the sport. Bouts no fan would ever tire of talking about.

'I always respected him as a champion and a man,' said Frazier. 'His way of living is his way and my way of living is mine. But you always have to watch him. When you walk away from him, walk backwards!'

After the interview ended, Tompkins asked Ali where he was headed next. At that point, he produced a notepad on which were written an alphabetic list of countries he wanted to visit to promote a worldwide organisation he intended to start to protect the human rights of children. As he scrolled through the nations, he stopped and asked, 'How do you pronounce that?'

Unsure whether Ali was mocking or serious, Tompkins read out, 'Vietnam.'

* * *

Ahead of his attempt to wrest the heavyweight title from Larry Holmes in Las Vegas, Gerry Cooney set up training camp at the Canyon Hotel in Palm Springs. Muhammad Ali paid a visit to the challenger on 10 May, accompanied by his fabled cornerman Bundini Brown and Harold Smith, still awaiting sentencing for ripping off Wells Fargo.

'Gerry Cooney is not the white boy,' said Ali. 'He's the right boy.'

Many who had come to camp to watch the Long Islander work out quickly turned their back on the elevated ring to line up for an autograph from the esteemed visitor. One man nearly fainted when offered the chance to shake Ali's hand. When Richard Hoffer, a reporter from the *Los Angeles Times*, mentioned his enduring popularity, Ali quipped, 'It's bad now, think if I'd have beaten Holmes!'

Then he launched into a recitation of his plans for the future.

'Spiritual life is the thing,' he said. 'King of Arabia called me. President of Bangladesh. Starting a big evangelism programme, explaining Islamic faith. One billion Muslims in the world. Four billion people. One billion Muslims. Boxing made me popular, but this is my real job, working for God.'

If that sounded like a man set to live the rest of his life as a missionary, Ali quickly contradicted himself.

'I got to stop travelling actually,' said Ali. 'Been home 30 days, most I've ever been home. Too much travelling. I like to cut my own grass, do the dishes, go shopping, simple stuff. Take my children to school, talk to my mother on the telephone. Simple things.'

Hoffer asked if he cut his own grass.

'Sometimes I want to,' said Ali.

* * *

On 4 June, a photograph of two of the most famous people on the planet flashed up the wire services in newspaper offices across the world. It showed Pope John Paul II and Muhammad Ali, each with pen in hand, signing autographs at a table. Both men looked serious and focused as they exchanged copies of each other's signatures. It was quite a shot. The pontiff, a promising soccer goalkeeper in his youth, alongside the retired boxer visiting Rome, the city where he had won Olympic gold in 1960 and launched himself upon the world all those years earlier.

Here was a picture that appeared to symbolise the next step in Ali's career. The best-known Muslim on earth visiting the leader of the Catholic Church in the Vatican, his new status as some sort of unofficial roving global ambassador of peace obvious from the fact he'd been granted a private audience in the pope's personal quarters.

Although the Louisville home of his childhood was Baptist, Ali knew well the significance of that papal honour. When a student at Central High School, the then Cassius Clay worked part-time for the Catholic Sisters of Charity at the Nazareth College library. His host knew the merits of having this high-profile visitor too. A year earlier, the pope had been the victim of an assassination attempt by the Turkish terrorist Mehmet Ali Agca. For him, a photo opportunity with Ali represented an ecumenical message to Islamic countries.

Not that Ali quite got that memo.

'I told the pope that he ought to take all the white statues out of the churches,' he said. 'All this is heavy. I hope the pope will come out and do this. You know how it says in the Bible, in Exodus 20, chapter 4, they shall not make any graven images. All the white statues are wrong, they're graven images. The pope wants me to come back to discuss that.'

* * *

Forty-eight hours later, Ali stepped off a plane in Cedar Rapids, Iowa. The Advisory Committee for Economic Growth, a local non-profit, had invited him to the midwestern city to assist their efforts to raise money for a cultural achievement centre for disadvantaged youth. At the Five Seasons Centre, a crowd of just over 500 turned up to see him – smaller than organisers had hoped for but still a decent turnout given how hastily arranged and poorly promoted the so-called 'Ali Extravaganza!' had been.

For instance, when 27-year-old Steve Eden, the national Golden Gloves champion at 178 pounds just two years earlier, climbed through the ropes for a proposed two-round exhibition, Ali was still wearing the trousers of a suit and a dress shirt with the tie recently removed. Hardly ideal, but they worked with what they had.

As he readied himself in his corner, Ali put on his game face, yelling 'I want Steve!' and gesticulating with his fists. These were the tone and actions of a man trying to convince a small but delighted audience he was taking this as seriously as a championship bout. Eden, in proper boxing attire, made the early running, taking the fight to his opponent in business casual and Ali shipped a couple of blows before returning fire.

'Ali's boxing skills were still intact,' said Eden. 'He picked me in the second round with a three or four-punch combination.'

Eden and Ali talked boxing afterwards and the recently retired amateur went home with an autographed photograph inscribed with the words, 'I'll get you next time, Steve!'

From there Ali went to his hotel, where he was scheduled to perform a 60-minute magic show for an audience of children. Ali sat cross-legged on the carpet, surrounded by boys and girls relishing his every move, for two and a half hours.

'As he was getting ready to go up to his room for a well-deserved rest, one little girl gripped his hand,' wrote Mike Chapman in the *Cedar Rapids Gazette*. 'He looked down at her, a white child perhaps three or four, and she said, "Hi Muhammad," in a very sweet voice. He gaped at her, smiled widely, then bent over and picked her up. She hugged him and he giggled, looking at me. "Hey, Mr Newspaperman," he said, "Where is your photographer now? You need to get a picture of this." He held her cheek to cheek.'

En route to the airport at the end of his visit, Ali asked how much money his trip had raised. One host confessed to having just about broke even on the whole thing. At that point, Ali promptly tore in half the expenses cheque they had just given him to cover the cost of his travel.

'Muhammad,' said one of the organisers, 'you can't do that!'

'Yes, I can,' he said. 'It's my way of giving back.'

* * *

On 8 June, Ali filed a suit against his former promoter Don King in the Northern District Court of Illinois, seeking $1,170,000 he was owed from the Larry Holmes fight in October 1980. The litigation also requested statutory interest on the money and payment of reasonable attorney's fees.

'I think Muhammad Ali is one of the greatest fighters of all time,' said King. 'Far be it from me to say anything derogatory about him. But you must understand, he had to get a headline.'

* * *

Tickets for the first-ever Monday Night at the Fights at Duke's Country in Tulsa, Oklahoma on 19 July retailed for $15 each, didn't list any of the boxers due to get in the ring but did advertise a guest appearance by Muhammad Ali. When the box office wasn't ticking over as briskly as initially hoped, somebody involved decided to bend the truth and garner some free publicity. 'I just know he'll be doing an exhibition,' said Ken Murray about the prospect of Ali putting on gloves. 'It's to kick off the first of a series of Monday night fight cards.'

Ali touched down at Tulsa International Airport 24 hours before the show and appeared bemused by the prospect of donning gloves. 'This may come as a shock or a surprise, but there is no way I've come here to box,' said Ali. 'I was told I was coming here to help as a promotion. No one told me I was expected to get inside a boxing ring. I'm a world-class fighter and three-time heavyweight champion, I just don't jump into a ring with anybody. I'm 40. I know I look young and pretty – you heard about me being pretty. Now, you see it is true.'

When Ali turned up at the nightclub on Monday evening, J.V. Haney, director of athletics at Webster High School, and Bill Roller, a basketball coach, were waiting. Haney moonlighted for a local radio station and had been sent to get an interview. While he set up his equipment, Ali flopped down on a couch next to Roller and fell asleep. His travelling companions eventually roused him to do a five-minute on-air chat, and afterwards he sat back down and dozed off again.

Later in the evening, he apologised to Haney for giving such a brief interview, then invited him and Roller to the penthouse suite at the Excelsior Hotel once the fights had ended. When they reached Ali's room that night, they found a man in his element. 'There was a large circle of people, probably around 20,' said Haney. 'I pushed my way up to where I could see, and there was Muhammad Ali sitting cross-legged, barefoot in the middle of the room, and he had about 30 to 40 magic tricks spread out on the floor all around him. He was really good at it. I remember his hands being so fast. They were pretty good magic tricks. And he was having a good time doing it. He really was enjoying himself.'

Many guests were still there as dawn broke. However, aspects of the event at Duke's Country left a sour taste. 'This is the last time I'll be involved with boxing or promotion,' said Ali, before leaving Tulsa. 'I've had 28 years in boxing. Most boxers, after they retire, they hang around boxing rings and gymnasiums. There's nothing else they can do. I don't want that image.'

* * *

On a whistle-stop tour of Vancouver on 4 August, Muhammad Ali appeared on Gary Bannerman's radio programme, taped a segment for *The Alan Thicke Show* and sat for an interview with local columnist Archie McDonald. He was accompanied by Richard Hirschfeld, a lawyer from Virginia with a colourful past that included falling foul of the Securities and Exchange Commission for banking irregularities. It was whispered that Hirschfeld inveigled his way into Ali's entourage by falsely claiming to have once been John Wayne's personal lawyer.

Ali spent the visit to Canada talking up his burgeoning business portfolio, performing his default magic trick of making a handkerchief disappear, and preaching an old tune about religious imagery. 'People see that God is white, the last supper is all white, angels all white,' he said. 'It's wrong but nobody has yet brought this up.'

* * *

On Friday, 20 August, Mal Vincent, a journalist with the *Virginian-Pilot*, found himself driving through the backwoods of Virginia Beach in a convoy containing Richard Hirschfeld, Sheikh Mohammed Al-Fassi, some local grandee politicians and Muhammad Ali. This curious ensemble headed to the summer home of local developer Eddie Garcia to discuss plans for a proposed $44m 600-room hotel.

As the mayor, the politicos and the businessmen talked telephone numbers and toured Garcia's mansion, Vincent noticed that Ali was on the fringe of the conversations. Present but not central to proceedings and much, much quieter than the public persona Vincent knew from television over the previous decades.

'Would you like an autograph?' asked Ali, before handing Vincent a pre-written piece of paper with his John Hancock [signature] on it.

Several more times that afternoon, they went through the same routine and the journalist went home with four identical pieces of signed memorabilia. If a potentially enormous hotel development was massive news for Virginia Beach and should have been Vincent's main concern as a newspaper reporter, he was too taken with Ali to get caught up in the story.

'The Muhammad I met that day was shy, reserved and, to tell the truth, a little overlooked in the business atmosphere of that day,' wrote Vincent. 'He carried a small attaché case under his arm, which he seemed to value. When I asked him what was in it, he was eager to show me. He opened it and pulled out a coloured scarf. He looked at me as if he wondered why I didn't react. Pretty quickly, I picked up on the routine. He was doing a magic trick.'

Then he did more magic tricks. And more. And each time, Vincent feigned amazement while wondering what Ali was doing with these characters. Garcia had recently denied mob ties, Hirschfeld had cost a few wealthy Virginians a lot of money with his dodgy bank. And, even as America's newspapers salivated over the extravagance of the mysterious Sheik Al-Fassi's decadent lifestyle – the Boeing 707 he chartered supposedly cost $8,500 per hour to run – they had lately been reporting him also leaving a trail of unpaid bills in his wake.

According to Hirschfeld, the hotel would bring jobs and revenue to the city, and massive profits to the principal investors, including Ali. As a goodwill gesture, the sheikh donated $30,000 to various Virginia Beach youth groups.

'Sadly,' concluded Vincent, 'you got the idea that the Arabian group and the other "suits" trotted Ali around for his celebrity rather than his investments. And it was sad that, somehow, I got the idea he realised it. He was very sad at that time but he was not "out of it". You get the idea that he knew fully what was happening but couldn't always control or handle it.'

* * *

Twenty-four hours later, James C. Lytle, Mayor of Evanston, Illinois, welcomed Muhammad Ali, Sheikh Mohammed Al-Fassi and an entourage of five limousines to a luncheon in the back of his home on sleepy Central Park Avenue. Just over a week before, he'd received word that the Middle Eastern billionaire wanted to make Lytle's municipality, 12 miles from downtown Chicago, the latest recipient of his philanthropic largesse. For everybody else present, the money mattered much less than the presence of Ali.

'Ali could not have been nicer to everybody,' said Lytle. 'He spent most of the luncheon with the kids from the neighbourhood who came quickly to see what was going on. He took pictures with them. Played with them. At one point, he saw my mom, who was 82 years old at the time and about 5ft 2in. He just walked right over to her, picked her up off the ground and said, "Hello, little momma!"'

If elderly Althea Lytle was, like everybody else, immediately smitten with Ali, Al-Fassi was not making quite the same impression. He brought a retinue of 40, his wife was made to walk four steps behind him, and at one point he lay in a hammock between two trees as his bodyguards gently pushed it back and forth. He did hand over a cheque for $15,000 – $10,000 to go to youth employment initiatives, the rest to fund beautifying Evanston.

'Most cities I go to I find financial problems,' said Al-Fassi. 'So, I help them.'

That was not quite true. It took Mayor Lytle several follow-up phone calls and, ultimately, a threat to contact others in the Al-Fassi family before the sheikh finally made good on his promise to underwrite the $6,000 it cost to host himself and his travelling circus.

'The sheikh was the biggest jerk I've ever seen or met,' said Lytle. 'I wondered afterwards why Ali was hanging around with this guy. As far as I knew, Ali had money. He wasn't washed up and desperate like fighters sometimes are. He was just such a decent guy to everybody he met that day that it troubled me that he was hanging out with this sheikh. Maybe Al-Fassi had some other positive characteristics to him that people only saw in private. I certainly couldn't see them.'

* * *

On 20 September, the Metropolitan Museum of Modern Art hosted its first-ever fashion show when 800 invited guests got to see Rudolph Valentino unveil his new collection. Brooke Shields, Norman Mailer, Placido Domingo, Raquel Welch, Calvin Klein, Bianca Jagger and Mikhail Baryshnikov were among the great and good gathered for the occasion.

As they arrived in the building, some dawdled in the lobby to watch Muhammad Ali perform magic tricks, repeatedly making a swatch of orange chiffron appear and disappear. On the way out at the end of the evening, Ali, who'd watched the catwalk show from a front-row seat next to Klein and Jagger, returned to his earlier pitch to continue conjuring but assured reporters asking about a potential change of career that this was just 'a hobby'.

* * *

Nine thousand shoehorned into the Baltimore Civic Centre in Maryland for 'An Evening with Sugar Ray Leonard' on 9 November. A city was afforded the chance to pay homage to its greatest fighter in a show that included highlight reels, interviews with friends, family and rivals, and testimonies from Ken Norton, Marvin Hagler, Angelo Dundee and Matthew Saad Muhammad. When it came time for Howard Cosell, the master of ceremonies, to introduce Muhammad Ali, he described his old friend as 'the most important figure in boxing history'.

'Did you say most important *figure* in boxing history or did you say most important *n******?' asked Ali. The place erupted and that set the tone for his contribution, one journalist describing his performance full of one-liners as 'fattish and frisky'.

'After the Olympics, Ray asked me how he should go as a pro,' said Ali. 'I told him to get Angelo Dundee. He ain't a great trainer. He ain't a great manager. But he has the complexion and the connection to get the protection.'

More laughter. 'I too have an announcement to make. I shall return …' He waited a couple of moments as the audience audibly gasped at the prospect of him unretiring yet again then delivered the punchline, '… to California!'

* * *

A couple of days later, a sedan pulled into the car park of the Allen Park Youth Centre in north Miami, where Angelo Dundee was working his latest stable of fighters. A passenger in the front seat saw sports journalists gathered at the entrance and smiled. 'My writers!' said Muhammad Ali.

None of the scribes took offence. They had too much history with the man. Ed Schuyler from the Associated Press had given a farewell address on behalf of the media at his final press conference following the defeat by Berbick. The *New York Times'* Dave Anderson first covered him as the then Cassius Clay in March 1963.

Nineteen years later, Anderson watched a very different fighter change into his workout gear to train ahead of a tour of the Middle East that was scheduled to include three exhibition bouts. Dundee told the reporters his most famous charge had already trimmed nine pounds off his frame, was tipping the scales at 241 and doing two hours' walking per day to supplement his training inside the ropes. 'I'm so glad he's going on this tour,' said Bundini Brown. 'He's so miserable in LA. Now he has something to do.'

Ali was adamant this wasn't a comeback, merely a way to raise money to fund the construction of mosques in America to grow the Islamic faith. 'My life just started at 40,' said Ali. 'All the boxing I did was in training for this. I'm not here training for boxing. I'm going over to those countries for donations. When I get there, I'll stop the whole city. You don't hear nothin' about Frazier, or Foreman, or Norton, or Holmes, or Cooney. But when I get to those cities, there'll be three million people at the airport. They'll be on the sides of the road going into the city. Boxing's not popular in India, boxing's not popular in Saudi Arabia. I'm workin' for the mosques, but I'm workin' for boxing, too. I'm introducing boxing to all those people. I'm still workin' for boxing.'

Then somebody raised the issue of his own financial situation. 'I got bonds and investments,' he said. 'I don't want to comment [on] how I live. Too many people out there are unemployed. I don't want to brag how much I got but I'm all right. I'm building a hotel in Virginia Beach, I'm talkin' to the King of Sudan about an oil deal.'

When Anderson pressed him about the length of the trip, Ali's response, in content and delivery, was telling. 'I'll be gone ...' he mumbled, his words clinging together as cobwebs of dust do,' wrote Anderson. 'I'll be gone six weeks.' He was counting with the fingers of his right hand. 'I'll be back November 10,' he said. 'Yeah, November 10.' 'You mean December 10, don't you?' somebody suggested. 'Yeah,' he said, looking up. 'Yeah, December 10.' 'Then you'll be away about three weeks, not six weeks.' 'Yeah,' he said slowly. 'I'll be away three weeks.'

His confusion about the calendar was less troubling than the manner of his speech. Over the course of nearly two decades covering 32 of his fights, Anderson had never heard Ali slurring like this before. It was a troubling realisation as he watched him get in the ring and start taking punches to the headgear from 25-year-old heavyweight contender James 'Quick' Tillis.

* * *

Upon arriving at Dubai International Airport, Muhammad Ali put paid to rumours he had come to fight in the Middle East to ease his financial troubles. The purpose of the visit, he assured local media, was to raise money to build mosques in America, starting with a project in Chicago. Humble, charming and, inevitably, performing magic tricks, he lived up the advance billing of posters along the Dubai Creek Road advertising an opportunity to see 'The Greatest' fight at the Al Nasr Sports Stadium.

His travelling companions and opponents for the exhibitions were Jimmy Ellis, an old friend from Louisville who had briefly been world champion during Ali's enforced absence battling the US government over the Vietnam draft, and Reiner Hartmann, a 24-year-old German protégé who was Angelo Dundee's latest heavyweight project. At 41 and long retired, Ellis was getting a handy payday. For his trouble, Hartmann, boasting an unimpressive 6-2-1 record as a pro, was getting the inevitable spotlight that came from being in Ali's orbit.

The first exhibition against Ellis took place on Friday night, 3 December. If the attendance was enthusiastic, even at the sight of this heavier, slower version of the champ, one with severely diminished powers, the venue was far from full. 'There was no denying the admiration that Ali got from the crowd that was present at the stadium,' wrote Rangi Akbar in the *Gulf News*. 'After the bouts, he walked slowly towards the railings and fans were just content on kissing his hands. Nevertheless, one expected a much bigger attendance judging [by] Ali's worldwide popularity.'

It was a similar story two nights later when he took on Hartmann. A planned third bout was then cancelled due to poor ticket sales, and Emirati Juma Ganem, a spokesman for the promoter, said, 'It would be a rank injustice to a great boxer to make him work hard without having anyone appreciate it.'

ROUND TWO

1983

*Some have argued that boxing allows a few
disadvantaged or minority individuals an opportunity
to rise to spectacular wealth and fame. This does occur,
but at what price? The price includes chronic brain
damage for them and the thousands of others who
do not achieve wealth, fame or even a decent living.
Boxing seems to me to be less sport than is cockfighting;
boxing is an obscenity. Uncivilised man may have been
bloodthirsty. Boxing, as a throwback to uncivilised
man, should not be sanctioned by any civilised society*

Dr. George D. Lundberg, *Journal of the American
Medical Association*, 14 January

MUHAMMAD ALI turned 41 on 17 January. That afternoon, 23 Edmonton Oilers paid a visit to his home in Hancock Park, Los Angeles. The hockey players came bearing gifts, a Mark Messier stick autographed by the entire squad and a giant chocolate birthday cake in the shape of a boxing ring with gloves on top. 'I've never had so many white people in my house at one time,' said Ali. 'Any of my brothers on this team?'

At which point, Grant Fuhr, the goaltender who was the first black hockey player to win a Stanley Cup, burst into laughter.

The visit was arranged by Larry Messier, an uncle of the Oilers' centreman, and an old-school PR man culled straight from the pages of a Damon Runyon novel.

Weighing in at just over 30 stone, with a resume that boasted a stint as a bodyguard for Howard Hughes, Messier insinuated himself into Ali's inner circle when he came up with the idea of a range of commemorative gold coins with the boxer's face on them.

Somebody asked Ali to entertain the visitors, so he duly performed some of his magic, making a handkerchief and two balls disappear. The Oilers then gave a lusty rendition of 'Happy Birthday' and were sent on their way with one of his staple rhymes ringing in their ears.

> *'I love your company*
> *I admire your style*
> *But to give a gift so cheap*
> *Don't come back for a while.'*

* * *

The governor of the California Men's Colony, a male-only prison located north of San Luis Obispo, invited Muhammad Ali to speak to the inmates on Saturday, 29 January. Following lengthy introductions from various luminaries, Ali announced, 'This is my show.'

And it was. One thousand inmates hung on his every word as he recounted his journey from the early days as Cassius Clay ('some of you were probably free then!') to his embrace of Islam, name change and increased awareness of the world. At one point, he invited a prisoner up on stage to spar with him. 'Man, you are innocent,' said Ali as he threw combinations. 'Any man that comes up here and challenges me has to be crazy!'

He performed magic tricks, and some of his greatest poetry hits too.

> *'This is the legend of Muhammad Ali*
> *The best boxer there ever will be*
> *He talks a great deal and brags indeed*
> *Of a powerful punch and blinding speed.'*

Afterwards, Cheryle Johnson from the *Five Cities Times Press Recorder* of Arroyo Grande asked what the world's most mistaken impression of him is. 'I don't know,' he said, 'never thought about it.'

* * *

Trainer and major domo at the San Luis Obispo boxing club, Pat Murphy ran fight nights for the boys at the town's junior high school. On 9 April, Muhammad Ali turned up to watch and was eventually beseeched to get into the ring. For ten minutes, he regaled the crowd with practised one-liners from his repertoire ('I shall return!'), magic tricks and trademark braggadocio. They lapped up every drop and, eventually, he invited a young fighter to join him inside the ropes. The pair shadow-boxed, the teenager in T-shirt and jeans doing a passable impression of the Ali shuffle. 'Many memories come back to me when I watched them young boys fight,' he said. 'I saw some of my style in all of them. I saw one, he moved like me. I saw one, he clowned like me. And one of them was almost as pretty as me.'

* * *

On 11 April, *Sports Illustrated* published 'Too many punches, too little concern', a lengthy investigative report by Robert H. Boyle into boxing and brain damage. As part of his research, Boyle had sourced a Muhammad Ali CAT Scan performed at

New York University Medical Center in July 1981, when Ali had been declared fit and well. For the article, Boyle had the scan independently reviewed by Dr Ira Casson, a board-certified neurologist at Long Island Jewish Medical Centre. 'I wouldn't have read this as normal,' said Casson. 'I don't see how you can say in a 39-year-old man that these ventricles aren't too big. His third ventricle's big. His lateral ventricles are big. He has a cavum septum pellucidum.'

Boyle reported a growing body of medical evidence that boxers exhibiting cavum septum pellucidums were also experiencing neurological difficulties.

The magazine reached out to Ali and asked him to undergo a fresh battery of neurological tests to set the record straight about the anomalies in what doctors deciphered from his CAT scan. He refused.

* * *

Standing in the Smoky Hills of the Great Plains of Kansas, flush by Interstate 70, the 2,000-mile highway that runs east-west, bisecting middle America, Bunker Hill is a glorified truck stop, long-haulers lured off-road by the Bear House Café, offering hearty fare and an entertaining backstory. Its name derived from a pair of caged animals that reputedly once stood sentry from their perch in the gas station next door.

On 13 April, Lee Modlin turned up for her first-ever shift waiting tables at this roadside landmark. That was the Wednesday morning when Modlin, patrolling the counter, notebook and pencil in hand, discovered Muhammad Ali sitting there next to his secretary/book-keeper Marge Thomas. 'I about died,' she said. 'He was real nice and real sweet.'

Soon, diffident truckers and shy kids pressed into service by starstruck parents milled around the boxer proffering snatches of paper and pens. As was always his wont, the bigger the audience got the more animated Ali became, eventually ignoring his freshly delivered soup and climbing out of his seat to shadow-box the more courageous customers, offering combat tips to some, savage put-downs to others.

Following a visit to Chicago to lend his celebrity to the campaign to help Harold Washington become the first black mayor of the city, he had decided to head back to his home in Los Angeles by driving cross-country. Accompanied only by Thomas, a wily accountant who had turned around Ali's traditionally porous finances, he set off on this epic trip in his distinctive 1978 Stutz Bearcat.

Strikingly silver grey in colour, the chrome features on the exterior were gold plated and it had cost him well over $100,000 (around $300,000 in today's money). The Bearcat was flash, fashionable and, under the circumstances of an odyssey through flyover country, prone to be faulty.

They had been just outside Bunker Hill when the water pump went. While mechanics, including Modlin's husband, at the Tri-States Truck and Trailer sales and repair shop worked to get the car back on the road, the locals informed him their tiny hamlet was still 400 miles from Denver. 'Man,' said Ali, shaking his head. 'I'm right in the middle of nowhere!'

* * *

Twenty-four hours later, the water pump gave up again, so Ali and Thomas pulled into the Colorado mountain community of Silverthorne (pop. 3,000) when they saw a Chevron sign. For the second day in succession, he went in search of a mechanic and wreaked a little havoc. Brad Johnson was at the news desk of the *Summit Sentinel* when he got a tip-off. He was so dubious that, on arriving at the garage, the first thing the reporter asked was, 'This may sound stupid, but is Muhammad Ali here?'

Johnson found him in the service area sparring, trash-talking, putting on a show. He posed for photographs with Keith Bouma, the man working on his car, warning him, 'That's the closest you'll ever get to laying a hand on me!' When it became apparent the water pump repair was going to take time and the remote gas station wasn't going to yield any sizable audience for his antics, Ali agreed to visit nearby Summit High School.

Hundreds of students were brought to the gym for a question-and-answer session, during which Ali announced grand plans to bring 300 kids on a 15-nation tour to promote the fight against world hunger, and then wowed them by unfurling a wad of $100 bills. Afterwards, he returned to the garage, climbed into the Stutz Bearcat and declared, 'The way things are going, I'll only get another 300 miles before I'll have to pull over again.'

* * *

The day before he was scheduled to defend his World Boxing Council heavyweight title against Tim Witherspoon at the Dunes Hotel and Casino in Las Vegas, Larry Holmes was asked about the arrival of Muhammad Ali into town. Rumour around the slot machines was the promoters had drafted Ali in to lend glamour to a lacklustre promotion that, even with Michael Dokes defending his WBA heavyweight crown against Mike Weaver on the undercard, was failing to grasp the public imagination. One reporter mentioned Ali getting $1,200 just to hang around the event. 'I don't want to talk about that,' said Holmes. When the journalists raised the issue of the persistent chatter about Ali slurring his speech, he wouldn't be drawn on that either. 'Ali's always talked low to me,' said Holmes. 'His voice is lower than it was in 1971, 1973, 1975. It's more slow and softer. He's hard to understand. But I don't look for him to stumble when he walks and stutter when he talks. He's my friend, he's a man I love and respect. I don't look to see if he's shaky, if he's punchy, if he's broke.'

Ali had arrived in from Los Angeles on 18 May, 48 hours before the first bell. His walk through the Dunes drew the type of excited crowds that had largely been ignoring Holmes et al. all week long. 'The promoters sent for me,' said Ali, speaking in a room overlooking the car park where he had been embarrassed by Holmes in 1980. 'The fight is dying. I've come here to promote. I am boxing. Not just in Vegas, where people are fight fans. It's the same way in China, Morocco, Algeria, and black Africa. Muhammad Ali is boxing.'

He certainly gave enough interviews to generate column inches. Dave Kindred, a veteran journalist Ali always trusted, got a one-to-one chat. Present for the Holmes destruction and in the Bahamas for the even more unnecessary defeat by Berbick 14 months later, Kindred hadn't heard Ali speak since the aftermath of that loss. 'His voice is a mumble,' wrote Kindred. 'It's as if the voice were an attic with all the words lost in the dust of time. You want him to sparkle. You want him to be fun. You want him to be what he was before a thousand punches hit him.'

After Kindred asked how he was keeping busy, Ali produced a sheet of paper. On it, there was a primitive drawing of an aeroplane over the words, 'Children's Journey for Peace', and he started a spiel about a plan to bring 50 children from 50 countries around the world visiting kings, presidents and sheikhs. 'We'll be making the announcement of the journey in six to eight weeks at the United Nations,' he said. 'It will cost $2.5m. Sheikhs of Arabia will donate money. Certain people will donate the aeroplane. It's going to be something, man. Beautiful. Powerful.'

At one point during their conversation, Larry Holmes wandered over to the table. They had a mock-angry encounter for the benefit of other diners, with Ali demanding a rematch. As he readied to leave, Holmes leaned over and whispered to the man for whom he had once been a sparring partner, 'One champ to another champ, you'll always be the greatest. I'm just the latest.'

* * *

Muhammad Ali arrived at the Mission Valley Centre in San Diego on 3 June, later than advertised, in a Rolls-Royce convertible. Then, he sat in the open window of a bookstore at the mall to promote *Prayer and Al-Islam*, a book written by Wallace Muhammad, who had succeeded Ali's spiritual mentor Elijah Muhammad as leader of the Nation of Islam in the mid-1970s. He also signed autographs. Many, many autographs. Some walked away with just his signature scrawled across a poster, a scrap of paper, a book or even boxing gloves, others with more profound messages. 'Service to others,' he wrote for one lady, 'is the rent we pay for our room in heaven.'

In the midst of it all, Ali never forgot why he was there, giving the book, piled high in the window alongside John Le Carre's *The Little Drummer Girl*, the hard sell. 'This book is the best book in history other than the holy grail,' he said. 'It's meaningful to everybody. If you have economic problems or financial problems or social problems, you can solve all your problems if you read this book. Just read one page, you'll see.'

Like a politician on the stump, women pressed children into his arms. Unlike a politician on the stump, he was speaking so softly journalists had to hold microphones up to his mouth so they could hear him properly. 'When I was boxing, I was campaigning,' explained Ali when they questioned him about his subdued demeanour. 'I was my own greatest promoter. You see, there was a method to my madness. You see the real Muhammad Ali now. Look at these people.

'They don't look at me as just another athlete. They look at me like I'm the president of a country, a world leader. I'll be in Manchester, England next week and then Arabia and then lower Pakistan. I tour the whole world.'

* * *

Forty-eight hours later, he touched down in Jackson, Mississippi, his arrival causing turmoil at the airport, where he was besieged by fans. When he reached his hotel downtown, he stopped and did a double-take of one of the employees. 'You look like Joe Frazier!' he said before getting into his boxing crouch and unleashing a few combinations. 'You still the greatest, Champ!' said the bellman.

Local journalists were invited up into his room, where he did magic tricks and reflected on the nature of fame, one minute telling them he craved anonymity, the next claiming he kind of enjoyed the recognition. When pressed about the controversies that dogged his career, however, he was unequivocal. 'I'd do it all exactly the same,' he responded. 'Because all the things that ever were bad turned out to be good.'

He had come to Jackson to remember Medgar Evers, a civil rights leader shot dead in the driveway of his Mississippi home in 1963 by Byron de la Breckwith, a Ku Klux Klan member. Evers' brother Charles succeeded him as field director of the NAACP and organised an annual commemoration of his life and work called 'The Medgar Evers Homecoming', a staple in America's social justice calendar.

On 5 June, Ali climbed into a convertible to be driven in the official parade through the city of Jackson. A crowd of 4,000 lined the streets to greet an eclectic line-up that also included BB King, the actor James Earl Jones, Reverend Jesse Jackson on horseback and former Governor Ross Barnett, a notorious segregationist who was in charge at the time of the assassination, in a limousine. His presence was supposed to speak to the new era in the state's race relations.

Asked by a reporter if his participation in a parade with so many prominent African-Americans signified a change of heart on his own behalf, Barnett answered, 'A change? In what? I ride with n*****s every day.'

* * *

On 12 June, the night he was to square off with Muhammad Ali at Northlands Coliseum in Edmonton, Dave Semenko realised he had neglected to buy proper boxing shoes and suitable attire for his ring walk. So, he ferreted out an old pair of black hi-tops and grabbed a crimson and silver terry towel bathrobe. Moments before the first bell, his cornerman Rocky Addison was still cutting the sleeves open, trying to get the robe off over the 16oz gloves, even as an angry Ali was being theatrically restrained by his seconds, to the cheers of the baying crowd.

The son of a Winnipeg plumber, Semenko was an enforcer with the Edmonton Oilers, serving as 'Wayne Gretzky's bodyguard', a punishing role in which the 6ft 3in heavyweight was charged with protecting the team's most prized possession from opposing goons. His hard-won reputation for dispensing retributive justice allowed pre-fight publicity to sell the charity event as 'the baddest man on the planet meets the baddest man on ice'. A whiff of pantomime about the billing. A touch more about the contest itself.

Ali wore a tracksuit he never took off, perhaps not wanting the fans to glimpse how the torso that once rippled with muscle now jiggled flabbily. With Semenko coming at him mullet-headed and bare-chested in sweatpants, there were moments when the encounter had the look if not the feel of a tawdry, bare-knuckle street brawl.

There has, perhaps, never been a serious athlete more willing than Ali to participate in freak shows in the name of entertainment, burnishing his legend or simply lining his pockets. Sometimes, even all three at once. On this occasion, he delighted the Canuck media by arriving in town and unveiling some doggerel about his opponent, the type of rhyme normally reserved for a Joe Frazier or a George Foreman.

'Ali comes to meet Semenko
But Semenko starts to retreat
If Semenko goes back an inch further
He'll end up in a ringside seat.'

Although a remix of an old standard (culminating in Semenko being launched, like so many others before him, into space as a satellite), locals still relished the Ali show. At a public appearance the day before the fight, he pretended to mistake a diminutive elderly lady for Frazier.

Six thousand fans paid between $9 and $40 into an arena that could hold nearly three times that, and instead of Angelo Dundee, Ali had Jan-Michael Vincent, star of *Airwolf*, then one of the biggest shows on American television, in his corner assisting Bundini Brown.

'He just moved around the dressing room with me,' said Semenko of when Ali came to see him before the fight. 'He had his hands in the air and had me throw punches to see what type of skill level I had, and he said, "We'll be fine". Then he went for a nap.'

Ali gave the crowd what they came for, delivering plenty of verbals and allowing the local hero latitude to punch without ever taking any serious hits. He produced a few renditions of his trademark shuffle to inevitable cheers but, right at the end of the third and final round, Semenko caught him on the head. In the manner of a performer who knew his lines, Ali pretended to go wobbly kneed then unleashed a flurry of his own, bloodying Semenko's nose. Moments later, the referee declared the bout a draw.

'I'm not here for the money because you couldn't afford to pay me,' said Ali. 'I'm here because you all have followed me over the years and you can tell your grandchildren you did see him.'

* * *

On 19 July, Champion Sports Management Inc. was incorporated in the state of Virginia, promising to eventually offer common stock in an outfit designed to develop and train professional boxers. Those involved as vice-presidents included Earnie Shavers, Angelo Dundee, Larry Holmes, Eddie Futch and Muhammad Ali. Among the directors listed were Richard Hirschfeld, now styling himself Ali's attorney, Jabir Herbert Muhammad, Ali's manager, and Wilhelm Wolfinger, an owner and board member at the Tajir Institute Establissement of Feldkirch, Austria.

As co-chairmen of the enterprise, lending their reputations to the project, Ali and Holmes would receive annual salaries of $78,000 each, rising to six figures when expenses were factored in. If that type of financial arrangement seemed almost too good to be true, the involvement of a European company that usually dealt in oil was also so odd that it gave some the immediate impression this whole farrago was not quite on the up and up.

* * *

On 5 August, Muhammad Ali touched down at Heathrow Airport in London. As he made his way through the terminal, he stared straight ahead, never smiled and ignored the many questions reporters threw at him. Most had to do with rumours of his cognitive decline. 'I feel fine,' he said, finally, in a voice journalists found difficult to hear. 'I'm just a little overweight. I'm glad to be in Britain. I'm looking forward to meeting all my fans.'

The low-key performance – the only time he seemed like himself was when a bunch of schoolchildren approached him – prompted a welter of negative newspaper headlines. 'Ali's shuffle has slowed to a crawl,' shouted the *Daily Mirror*. 'Enter Ali, the incredible hulk,' said the *Liverpool Echo*. He responded to the criticism by pointing out he hadn't slept for two days before flying across the Atlantic.

He had been greeted off the flight by James Hunte. A city councillor in the West Midlands, Hunte had invited Ali to open a multiracial community centre that would bear his name in Handsworth, a troubled area of Birmingham infamously marred by nights of rioting against police the previous summer. There was more bother when Ali turned up to conduct the opening ceremony. A crowd of over 1,000 youths gathered outside, and when he finally arrived, many tried to surge through the doorway to get in. As officials and police blocked their path, fights broke out and Ali had to shelter in a side room while calm was restored.

Even during the formalities, there was more consternation. Hunte was booed by some of the audience, and when Ali finally spoke, he cautioned, 'That sort of thing looks awful bad for black people. When I used to say, "I'm the greatest", it was not just because I was boasting. I meant "*we* are the greatest". I am a real freedom fighter. I may be rich and famous but I'm still 100 per cent black.'

The rest of his stint in the English Midlands was much more pleasant. He spoke at Birmingham's Central Mosque in Belgrave Middleway, the largest in Western Europe when it opened eight years earlier. He was fitted for a wool and mohair suit by Ahmet Yusuf, a tailor who offered to make it for him to give thanks for his visit. There was the obligatory promo shot with a local boxing prospect, Mark Sherrington from Chelmsley Wood, and several babies were pressed into his arms to be kissed, even when walking through a factory in Smethwick.

Wherever he went, and no matter how enthusiastic he seemed – several times he started shadow-boxing with gangs of youths on the streets – questions about his health lingered. Eventually, he addressed them. 'I have got the world's press trying to make me out to be crazy,' he said. 'I have had a good laugh about it and said an extra prayer to Allah.'

That seemed reasonable enough, especially given the hectic nature of his schedule during his six days in Birmingham. More troubling perhaps was one throwaway quote to a reporter from the *Daily Star*: 'All the time I've been in England my phones have been tapped,' said Ali. 'The [US] president [Ronald Reagan] has ordered a special watch on me. They know I'm the leader of a billion black people. They are the president's men and they have a file on me at the Pentagon six feet high.'

* * *

On 20 September, the World Boxing Council held a black-tie dinner at the United Nations in New York to celebrate its 20th anniversary. Hosted by WBC President Jose Sulaiman, the event attracted nearly two dozen present or former world champions. Among the star-studded line-up were Larry Holmes, Joe Frazier, Ken Norton, Bob Foster, José Torres, Carlos Monzón, Emile Griffith, Nino Benvenuti, Sugar Ray Leonard, Thomas Hearns, Carlos Ortiz, Alexis Arguello, and Muhammad Ali.

Even in such heady company, nobody received more attention upon his arrival that evening than Ali. When each champion was asked to name the greatest champion of the last two decades, the so-called 'champ of champs', Ali easily topped the poll. Fighters justified their selection in different ways. Hearns said it was Ali who inspired him to become a boxer, Arguello cited the fact he gave all subsequent boxers the chance to be what they are, and Frazier mentioned how, more than anybody, his great rival had 'fought 'em all'. 'Ali brought his own style into boxing,' said Emile Griffith, a two-time middleweight and three-time welterweight champion from 1961 to 1968. 'His best fight was in Manila when Frazier couldn't come out for the last round. That night, both were really trying to hurt each other. Ali was never the same after that fight.'

* * *

The crowd gathered at the Kalamazoo Boxing Academy in Michigan had been told Muhammad Ali's appearance would start at 1pm on 28 September. It was past 5pm when he strolled in with a fanfare: 'I told you I was coming to town! Am I here?'

Suddenly, the audience sensed it had been worth the wait. Quickly, he swapped his suit for shorts and a T-shirt, then climbed inside the ropes to spar with Battle Creek heavyweight Kevin P. Porter, a 25-year-old with two wins from two pro outings. 'He's still quick,' said Porter after the session ended. 'He's still got a little bit in the right hand and the reflexes are still there. I don't know about his conditioning and power.'

When Ali had showered, reporters corralled him in an office belonging to Henry Grooms, Porter's trainer. 'If I was 30lbs lighter, I could take the crown,' he assured them. Deadpan.

Even though he was down to fight an exhibition on one of Grooms' cards at the Wings Stadium in Kalamazoo on 28 October, nobody was buying that story. Not in the condition they found him. 'Yesterday's experience did nothing to brighten Ali's fading image,' wrote John Singler in the *Battle Creek Enquirer*. 'The rumours about slurred speech are not rumours at all. They are fact. At one point, Ali's left arm began to quiver as he reached for a beverage. Ali is not ageing gracefully. But the saddest part of all this is that they are planning to shove him into the ring for an exhibition bout in a shameful attempt to hype the gate. On a day such as this, the prospect of Ali fighting in an exhibition seemed less incredible – but no less repulsive.'

The exhibition bout never happened.

* * *

By 9am, over 500 people had gathered at the Mathews-Dickey Boys' Club boxing gym on North Kingshighway in East St Louis to meet Muhammad Ali. Some bought copies of Wallace Muhammad's *Prayer and Al-Islam*, all lined up for an autograph. Perched behind a desk, Ali didn't seem his usual self. Quiet. Not alert. Barely speaking. His diminished persona worried onlookers, although those in his entourage claimed he'd been sick for the previous 24 hours. 'I'm Sonny Liston's nephew,' said Richard Shelton, a 20-year-old lightweight, when he sidled up for his audience. And Ali immediately, from some place, found energy, rose from his seat, and started delivering slow-motion punches either side of the young man's delighted head.

He climbed into the ring as well, pulling on a pair of boxing gloves but staying in his business suit as small children orbited his enormous frame and tried to land haymakers on his legs. He had arrived in St Louis on Friday, 8 October. Over the next 24 hours, he made public appearances at bookstores to promote *Prayer and Al-Islam* and spent several hours signing autographs outside an ADC and Food Stamp Centre on Collinsville Avenue.

Due to ill health, he had to cancel a number of promised engagements and never really looked like himself for the duration of the trip. About the manner in which he departed the Mathews-Dickey club, Neal Russo of the *Post-Dispatch* wrote, 'Ali seemed dazed, his speech was slurred and he had to be held up as he was escorted to his car.'

* * *

Muhammad Ali was among the esteemed guests at Esquire magazine's 50th birthday party at the Four Seasons in New York on 7 November. The final edition of the year was a tribute to 50 people who made a difference in American life. As he sipped a Diet Coke, Ali confided that he had no idea why he was picked, except, 'Beauty is in the eye of the beholder'. Other living honorees who attended were Carl Bernstein, Ralph Nader, William S. Paley and Betty Friedan.

Bob Greene, the Chicago-based journalist, had been charged with writing a feature about Ali for the commemorative publication. When he first called up to broach the idea, Ali was unreceptive, asking how much he was going to be paid. 'You're just using me to sell magazines,' he said. 'You just want to put me on the cover.'

* * *

'I am coming back,' declared Muhammad Ali at a press conference in the Starlight Roof supper club at New York's Waldorf-Astoria on 15 November. 'You thought I was washed up. You all said, he's old, he can't talk anymore! I'm making my comeback. I will now fight in another arena, however, and my opponent will be hunger. I'm fighting hunger. All my life I wanted to do something big like this and I say this is a much bigger arena in life than a boxing ring. I'm dealing with different people now. Not the flat-nosed boxing type.'

While his personal fight against hunger would be funded by a commemorative coin with Ali's image on it, set to retail by mail order for $45, most reporters took away an abiding impression from this encounter that the star attraction appeared in better fettle than advertised. He spoke well and looked leaner than for some time. The Associated Press described him as 'gregarious, articulate and witty'. In the *New York Daily News*, Bill Gallo, an experienced Ali correspondent, reckoned 'the improvement in his appearance and his speech was remarkable'.

* * *

'So, it was heartbreaking to find the rumours confirmed,' wrote Gary Wills in the *Miami Herald* on 8 December of a recent encounter with Ali. 'My wife and I, talking to our hero recently in New York, could not believe how the tongue had slowed, the eyes dimmed. This was the man as quick, once, with his tongue as with his fists, the wittiest and prettiest of fighters as well as the best. We, like most fans, did not want to believe it. But the facts had to come out. His brain was damaged in the ring.'

* * *

Muhammad Ali walked through the exercise yard on the rooftop of the Metropolitan Correction Centre in San Diego. First, the inmates stared. Then, they started to applaud and cheer. Eight days before Christmas, Ali unpacked a plastic box, readied himself to do magic and then said, 'I'd like to thank you all for coming.' The audience loved that one. Some, however, were not so impressed with his disappearing handkerchief routine. 'If you're so good,' shouted one prisoner, 'I got 20 years you can make disappear.' 'I'll do you better than that,' responded Ali, shaking his fist in mock anger. 'I'll make you disappear.'

Over the course of two hours, he performed many tricks and then started to show them how each one worked. 'Look how easy you've been tricked,' he warned. 'If I can trick you, think how easy the devil can trick you.'

ROUND THREE

1984

*I saw him once at eight o'clock in the morning, leaning
in a doorway on East 45th Street, painfully signing
autographs and staying there until it was after nine and
then leaving only when he was pulled away*

Jimmy Breslin, *New York Daily News*, 20 September

ON 2 January, Impact on Hunger, a Massachusetts-based non-profit, released a letter calling on world leaders to end death by starvation on the planet. Among the notable signatories were former presidents Jimmy Carter and Gerald Ford, former West German Chancellor Willie Brandt and the boxer Muhammad Ali.

* * *

The cake in the offices of Korbin Securities read, 'Happy Birthday Muhammad Ali! Good luck with Champion Inc'. Forty-two years after his birth in Louisville, Ali was in Rochester, New York on 17 January to promote the initial public offering of stock in Champion Sports Management Inc., the now full name of the operation.

Six months after the company was first mooted, Korbin Securities was charged with taking Champion public and raising $5m. A glossy 27-page brochure advertised plans to build an 88-

acre facility in Virginia Beach and to recruit, train, develop and promote the best young fighters in the country. 'I'll be adviser, promoter, visit training camp, visit each fighter, get into the ring with heavyweights,' said Ali, wearing prescription sunglasses and talking in a slow, deliberate drawl. 'Too many boxers come out of their careers broke. The managers and promoters continue on with other boxers but a lot of the boxers who quit don't have any money. We will train and promote boxers and assure them of receiving a percentage of their winnings. We're going to train people to be little 'Greatests'. We're just going to run a nice clean operation.'

Paul Lucci, a young stockbroker and inveterate fight fan, was thrilled to meet his hero and helped out when Ali had issues recalling certain details of his own sporting life. 'He was struggling with opponent names, fight dates, locations, and I was filling in the blanks for him,' said Lucci. 'He noted to me that he appreciated that. Right in the middle of the meeting, we guided him into an unused office where he could lie down for an hour or so.'

When reporters asked why Champion Inc. had chosen to use this particular brokerage, they were told that Richard Hirschfeld, Ali's attorney, had an excellent relationship with the company's Securities and Exchange Commission attorney.

* * *

For a 22 January article about the plight of Sugar Ray Seales, a former middleweight contender battling blindness due to two detached retinas, and the dangers of boxers going on too long, the *Washington Post*'s David Remnick interviewed Angelo Dundee. 'There ain't a thing wrong with Muhammad Ali,' said Dundee, responding to reports about his most famous charge's decline. 'When I'm with him, it's a joy. All that stuff about him being punch-drunk is baloney. We had him in our house three months ago. My wife Helen cooked some Irish stew and Ali just sat here with us, talking about boxing. He's fine.'

* * *

Larry Merchant, HBO boxing commentator and *New York Daily News* columnist, bumped into Muhammad Ali before the Tim Witherspoon-Greg Page fight for the WBC title at the Convention Centre in Las Vegas on 9 March. He thought Ali looked much thinner and had the gait of 'an arthritic old man'.

Next day, Merchant was on the same flight as Ali where he watched him entertain Sugar Ray Leonard with magic tricks and heard him recite lyrics from *Buck White*, the Broadway musical he'd briefly starred in way back in 1969. Positive signs. So too the testimony of a German reporter who told him Ali had recited a rhyme to him he'd first taught him in German 13 years previously.

When Merchant asked Ali about his health, his answer was to meditate on his influence on the sport and to unfurl photographs of himself with famous people, such as the pope. 'He walks slowly because there is no place to go he hasn't been,' concluded Merchant, 'and because the crowds that wanted to touch this breathtaking butterfly have never let him walk fast.'

Once they arrived back in California, Merchant accompanied Ali to the Joe Louis Memorial Gym in Santa Monica. There, he watched him work the speed bag and do light sparring, moving with a speed seemingly beyond him in civilian clothes. Merchant's ad hoc investigation also included garnering intelligence from unnamed members of the entourage. 'According to these friends, Ali gets $25,000 a month from his trust fund and his wife Veronica helps him spend it all,' wrote Merchant. 'He takes their two daughters to school every morning (he has four children by a previous marriage). Michael Jackson knocked on the door the other day and boogied in for a visit. Joe Louis was the world's guest. Ali is the world's host.'

* * *

In an appearance on British television on 4 May, Muhammad Ali explained the techniques behind his favourite magic tricks. While the audience loved it, his revelations cost him his membership of the British Magical Society. 'When Ali came to Britain several years ago, he did a number of magical items on some of his interviews and we decided it would be a nice gesture to welcome him to the Brotherhood,' said Barry Gordon, secretary of the 99-year-old society. 'Now, however, he has broken the cardinal rule of all magicians by exposing how the tricks are done, and we have decided to remove his name from our list of honorary members.'

Everybody else he met in England was happier to see him, especially in Birmingham. A year after his first visit to Handsworth, he went walkabout in the city centre. A BBC correspondent described him as 'dazed and listless' and looking like he was operating on 'showbiz autopilot' as he pressed the flesh, shaking every outstretched hand and smirking as a woman leaned in to kiss his cheek. The business at hand was picking up a new tracksuit to wear on a peace run around Edgbaston Reservoir, where dozens of children gambolled alongside him.

There were other sporting cameos too. At Edgbaston cricket ground, he watched Warwickshire entertain Surrey in the Britannic Assurance County Championship. Aside from posing for a photograph with the home side, he put on a Warwickshire jumper, donned pads and brandished a bat under the tutelage of England internationals Bob Willis and Dennis Amiss.

On Saturday, 5 May, he was Birmingham City's guest of honour at St Andrew's for the club's Division One football match against Liverpool, the newly crowned English champions. Wearing a suit and sunglasses, Ali was introduced to the crowd before the game, accompanied on to the field by councillor James Hunte, the local politician whose bold idea to name a community centre after the three-time champion had started something of a love affair between Ali and the locals. 'I'm glad to be back,' he said of his time in England's second city. 'It's just like being back home. I couldn't be received no better at home. I love it.'

* * *

Several hundred people gathered in front of the Kentucky Centre for the Arts in Louisville on 27 May, awaiting the Olympic torch as part of its 3,000-mile odyssey from New York to Los Angeles. At 12.35pm, Muhammad Ali's arrival prompted a surge of electricity through the spectators. 'Isn't this a great day for Louisville?' asked Mayor Harvey Sloane. 'He still floats like a butterfly and stings like a bee. Let's give the warmest welcome we know how to our own native son Muhammad Ali.' 'I didn't know I would have to speak,' said Ali, before informing the crowd that he had to look up what a kilometre was when he heard that's how far he had to carry the torch. 'If you'd told me 20 years ago I'd still be participating in the Olympics, I'd have said you're crazy. They say how time does fly. Now I know what they mean.'

Rain started to fall as they waited for the relay team to reach the city but the weather didn't dampen the spirits any. To pass the time, the crowd started chanting 'Ali! Ali! Ali!' Finally, Bryce Kurfees hove into view, bearing the two-and-a-half-pound butane-powered torch that he duly passed off to Ali. The 1960 Olympic light-heavyweight champion headed west on Main Street, south down Sixth Street and on to City Hall, where his initial fast-paced jog slowed to something more like a fast walk. 'A couple of dozen people ran the route with Ali,' wrote Alan Judd in the *Louisville*

Courier-Journal, 'and the run seemed to take less of a toll on them than it did on him.'

In front of the Louisville Galleria on Liberty Street, a photographer on a passing truck shouted, 'Champ, you're the greatest!' 'You're smiling because you're riding,' responded Ali.

As he neared the intersection of Third Street and Muhammad Ali Boulevard (the street named in his honour back in 1978), Ali quickened his pace before passing the torch to Melinda Warren. For the next half-hour, he signed autographs, posed for photographs, sparred game young men and kissed babies. When every request had been satisfied, he declared, 'I'm an old man.'

* * *

'This is the greatest cookie of all time,' said Muhammad Ali at a 5 June event in Atlanta to publicise the launch of 'Champ Cookies' in the Georgia market. 'I don't sign my name to anything that isn't the best. This cookie is good. If you eat one, you end up eating the whole bag.'

Having been available in the DC and Los Angeles markets since 1982, his brand of cookies was going nationwide, retailing for between $1.99 and $2.25 per bag. 'I just received a call from Nigeria,' he said. 'The government there is considering backing the cookie there. We are also considering the Bahamas, Saudi Arabia, Jamaica, wherever Muhammad Ali is known. Even Peking is considering carrying the cookie.'

* * *

On 3 July, a judge in Allegheny County, Pennsylvania, delayed for 48 hours the foreclosure sale of a three-bedroom house in Mount Lebanon that belonged to Muhammad Ali and his first wife Belinda. The court filing claimed Ali owed more than $32,000 in principal and interest on the property in suburban Pittsburgh.

* * *

Ahead of an Independence Day Parade in Washington, DC, over 200 people gathered in front of Frederick Douglass' stately home. Warith Deen Muhammad (formerly known as Wallace), leader of the now more mainstream American Muslim Mission, had called a press conference to dissociate his movement from Louis Farrakhan, leader of the latest iteration of the Nation of Islam, which ten days earlier had called Judaism 'a dirty religion'. In town to be grand marshal for the parade, Muhammad Ali was among those present and after initially refusing to speak on the issue, he eventually responded to reporters' questions. 'We're here to explain that we're not him,' said Ali. 'I'm not with Farrakhan. None of these people are with Farrakhan. You want the people to believe that his beliefs about Jews and other things are our belief. You want the masses of people who are going to convert one day to think that this is a Muslim, one that's radical, one that's not Godly, one that's not Islam.'

* * *

Wearing an impeccable white suit, Muhammad Ali cut a pathetic figure during a ten-minute appearance on an episode of *Late Night with Letterman* that aired on NBC on 9 July. His delivery was slow, the voice almost too low for microphones to pick up and David Letterman, his first time interviewing the fighter, struggled to build a rapport with the guest he introduced as 'the most famous man in the world'.

Ali smiled a lot but mumbled most of his answers, although the audience loved it when, after a request to do magic, he pretended to levitate Letterman's mug before shouting, 'April Fool'. During the second half of the interview, things got really excruciating. 'We have 19 unknowns,' said Ali when he started to talk about Champion Sports Management. 'Our job is to make them knowns.'

Then, Ali grew animated as he introduced his entourage in the audience, most notably Tim Witherspoon, the WBC heavyweight champion, the now ubiquitous Richard Hirschfeld and former world light-heavyweight champion Eddie Mustafa Muhammad. They were all sitting, alongside Ali's daughter Maryum. Having allowed him to promote Champion, Letterman asked whether he now had any relationship with Larry Holmes, and evincing a speed that made a mockery of his earlier faltering appearance, Ali made to run off the set.

Letterman tossed a few softballs about the nature of their friendship before delving into how Holmes' proposed fight against Gerrie Coetzee wasn't going to happen because of a disputed contract he had signed with Champion. Uncomfortable with the questions, and savvy enough to know it was the subject of ongoing legal action, Ali invited his lawyer out of the audience. Moments later, Hirschfeld was sitting next to him on stage, giving lawyerly answers to leading questions about the situation.

As Hirschfeld spoke, Ali started grinning like a child and pointing towards a monitor in front of the pair of them, asked his legal adviser, 'You ever see yourself on television? All the people in Virginia Beach are watching.'

* * *

At a press conference in Pittsburgh on 11 July, Muhammad Ali announced he was reopening his fabled Deer Lake training camp in Pennsylvania so he could work with the next generation of fighters under the Champion Sports Management umbrella. Eddie Mustafa Muhammad would be the biggest name in the stable but they were also looking at Tim Witherspoon and any notable prospects emerging from the Los Angeles Olympics. 'I got so much out of boxing, did so much for boxing,' said Ali. 'I am boxing. I didn't think it would be right to start something new.

I'll just take up what I know best: boxing. I'll probably be working out with champions for the next ten years.'

Although reporters present remarked Ali was speaking slower than normal, he was in good form, touching on a range of topics. He assured them he'd be giving 40 per cent of his time to the sport from now on, wondered about age getting to Larry Holmes (the reigning champion was then 35) and dismissed recent newspaper articles calling for boxing to be outlawed. 'I think the only reason people want to ban it – I hate to say this – but it's racially motivated,' he said. 'Blacks are dominating. Black boys can come out of jail or off the streets, go into boxing and in three or four years of good fights be worth about five million. It helped me, made me what I am, and it will make thousands of boys in the future who will take it up. When there were all white champions and contenders in boxing, there was no movement to stop it. Now they're trying to stop it. I may be wrong but that's all I can see.'

Angelo Dundee was in the room too, recounting a recent evening at a fight night in the Los Angeles Forum where he witnessed the positive impact being around boxing had on Ali. 'He's got two diseases,' said Dundee. 'Hypoglycemia and boredom. If he would do something like that, it would really juice up the youngsters. He's just got nothing to get excited about. He loves boxing, loves boxing people and loves the media. He can talk to boxers and motivate them. There's no better motivator than Muhammad Ali.'

* * *

Muhammad Ali walked into the press conference at the Tavern on the Green at Central Park on 12 August and, with a tell-tale smile breaking across his face, said, 'I'm here to announce my comeback.' He wasn't. But it made for a more dramatic entrance than admitting he had come to promote the launch of a new cologne bearing his name. Eau d'Ali, produced by Acardyl Products across the river in Newark, would be hitting department store shelves by Thanksgiving and retailing for $24 per two-ounce bottle. 'I predict it will be the greatest thing of all time,' said Ali. 'I checked it out. I smelled it. I tried it on. I'm behind it 100 per cent.'

* * *

The scene was the US District Court in Manhattan on 24 August. 'Are you the greatest of all time?' asked Stanley Sacks, attorney for the defence of Muhammad Ali. 'Objection! Irrelevant!' interjected Margaret McQueeney, attorney for the Securities and Exchange Commission (SEC). 'I don't think it's irrelevant to the witness,' overruled Judge Robert J. Ward. 'I think so,' said Ali when he was finally allowed to answer.

The SEC had charged Champion Sports Management with deceiving investors by disguising a $600,000 loss as a loan to make their stock look a more attractive prospect. The SEC wanted Judge Ward to bar Champion and its president, Richard Hirschfeld, from committing future fraud. Lawyers for the company argued they had already returned $1m to investors. Not named in the suit, Ali, as somebody closely associated with the outfit, wanted to clear his name. 'It'd be low, dirty, cheap and I can't believe I'm being tried for something like this,' said Ali. 'We're trying to help people, not defraud them. We are trying to help boxers and better the sport and knock out much of the criminal action. Take boys off the street and help people, not defraud them and rob them. I wouldn't dream of violating the law because they call me the most recognised person in the world.'

When McQueeney handed him the 27-page brochure that contained false information to lure investors, Ali confessed to never having read the publication. 'I only read the Holy Koran, parts of the Bible and the sports pages,' he said.

Growing frustrated with Ali's inability to answer questions about the business operations of Champion, Judge Ward loudly demanded to know, 'Who handles the money?' 'You scared me, judge,' said Ali before answering that Richard Hirschfeld was the money man and somebody he regarded as totally 'trustworthy'.

The SEC investigation had uncovered that money to fund the proposed training camp in Virginia had come from Wilhelm Wolfinger, a financier from Austria and longtime associate of Hirschfeld. Wolfinger had got involved as a 'quid pro quo' for Ali helping him to set up an $800m oil refinery deal in Sudan. Ali had made the introductions to influential people in the African nation as requested and, by one account, was supposed to be earning $20,000 a month on a retainer from the European.

While defence lawyers argued the SEC suit had effectively killed off Champion's chances of surviving as a business, Judge Ward's decision was to injunct the company and Hirschfeld, noting it was the third time he'd committed SEC violations and predicting he would do so again. 'Defendant Hirschfeld's knowing and wilful conduct in this case, together with his past conduct and ongoing involvement with public companies,' said Ward, 'demonstrates that there is a reasonable likelihood that Hirschfeld will commit further violations of the antifraud provisions of the federal securities laws in the future.'

* * *

On 6 September, Muhammad Ali checked into Columbia Presbyterian Medical Centre in New York to undergo neurological tests. Somehow, in the media capital of the country, his presence there remained a secret. After five days, he checked out and flew to West Germany on a business trip. The story of his hospital stay leaked when he was in Europe after one of his travelling party, Dr

Martin Ecker, a consultant radiologist and relative of Hirschfeld, mentioned it in a radio interview.

Upon his return to America on 19 September, a phalanx of journalists was waiting at Kennedy Airport. 'You're the greatest!' shouted a fan. 'Of all time!' responded Ali, and then he started a brief chant of that very phrase. But, when the crowd had dwindled, he spoke candidly to a couple of reporters, asking them, almost plaintively, 'What do you think is wrong with me?'

From the terminal, he went straight back to the hospital on the Upper West Side for more tests and treatment. Except now, the world was watching and anxious for updates. Eventually, Dr Stanley Fahn, the neurologist handling his case, spoke to journalists gathered at the facility. He explained Ali was not suffering from Parkinson's disease but from Parkinson's syndrome, an umbrella term covering a range of neurological difficulties that cause slurred speech, tremors and problems with gait and posture.

All of those were evident to anybody who had crossed paths with Ali at any time over recent years. Fahn even confessed that members of the former champion's inner circle told him they'd witnessed disturbing signs from as far back as the Larry Holmes fight in 1980. However, he was also confident the patient would improve after being prescribed Sinemet, a form of the drug L-Dopa, and Symmetrel, both of which worked together to alleviate the symptoms. 'He's got a problem with his brain in terms of motor control,' said Fahn. 'We expect he'll respond to medication. After the medication, he should live as normal a life as possible.'

During his stay at Columbia Presbyterian, Ali received over 200 telegrams, including messages from President Mobuto of Zaire and President Ferdinand Marcos of the Philippines. There were ten baskets of fruit, phone calls from Sugar Ray Robinson, Sugar Ray Leonard and Joe Frazier, and so many bouquets of flowers that he asked the nurses, 'Who died?'

'He spoke somewhat slurred but not badly,' said former heavyweight champion Floyd Patterson after visiting. 'I could understand everything he said. He seems happy. He seems content.'

Fern Isaacson, a 25-year-old outpatient suffering from connective tissue syndrome, a condition that had seen her hospitalised 39 times in four and a half years, was granted an audience with Ali. He signed his name in thick, bold letters across the front of her neck brace. 'He gave me a kiss,' she said, 'and he hugged me and showed me magic tricks.'

When told about the crowds gathering outside amid growing concerns he was near death, Ali went downstairs to talk to the media. Reverend Jesse Jackson, visiting that day, accompanied him. A photograph of that moment flashed across newspaper wires showing a mysterious figure lurking in the background. Lunatic conspiracy theorists came to believe the face was that of Elvis Presley, a rumour that gained such currency that Larry Kolb, a recent recruit to Ali's entourage and the man lurking in the shot, had to appear on American television to debunk the myth. 'I'll whip this thing,' said Ali to the reporters. 'I'll whip it. I'm not scared. They could tell me tomorrow, "Ali, you have cancer of the heart, you've got six months to live." And I'll say, "I'm glad." I had a good life. I was good to people and I'll be glad to meet Allah. I came out to show you I'm still the greatest of all time.'

Questions about whether his deterioration was caused by staying in the ring too long were not discounted. 'I've been punched a lot of times,' he said. 'I've been in the boxing ring now for 30 years and taken hard punches in fights, also in training preparing for fights, so there's a great possibility things could be abnormal.'

He also mentioned he hadn't been sleeping enough, managing five hours per night when he needed eight, and speculated that his problems could stem from a motorcycle accident 11 years previously in which he'd suffered a blow to the head. Meanwhile, Jackson asked for people everywhere to 'cross lines of religion and race and pray for him so he can realise a quick recovery.'

* * *

Within hours of being discharged from Columbia Presbyterian on 21 September, Muhammad Ali flew to Khartoum to celebrate the first anniversary of President Gaafar al-Nimeiry imposing Sharia Law on Sudan. Ali stood with al-Nimeiry as they applauded a mass march through the streets of the capital designed to reiterate support for his controversial decree. It had provoked a rebellion in the largely Christian south of the country and a conflict that would endure for decades. 'Western news media circulated distorted reports to give an indication I would not be able to travel to Sudan to take part in this Islamic gathering, which aims at bolstering our faith,' Ali told the official Sudan News Agency. 'I now have felt peace and security since my arrival in Sudan.'

Having mentioned he was determined to spread the word of Islam as long as Allah kept him healthy, he also claimed there was great support in America for Sudan's efforts to become an Islamic republic and that the religion was winning scores of new converts in his homeland every day.

* * *

Jerry Zerg, a GOP – Grand Old Party – candidate trying to unseat Henry Waxman, Democratic incumbent for California's 33rd congressional district, hosted a gathering for prominent black Republicans at his house in Hancock Park on 1 October. Muhammad Ali was the star guest, his presence generating international headlines when he endorsed not only his neighbour but also the re-election campaign of Ronald Reagan. 'He's keeping God in schools,' said Ali. 'And that's enough!'

When pressed on his preference for Reagan over Walter Mondale, especially since he'd supported Jimmy Carter just four years earlier, Ali claimed to know nothing about the Democratic challenger. He also admitted that he'd be voting for Reverend Jesse Jackson, defeated by Mondale in the primaries, if he was still in the race – or any black candidate for that matter. 'They all looked alike to me,' he said of the remaining options. 'Wallace Muhammad, the leader of all Muslims, says Reagan is our man.'

That detail didn't make it into all the news stories of the evening, nor did all reporters comment on Ali's parlous condition at the event. 'Ali seemed tired and weak during Monday night's appearance,' went the dispatch from the UPI. 'He stumbled over his words and at times appeared disoriented.'

Across New York, New Jersey, Pennsylvania, Ohio and Michigan, billboards emblazoned with 'We're voting for the man!' soon appeared. They showed President Reagan throwing a playful punch at Ali while Joe Frazier and Floyd Patterson look on.

* * *

On Saturday, 27 October, over 500 people gathered outside Shake and Bake Family Fun Centre on Pennsylvania Avenue, the heart of black Baltimore, to witness the arrival of Muhammad Ali, accompanied by Eddie Kendricks, formerly of The Temptations. 'Ali! Ali! Ali!' reverberated once spectators caught sight of the headline act. He gave a speech that drew laughs then invited 20-year-old Wade A. Johnson, a local Ali impersonator, up on stage to mimic one of the fighter's encounters with Howard Cosell.

After that, Ali invited the crowd inside but only half took him up on the offer. The others didn't have the price of admission. 'Please come out and sign an autograph,' shouted Dorothy

Satterfield. 'We don't have $5 to get in. We live in the ghetto. We don't have the money to come inside.'

Later in the day, he recorded an episode of a show called *People are Talking* for Channel 13. Before going on, he performed magic tricks in the green room for local reporters covering his visit to the city. 'He moves like a man in syrupy slow motion, and his speech is slow and slurred,' wrote Michael Olesker in the *Baltimore Sun*. 'He is a kind of swollen presence that reminds you of Elvis Presley when it all began to end for him.'

Yet, Olesker was impressed too by how incredibly patient he was with a public pressing demands on him at every moment. And by his wit. Witness the exchanges as he departed the television studio through a sea of people.

'How do you stay so young-looking?' asked a woman.

'Oil of Olay,' replied Ali.

'How is your home life?' shouted someone.

'I don't know,' he answered. 'I'm never home.'

* * *

At the Macedonia Missionary Baptist Church in Mt Morris Township, Michigan on 31 October, Reverend Jesse Jackson was asked about Muhammad Ali endorsing President Reagan's re-election and allowing his image to be used on campaign posters. 'He has Parkinson's syndrome,' said Jackson. 'He's not thinking very fast these days. He's a little punch-drunk.'

* * *

Muhammad Ali arrived in Lagos, the capital city of Nigeria, on 10 November for the finale of Expo Africana 84, the continent's largest music festival. Thousands greeted him at the airport and, quelling recurring rumours about his demise, he assured everybody he felt cured already. When asked why he had voted for

Ronald Reagan in the presidential election, he quipped, 'I chose the better of the two whites.'

* * *

In the 17th floor dining-room of the Downtown Athletic Club in New York on 19 November, Muhammad Ali was presented with the organisation's Rocky Marciano Memorial Award for being a champion in and out of the ring. 'I travel around a lot these days with my fighters,' said Joe Frazier. 'But when they asked me to come here tonight, I said, "You don't have to ask me, just tell me where to be and when." We had some wonderful days. No other man deserves this honour tonight but him. Congratulations. I'm here to pay him great respect.'

Ali told reporters he had to take Sinemet and Symmetrel three times per day, and admitted, 'I'm lazy and I forget.' But he also went into detail about his punishing travel schedule to demonstrate how reports of his physical decline were exaggerated, and held forth on the enduring power of his celebrity. 'I'm more celebrated, have more fans and I believe I am more loved than all the superstars this nation has produced,' he said. 'We have a saying, "Him whom Allah raises none can lower". I believe I have been raised by God. You think the spiritual world is not big. Turn on any television any Sunday and watch Oral Roberts or Billy Graham. You know Jimmy Swaggart? He can preach. If I had to pay for my press, it'd cost me $100 billion. I am a master at staying in the news. When I was in the hospital, headlines. When I checked out of the hospital, headlines. I mean, front page. Do you think I'm dying?'

Loath to dismiss the idea that punches to the head contributed to his condition, Ali lamented the fact he wasn't doing more to keep in shape. When a journalist complained he was talking too softly, he broke into a shout and refused invitations to advise

Larry Holmes and Sugar Ray Leonard (recently unretired) to hang up their gloves. And as for Reverend Jesse Jackson describing him as punch-drunk for supporting Reagan, he took the higher ground. 'To run for the office of president,' he said, 'you have to be diplomatic. I'm going to make no comment about him. He's my brother.'

Regarding all those who questioned his endorsement of the president getting a second term, he was unequivocal. 'Why pick on me? He fooled the whole country, 49 states. Reagan is the best man and Russia is afraid of Reagan.'

The quote of the evening may have belonged to Frazier. The man on the receiving end of so much verbal abuse and name-calling back in their pomp broke out a rhyme of his own.

> 'He floats like a butterfly
> And stings like a bee
> But he could never forget Joe Frazier
> That's me!'

* * *

On 12 December, Muhammad Ali filed suit against the Federal Government and the World Boxing Association, seeking to have his title restored for the 1967–70 period and to recover earnings lost due to his ban from the sport. Ali requested any reference to his 1967 conviction for refusing the Vietnam Draft (since overturned by the Supreme Court) to be expunged and for him to receive $50m in compensation.

Although the primary motivation, his lawyer said, was to remove the 'stigma', Ali also pledged to donate 'a substantial portion' of any money received to Vietnam veterans and their families.

ROUND FOUR
1985

He's completely bored; he's not the same guy. He loved what he used to do, that instant light–up. He cannot capture what he had before

Angelo Dundee, Miami, 6 May

AN ESTIMATED 100 people paid $25 each for cocktails and hors d'oeuvres in the company of Muhammad Ali at the Pontiac Silverdome just outside Detroit on 17 January. All proceeds went to the Youth Development League for underprivileged children in the city.

'How old are you?' asked one woman.

'I'm 49 today!' said Ali.

'You don't look 49,' she responded.

He had just turned 43.

* * *

Muhammad Ali was an hour late for his appearance at Walbrook High School in Baltimore on 29 January. A thousand students gathered to hear him talk about world hunger, each donating tinned goods as part of a food drive. In an hour-long speech, he extolled the virtues of education and even introduced a mystery guest. 'Is it Prince?' he asked the frenzied crowd. 'Is it Michael Jackson?'

It turned out to be Ernest Thomas, star of the ABC sitcom *What's Happening?* Not quite the same wattage. His show was no longer on the air but most of the boys and girls recognised Thomas from television and that was perhaps enough. They cheered accordingly. 'I always wanted to see Nat King Cole in my school, Sugar Ray Robinson or Joe Louis,' said Ali. 'It's a treat for me to come in your school and for you to see I'm black like you.'

His performance at nearby Douglass High School the same day went less smoothly. Having scarcely touched on world hunger in his presentation, preferring to spend the time joshing with Thomas and his entourage, the floor was opened for questions. A 17-year-old named Steven Yelity raised his hand and asked, 'Mr Ali, is it true you campaigned for Ronald Reagan in the '84 election and if so ...'

That was as far as he got. Ali moved towards the microphone and replied, 'I'm not answering that question. We're here to talk about hunger, not politics.' 'Why did you come to Douglass?' asked Yelity. 'Who else are you asking to help in this world hunger thing?'

Ali stared down at the student, who was 5ft 9in, weighed 240lbs and wore thick glasses because he was legally blind, and quipped, 'I can tell you ain't hungry, that's for sure.'

The whole auditorium laughed at the cruel jibe. A teenage boy already the butt of too many jokes about his weight and eyesight was mortified. 'Cheap shot, champ!' shouted Madeline Topkins, an English teacher. 'Cheap shot at a teenager. Steven can out-think, out-write and out-read anybody on that stage.'

Two days later, Michael Olesker of the *Baltimore Sun* tracked down Yelity to see how his moment in the spotlight had affected him. 'I'm the most disliked kid in the school now,' he said. 'I used to be Steven Yelity, nobody. Now, I'm Steven Yelity the person who assaulted Muhammad Ali. I just thought it was unfair of him to come to us and then just make jokes. Why isn't he marching in Washington, talking to all those Republicans he supported last summer? That's all I wanted to ask. And his response was to humiliate me.'

Two months later, the Philosophy Club of Morgan State University gave Yelity an award to recognise his 'critical thinking'.

* * *

At 2am on a February morning in West Beirut, Muhammad Ali and his entourage stood outside the Summerland Hotel, a place so war-torn that its manager boasted every mirror and window had been shattered at least once by bullets or shells. A pair of battered Mercedes driven by men wearing keffiyehs and toting kalashnikovs pulled up and opened their doors, as arranged. After the convoy negotiated its way past the first heavily fortified checkpoint, there was another stop so everybody could transfer to a Volkswagen bus and a Chevy for the next leg of their journey into the Lebanese night.

Ali and his fellow travellers kept waiting for blindfolds that never came and, eventually, the cars stopped outside a dimly lit, shabby villa. At the door, a friendly man welcomed them with glasses of juice and a plate of dates and invited them to sit. His name was Ibrahim Al-Amin. Days earlier, at the al-Ouzai Mosque in the city, he had proclaimed the existence of Hezbollah to the world, outlining a manifesto calling for the obliteration of Israel and promising 'to expel all Americans and their allies from Lebanon, putting an end to any colonialist entity on our land'.

Oblivious to the disturbing realpolitik, the most famous American on earth sat across from Al-Amin, the new face of Shi'ite fundamentalism, and argued for the release of four of his compatriots then being held hostage in south Lebanon. Al-Amin feigned ignorance about the plight of the quartet but, contradicting himself, also assured Ali their liberty might be possible if the former boxer could secure the release of several hundred Shi'ites being held in Israel. He even handed over a list of names to make it easier to plead their case.

A trip to the then most dangerous city on earth had been suggested to Ali by a most unlikely source. Months earlier, during a visit to Ronald Reagan at the White House, the former boxer had been deliberately waylaid in the West Wing by vice-president George H.W. Bush and, according to Larry Kolb, Ali's friend and adviser, the former director of the CIA made a very specific request of the three-time heavyweight champion.

'We'd like you to use your status as a respected Muslim to enter into a secret dialogue with the Ayatollah Khomeini to try to procure the release of the American hostages held in Beirut,' said Bush. 'This will have to be done without any trace of White House support.'

Spending time in a place where a daily ceasefire existed until midday so women could get home safely from the markets before fighting resumed left a mark on Ali. 'I'm just leaving Lebanon for Zurich, and I wanted to drop you a note,' he wrote in a letter to Gene Kilroy, his long-time confidante, on 20 February. 'When you hear bombs go off around you, it makes you think how much you like to be with the people you care about. I hope to see you soon, but in the meantime, I want you to know that I appreciate your loyalty over the years.'

* * *

Fourteen years after their first encounter at Madison Square Garden, Muhammad Ali and Joe Frazier returned to the scene of the fight on Friday, 15 March for the finals of the Golden Gloves, where a 17-year-old future world champion named Riddick Bowe showcased his knockout power. The litany of icons at ringside also included José Torres, former light-heavyweight champion, and Floyd Patterson. When the luminaries were introduced to the crowd, the most raucous reception was reserved for Ali. Even in exalted company, his erstwhile peers came to pay homage. 'Hey, we're huggin' cousins,' said Frazier as he wrapped Ali in a warm embrace backstage at the Penn Plaza Club. 'I admire you greatly,' said Patterson as he looked Ali in the eyes. 'Champ,' said Jose Torres, 'there was never anyone like you.'

Bill Gallo, veteran cartoonist and columnist with the *New York Daily News*, was on hand to chronicle the meeting of champions in a corner booth. He and Ali had such a long-standing friendship that they could joke about the time before Ali-Frazier III when Gallo depicted the then overweight fighter with a belly so expansive he had to carry it around in a wheelbarrow. Gallo handed Ali a piece of paper and asked him to list his top ten heavyweights of all time. 'I have never done this before,' he said. 'But I thought about it plenty.'

Then he wrote, in order of greatness, Jack Johnson, Joe Louis, Rocky Marciano, Ezzard Charles, Jack Dempsey, Gene Tunney, Joe Frazier, George Foreman, Sonny Liston and Floyd Patterson. When somebody pointed out that he'd omitted Larry Holmes, Ali quipped, 'He's number 11.'

As a long-time watcher of Ali, Gallo spent his time in Ali's company gauging the true nature of his condition. 'An hour before the others arrived, it was Ali and me, one on one, talking freely, no halting of speech, no slur, and as alert and bright as a penny,' wrote Gallo. 'It was good to see him this way, although not everybody did since by the time he made his appearance in the Garden ring, a medicinally induced lethargy was noticeable.'

* * *

Muhammad Ali touched down at Miami International Airport on 20 March, greeted by a scrum of media and Angelo Dundee. He had returned to the town from which he had once launched himself upon the world to speak at a charity roast of his former trainer, a fundraiser for the head trauma unit at the city's Bon Secours Hospital. 'I'm gonna burn the roast,' he declared as one woman spun the wheelchair in which she was pushing her mother in order to see Ali in full baby-kissing, autograph-delivering mode. 'These bones are not dead,' Dundee told a journalist. 'See what I mean.'

When he turned away for a second, Ali gently blew on the strands of hair straddling across his trainer's scalp. Dundee reached up to scratch his head, oblivious that this was the handiwork of his most famous fighter. 'Throughout the airport, a loose crowd swirls like a whirlpool around the man with a slight paunch, little coils of grey on the temples, the subtlest of half-smiles still in bloom,' wrote Peter Richmond in the *Miami Herald*. 'Some charge up and pump the hand. Others are too bashful. They offer blank sheets of paper as if proffering a bad report card to a parent.'

A new member of his entourage that day was Gary Catona, a recently hired voice and speech coach. His positive impact could be gauged by the fact Floridians found Ali to be something like his old articulate self, albeit at a lower volume.

At the Bon Secours Hospital, he visited a stroke victim who had communicated that his greatest wish was to meet the former heavyweight champion. Seeing the condition of the stricken man, Ali got down on his knees and spoke gently into his ear for 15 minutes. 'There weren't any media there,' said Dick Satterfield, an employee of the hospital. 'This was the act of a kindly man.'

At a get-together before the beginning of the roast proper – for which patrons of the Doral Hotel paid $150 per seat – Ali appeared more subdued. Indeed, as he listened to Mr T (then in his pomp as star of TV's *The A-Team*) complaining about people wondering if his gaudy jewellery was real gold, he quipped, 'I thought I could talk but you're the greatest of all time.'

When the microphone was eventually thrust into his hand, Ali was somehow invigorated and rather than eviscerating Dundee he told the story of their relationship. It ran from their first meeting at the Columbia Hotel in Louisville when the 16-year-old Cassius Clay called the trainer – in town working with Willie Pastrano, the future light-heavyweight champion – from the lobby to tell him he was going to be the greatest fighter of all time. 'I remember putting my hand over the receiver,' said Dundee, 'and tellin' Willie, "There's some kind of nut on the phone."'

* * *

A sold-out Madison Square Garden echoed to 'Ali! Ali! Ali!' as he walked towards the ring on 31 March. It was just like the nights of old except he wore a blue dress shirt and a dickie bow as the outside referee for a new WWF (World Wrestling Federation) event called 'Wrestlemania'. The rest of the crew included Liberace (official celebrity timekeeper), Cyndi Lauper (managing one of the distaff competitors) and Billy Martin, former manager of the New York Yankees. None got the response afforded Ali during his introduction. 'When the show started,' said Hulk Hogan, 'and I saw Muhammad Ali was there, and Billy Martin, and the Rockettes, and all these actors, I said, "Holy shit! This is huge!"'

One million-plus fans watched the matches live at closed-circuit arenas around the country. As outside referee, Ali's function was to maintain order during a bout pitting Mr T and Hulk Hogan against Rowdy Roddy Piper and Mr Wonderful (Paul Orndorff). A tall order. Once things went awry during the showdown, Ali got involved, repeatedly throwing punches at Piper before manhandling him out through the ropes.

* * *

The morning after 'Wrestlemania', Muhammad Ali touched down in Galveston for three days of events to raise money for the proposed building of a memorial to Jack Johnson, the former heavyweight champion and the Texan city's most famous son. 'Jack Johnson was the greatest boxer, to me,' said Ali. 'You may be surprised at me saying that – of all time. He wasn't just a boxer, he was a freedom fighter. He fought in a time when black people weren't even free enough to walk on the same side of the street as the white people. He fought for his beliefs. He married a white woman when a black man couldn't look at a white woman. The Ku Klux Klan would kill and lynch people. He would drive up and down the boulevard in his convertible, a black beret on his head, a cigar in his teeth and two blonde, blue-eyed women sittin' next to him. He was one *ba-a-a-ad* man.'

On his second day in town, Ali toured the Shrines Burns Institute, spending an hour making children smile, handing one little girl an autographed note that read, 'Love Always', accompanied by a smiley face. 'We've seen a lot of celebrities come to town, but a lot just don't think about the children,' said a spokeswoman for the hospital. 'The kids were just absolutely knocked out.'

While the purpose of the trip was to lend his celebrity to a fundraising 'Night at the Fights' at the Moody Civic Centre, Ali, of course, found time to be sidetracked. Walking through the San Luis Hotel, he spotted Jeffery 'Chill' Alexander from Cisco Junior College, in town for a student government convention. 'That guy looks just like Joe Frazier,' he shouted before walking towards Alexander, throwing jabs.

Ali had chosen his target wisely. Alexander started to throw fake punches back in his direction and to mouth off too. 'I just played along with it,' said Alexander. 'I started jabbing at the air, too, then I leaned against a wall and said, "Rope-a-dope, rope-a-dope," and he tapped his fists against my head real fast. It was pretty cool.'

Moments later, Alexander and his travelling companion were carrying Ali's bags up to his room, where the NCAA college basketball championship game between Villanova and Georgetown had just started on television. They were invited to stay and watch with Ali. 'I don't even remember if we really had a specific conversation; it was just guys watching a game,' said Alexander. 'That was the best part – it wasn't like he was on a pedestal or anything, he was just hanging out with us. I was just in awe of how big he was. We were just so little, so small compared to him.'

Like everybody who spent time around Ali, they were inevitably exposed to the full legerdemain of his magic act and the student interlopers were still in his entourage as he did a press conference with Sugar Ray Leonard, another celebrity attendee, to promote the Johnson project. Alexander's final interaction with him took place in the corridors of the San Luis Hotel. 'Ali snuck up behind me and did something with his hand, rubbing his fingers together,' he said. 'And when I turned around because it startled me, he's standing there and he leans in and says, "That's what a butterfly sounds like."'

* * *

Before Marvin Hagler took on Thomas Hearns in 'The War' at Caesar's Palace, Las Vegas, on 15 April, a roll call of ex-champions was introduced to the crowd. Each got an ovation but the reception for Muhammad Ali was very different. Sixteen thousand fans chanted 'Ali! Ali! Ali!', the chorus going on so long that he lifted his finger to his mouth to urge them to stop.

* * *

Jim Cassidy was a boxing fan who would end up promoting fights in upstate New York. When word reached him on 27 April that Muhammad Ali was visiting Rochester City Hall, he went straight there. In town to drum up interest in a WBA heavyweight title fight between Tony Tubbs and Greg Page taking place down the road in Buffalo two nights later, Ali posed for photographs with Don King and Mayor Tom Ryan. Then he met Cassidy. 'I go there and didn't have anything for Muhammad to sign, but I did have a $20 bill in my wallet,' said Cassidy. 'I thought, "Couldn't be better spent than to have him sign it". It's been one of my greatest treasures.'

The Tubbs-Page fight at Memorial Auditorium was such a non-event that, growing quickly tired of the lack of action, the crowd started booing then regularly segued into 'Ali! Ali! Ali!' During the eighth and ninth rounds, Ali rose to his feet and joined in the chant. Between the 10th and 11th, he climbed through the ropes and briefly shadow-boxed across the ring. His performance drew the loudest ovation of the night.

* * *

On 28 April, a headline on the front page of the *New York Times* read, 'AGE HASN'T COOLED THE FIRE INSIDE ALI!' Beneath was a lengthy feature by Ira Berkow, a veteran sportswriter whose career covering the fighter stretched back more than two decades.

Berkow had visited him at his Los Angeles mansion earlier that month, arriving on a morning when Gary Catona had just finished up the now daily one-hour voice lesson. 'Muhammad never really had strong vocal muscles,' said Catona. 'He used to scream out his words. His normal speech was never a normal speech. It's like building body muscles, you've got to work at it. He sings the sounds of the scales. "Ah! Ah! Ah! Ah!", his voice rising at each "Ah!"'

For Berkow, Ali delivered one-liners from his back catalogue and performed magic tricks. When the house phone went, he answered, 'City morgue!' There was less joking when he was asked about his health. 'I don't feel sick,' said Ali. 'But I'm always tired.'

Touring the residence, he showed Berkow some memorabilia. A LeRoy Neiman painting, a pair of gloves signed by Sylvester Stallone and addressed, 'To the champion of champions', and a robe on which multi-coloured sequins spell out the words, 'The People's Champion', a gift from Elvis Presley. 'What am I doin' now, oh, I'm so busy,' he said as he sifted through letters from fans in England, Germany and Bangladesh. 'I'm busy every day. I've got all this mail to answer – they're startin' fan clubs for me all over the world, in Asia, in Europe, in Ireland, in China, in Paris. But my mission is to establish Islamic evangelists, and to tour the world spreadin' Islam.'

* * *

Muhammad Ali arrived at the Great Mosque of Xi'an in China on 17 May, stopping to pray at a site where Chinese Muslims first built a place of worship in 742AD. 'To be there with my brothers,' said Ali, 'people so different and from so far away, was unforgettable.'

His co-religionists besieged him for autographs and Imam Ma Liangji summed up what his visit meant: 'Muhammad Ali has won fame for Muslims the world over. And Chinese Muslims take great pride in his achievements. We wish him good health and greater contributions to Muslim solidarity and world peace.'

Following an official invitation from Deng Xiaoping, leader of the Chinese government in Beijing, whom he had met on a previous visit in 1979, Ali embarked on an 11-day tour. Twenty-six years after Mao Zedong banned boxing due to its brutality and capitalistic overtones, he was tasked with promoting its resurgence. 'Ali, we warmly welcome you,' announced the front page of *Sport News*, 'the boxing king that shook the world, an outstanding black American.'

For his visit, a makeshift ring was erected at the Physical Education Institute in the Chinese capital and, once he'd taken off his jacket and tie, Ali fought five one-minute rounds against hand-picked students. He ran through the usual crowd-pleasing routine, unfurling windmill punches and even pretending to go down during an encounter with the smallest opponent. 'The coaches told us only to hit him in the stomach,' said one of the fighters. 'We were warned he is not in good health.'

Ali made all the right noises about his opponents. 'They've got great potential,' he said. They're not big but they can take a punch, and they are determined and courageous. I hope to come back with a programme to train Chinese boxers.'

Aside from boxing, he spent time at the Summer Palace but a trip to the Great Wall was worryingly cut short due to fatigue. At another press conference he signalled the end of the event by lapsing into a giant yawn, although not before delivering a knowing reference to China's strict one-child policy and the acknowledged preference of most families for boys rather than girls. 'When people ask how many children I have,' said Ali, 'I say one son and seven mistakes.'

* * *

Doin' Time opened in movie theatres on 19 May. A pastiche of the *Police Academy* genre, it is set in the John Dillinger Memorial Penitentiary – 'the only prison in the world where you break out. Laughing!' according to the tag line. At one point, the main character (played by Jeff Altman) gets into the boxing ring and, as he waits for the bell, hallucinates and pictures Muhammad Ali, accompanied by his fabled cornerman Bundini Brown, reciting, 'Float like a butterfly, sting like a bee'.

For this cameo, Ali received top billing in the credits of a film *TV Guide* described as 'wretched as they come, filled with numerous unfunny gags that follow the expected sexual, scatological, and foul-mouthed route'.

* * *

Mayor Tom Bradley of Los Angeles declared 20 May to be Muhammad Ali Day in the city. Two nights later, 650 people paid $500 a plate to witness Jose Sulaiman, president of the World Boxing Council (WBC), present Ali with the governing body's 'Lifetime Achievement' award at the Beverley Hills Hotel. Natalie Cole sang the national anthem and President Ronald Reagan delivered a videotaped message, assuring him, 'You will always be the greatest.'

Among those paying homage were actresses Bo Derek and Debbie Allen, as well as Olympians Mark Spitz and Edwin Moses. From boxing came Thomas Hearns, Marvin Hagler, Sugar Ray Robinson, Sugar Ray Leonard and Henry Armstrong. All proceeds went to Safety and Performance Advancement through Research (SPAR), a foundation at UCLA being funded by the WBC to use science to improve the health of fighters.

Bob Arum testified that he learned more about promoting from Ali than anybody else, Sugar Ray Leonard boldly declared himself to be prettier than his hero and Don King said the former champion was 'a great human being'. Journalists hoping for quotes from the guest of honour were disappointed when he was whisked past them by security.

* * *

In the first week of June, Muhammad Ali was in the Atlanta City Council chambers in Georgia promoting Champ Gourmet

Chocolate Chip cookies and explaining his decision not to sample the merchandise. 'I'm on a diet,' he announced. 'If I eat one, I'll eat 20.' Taking a shot at the long-established Famous Amos' brand, he added, 'There are a lot of cookies on the market but I'm the one that's famous. This is one of the few products I'd put my name on. I don't put my name on anything unless it's great. These cookies are the greatest of all times!'

He was sanguine about the prospects for the confectionery, pointing out that he merely needed 'all the people who heard my name to just buy one bag'.

* * *

Muhammad Ali was the keynote speaker for the Galveston Chapter of the NAACP's Freedom Fund banquet at the Holiday Inn at the Strand on 17 June. As part of the city's Juneteenth (federal holiday commemorating the emancipation of African-American slaves) celebrations, the theme was 'Stand up Black Americans – Love and Help One Another.'

Before an audience of 250, he betrayed no signs of health problems as he ran through the highlights of his career and his various struggles, pausing eventually to conclude, 'Maaan, that was some heavy stuff!'

He feigned surprise when organisers thanked him for giving his time to their cause for free and then delivered an old meditation on racial identity. 'There are still positive images of the term "white" and negative images of the term "black",' he said. 'I wonder how whites would feel if for hundreds of years, they only saw a black Jesus on the cross and saw pictures of the Last Supper with only blacks! I'm working to break down those white/black and superior/inferior images. What has really gotten me to where I am today is the fact I stood up for my people and what I believed in.'

* * *

At the Marriott Ballroom in Irvine, California, Robert Shannon made his fifth outing as a professional against Ralph Gutierrez. An undefeated super-bantamweight out of Edmonds, Washington who had represented the USA at the Los Angeles Olympics, Shannon cruised to a majority decision but the entire card was overshadowed by the presence in the crowd of Muhammad Ali, a friend of the fighter.

Afterwards, Ali went to Shannon's dressing room to congratulate the prospect on his night's work. There, he sat down at a table with a white cloth stretched on it and wrote, 'Muhammad Ali – After me, there will never be another. June 24 – 85'. Then, he drew a smiley face and a tiny boxing ring beneath it.

* * *

On 25 June, eight years and one week after they were married, Muhammad Ali and Veronica Porche (29), his third wife, filed for divorce in Los Angeles Superior Court, citing 'irreconcilable differences', claiming an amicable agreement had already been reached between the couple.

A statement was released to the press that read, 'Both parties maintain the utmost admiration, love and respect for each other. Our deep friendship remains intact. Muhammad and Veronica wish each other the best of luck and success and are pleased to have the public share this desire with them.' The couple's two children, Hana and Laila, were then eight and seven.

* * *

Muhammad Ali touched down at Ben Gurion International Airport in Israel on 27 June and announced he was there to negotiate the release of Shi'ite prisoners being held in the Atlit Detention Camp. 'I'm here to discuss the release and plight of 700 Muslim brothers of mine, who are detained here in Israel, with the proper authorities,' he told journalists. 'I have some ideas but I'm afraid I can't reveal them to you. I must first tell it to the proper people involved.'

When asked if he was also trying to simultaneously secure the release of 39 American hostages being held by Shi'ites in Beirut, Ali responded, 'I didn't come here for that.'

He met for 40 minutes with Israel's deputy foreign minister Ronnie Milo. Besieged by reporters on the way out of that meeting, Ali refused to comment on their conversation, saying only, 'I will not discuss what we talked about, it will ruin the plans.' For his part, Milo described Ali as a 'humanitarian American' and revealed that he asked him to use his influence to assist his own compatriots being held in Lebanon.

* * *

Joey Keene, a local middleweight with a 6–2 record, pummelled Salt Lake City's JJ Cottrell in the middleweight main event at the Western Idaho Fairgrounds in Boise on 23 July. The crowd of 1,700 included Muhammad Ali. Earlier that day, he made headlines by restating his belief that the campaign to ban boxing was racist. 'Unconsciously, I think it's a move because blacks dominate it,' he said. 'They sign contracts for $5m dollars. Two ghetto boys, who can't read and write, get into the ring and $5m! All of a sudden, the whites love us so much they want to protect us. What we need is more white champions and more white contenders who can make a good show. People love to see their own kind on top.'

Ali also sat for a live interview with local sports reporter Mark Johnson. When greeting him, Johnson pointed out a shaving nick had left more blood on his face than any of his fights. Ali responded by asking, 'Who are you? The local Howard Cosell!'

At the Fairgrounds, he got into the ring and shadow-boxed, to the usual raucous cheers. After a throng of fans delayed his exit from the arena, one of his entourage beseeched him to stop signing autographs so they could leave. 'Not until everyone gets what they came here for,' said Ali. He kept signing.

* * *

Ed Schuyler Jr of the Associated Press, who spent more than two decades covering Muhammad Ali's career, caught up with him in New York in the last week of August. A conversation between old friends. Ali boasted about stopping traffic in Harlem, recounted his trip to China and announced the formation of his official Muhammad Ali Fan Club. Members were to be known as 'Ali's Allies' and most of the fees they paid would be donated to charity to help the children of the world.

Ali dismissed Schuyler's concerns about his health, wishing people would worry more about the welfare of really sick people. He joked that he was just 'a washed-up old bum', referred to the peak of his fistic powers as 'the good old days' and declared, 'There's no one like me. I'll bet it'll be a long time before there's another me.'

* * *

Cus D'Amato's funeral took place in Catskill, New York on 8 November. Among the bouquets piled high, one contained a brief, significant note, saying, 'Cus, You were "The Greatest!"' Decades earlier, D'Amato had been in Indianapolis training Floyd Patterson when a brash teenager from Louisville then named Cassius Clay requested an audience and the chance to pick his brain. They had been friends ever since.

* * *

In his 16th professional fight, Cassius Clay stopped Archie Moore, the former light-heavyweight champion, a few weeks short of his 49th birthday, in four rounds. Twenty-three years later, on 9 November, Muhammad Ali was ringside at the Portland Sports Arena in Oregon, where the announcer for the evening was Billy Moore, Archie's son. After Moore invited the esteemed guest into the ring, Ali stalked the canvas, happened upon the promoter Paul Brown and declared, 'I want you!'

Within seconds, both men had taken off their sports coats, donned gloves and begun mock hostilities. 'One round, no bell!' shouted Ali.

After they'd put on a show for a few minutes, the bell did toll but Ali wasn't done. 'He called me n*****!' he roared, pointing out a white man in the audience – his next opponent. 'The fan crawled through the ring ropes, shook Ali's gloved hand, put on a pair of gloves and punched Ali in the mid-section,' wrote John Pisapia of the *Daily News*. 'Ali pulled a wicked uppercut from the fan's face and then landed a jab. Down went the fan. A few moments later, the bell sounded. The two touched gloves then returned to their previous spots – the fan to his folding chair and Ali to his place in history.'

* * *

James and Renita Dozier were browsing the Military TV and Stereo in Fayetteville, North Carolina on 23 November when Muhammad Ali walked in. The Rocky Mount couple, a pair of karate black belts, were thrilled to meet him. James Dozier informed Ali that throughout his own martial arts career, he'd adopted 'float like a butterfly, sting like a bee' as his motto. Ali had been making appearances at the chain of Military TV stores all through the state that month, leading to rumours he was actually a shareholder in the company.

* * *

The Christmas Eve crowd at Patsy Stone's Cosmetic Studios in Louisville were treated to impromptu poetry and magic when Muhammad Ali came in for a facial. 'I feel like I'm in a morgue,' he joked when Marilyn Williams, a beautician and former neighbour, draped him in a white sheet as he lay in the chair. 'I used to be so scared of him,' she said. 'But he's just a big baby.'

A photograph of that famous visage wearing a mask of white cream featured in newspapers across the world over the next few days. 'Louisville, I'm so proud to be from Louisville,' said Ali, who told employees he'd returned to spend the holiday with his mother, Odessa Clay. 'I've conquered the boxing world and when people think of the best one in the world, he's from Louisville!'

ROUND FIVE

1986

The right hand that once was a blur signed autographs
as laboriously as a child learning how to write. His
signature was barely legible. Mainly, he just stared
blankly as if a million miles away. He almost never
blinked, which was eerie

Bob Rubin, *Miami Herald*, 15 March

ON SATURDAY, 11 January, a photograph on the front page of the *Pittsburgh Post-Gazette* showed Muhammad Ali kissing Coretta King on the cheek at a press conference in Atlanta marking the start of festivities surrounding the first national holiday honouring her late husband, Martin Luther King. Ali had already been in town for over a week, at the behest of Don King. Always tuned to the cash-in frequency, the wily promoter had recognised the events surrounding MLK represented an opportunity to turn a buck.

King had pieced together a night of boxing at the city's Omni Arena, headlined by 'Terrible' Tim Witherspoon challenging Tony 'TNT' Tubbs for the WBA version of the world heavyweight title. In typically brazen style, he ran advertisements calling it 'KING'S DREAM', showing photographs of MLK next to the words 'I have a dream!' and himself alongside his infamous catchphrase, 'Only in America'.

To lend credibility, he had persuaded Ali to get involved, ostensibly as a celebrity sparring partner for both Witherspoon and Tubbs. In a classic boondoggle, one of King's spokesmen, Paul Sciria, even floated a groundless rumour that Ali was seriously considering another comeback and might be getting back in the ring too. Anything for a headline or a column inch.

That Ali was in no condition to spar was obvious when he entered the ring in Atlanta. The sight of the corpulent 43-year-old working out in a rubberised suit, a staple of his training routine in his pomp, was enough for the *South Florida Sun-Sentinel* to run an unflattering picture called 'Pant-A in Atlanta' and to wonder, 'Guess he needs the money?' 'Had you not known, you couldn't have known it was Muhammad Ali up there in the ring, his body hidden in a baggy blue sweatsuit, his face lost under a fighter's headgear,' wrote Dave Kindred. 'The man is 44 years old next Friday, the father of seven daughters and a son, three times a husband and three times the heavyweight champion. We were in a small room made into a fight gym, the lighting dim, cigarette smoke moving in the dark. You knew it was Ali because he had told you he would be there.'

Kindred and other witnesses knew what they saw in the downtown Marriott wasn't actual sparring, merely Ali lending his fading grandeur to a mediocre boxing promotion. As they sparred, Witherspoon pulled his punches, threw no headshots and after ten lacklustre rounds, put his arm around Ali and touched his cheek with his glove. It was the affectionate embrace of a 28-year-old who had spent his formative years watching the older fighter take on the world and the early stages of his own career as his sparring partner. 'How do you feel?' asked one of the reporters when they joined Ali in his hotel room afterwards.

The answer was mumbled, indistinct. 'Excuse me,' went the follow-up. 'With my hands,' quipped Ali, his eyes widening at his own gag. 'Seriously, though, how's your health?'

His response was to let his arms fall limp at his side, to close his eyes and let his head roll on the couch. 'Seriously, Ali?' 'Good enough to go a good nine rounds,' he replied.

Glimpses of the Ali magic endured outside the ring. He pinched a small child on the cheek at one training session, looked up at his dad and asked, 'This your boy? Ugly as you are!'

Aside from fleeting cameos of his old charisma, Ali did his bit to promote the fight. Having sparred both men, he told a press conference he was friends with the combatants (Tubbs had also been a sparring partner of his) so couldn't root for one over the other. But he did bring humour to his analysis. 'Tim, when you used to spar with me, you didn't talk,' said Ali. 'Tony, you didn't talk either. Now both of you are talking and making lots of money. Me? I'm unemployed! I'll see you both after the show.'

Evincing his capacity for exaggeration, something King was paying him to provide, Ali compared Witherspoon to Sonny Liston and Tubbs to himself. If those were not analogies any serious-minded analyst was bringing to bear on this contest, the crowd in the Omni Arena were thrilled when Ali walked towards his seat on fight night. Beseeched at every turn by fans desperate to reach out and touch the hem of his black tuxedo, the ex-champ heard 'Ali, Ali, Ali' echoing through the chamber.

All similarities with great boxing nights ended about there. 'King put on seven fights with out-of-shape heavyweights who weighed an aggregate of 3,212 pounds,' wrote Jack Newfield. 'Every fight stank. The night began with about 5,000 fans, but only about 300 remained when the last bout ended at 1am. Anyone who ever wanted to make a documentary about what's wrong with boxing should have had a few camera crews shooting this *Animal House* card.'

* * *

At the Primary Children's Medical Centre in Salt Lake City, Utah on 24 January, Muhammad Ali spent three hours visiting patients and performing magic tricks by the bedsides of those who were unable to get up and watch him put on a show. 'Are you a wrestler,' asked one boy. 'No, I'm an old fighter,' replied Ali. 'Then fight me!' said the boy.

Ali smiled.

* * *

Muhammad Ali met Wanda Bolton in 1973 when he was 31 and and she was a 17-year-old high school senior visiting his training camp in Deer Lake, Pennsylvania with her parents. A relationship ensued, she became pregnant and gave birth to a daughter, Khaliah, in 1974. Eleven years later, the former Wanda Bolton (now going by the name Aaisha Ali) sued the father of her daughter for paternity and child support, claiming the couple had been married in Florida in 1975 in an Islamic ceremony not recognised by the American legal system.

On 28 January, the case came before Judge Stephen Lachs in the Los Angeles Superior Court. The hearing was an acrimonious affair as attorneys for Ali, Aaisha Ali and Ali's third wife Veronica, represented because her divorce agreement was questioned in the suit, did verbal battle.

The warring parties created a soap operatic scene, with Aaisha and Veronica pacing up and down outside the courtroom for much of the heated proceedings while Ali sat in the back row with his 11-year-old daughter Khaliah, spending the entire episode cuddling and whispering to her.

Eventually, it was agreed that Ali would set up a trust fund worth $200,000 to cater for his daughter over the next ten years, pay for her medical insurance and give her mother $5,000 from the sale of the $660,000 house he had shared with Veronica. 'I want to take care of all my kids,' said Ali as he cuddled Khaliah some more while talking to reporters.

* * *

At a press conference at the Beverley Wiltshire Hotel in Los Angeles on 6 February, the Children's Peace Foundation announced plans for Muhammad Ali to lead a Children's Peace Journey to Britain, India, the Soviet Union, China, the Vatican and the United States later in the year. Setting out from Washington, he would be accompanied by 50 children selected from 50 different countries on a trip designed to 'stop the nuclear arms race and work towards peace'.

'I'm fighting another tough fight,' said Ali.

* * *

Wearing a pinstripe suit and patent leather shoes, Muhammad Ali arrived at the Virginia State Capitol in Richmond on 13 March to meet Lieutenant-Governor L. Douglas Wilder, then the highest-ranking elected black official in the country. 'I haven't met many black governors,' he said as they toured the building, accompanied by a phalanx of reporters and a burgeoning crew of civil servants, all caught up in the force field that was Ali barrelling through any place. 'I'm unemployed and looking for another job!' shouted Ali when he sat in the chair from which Wilder presided over the state senate. 'Maybe I'll run for governor.'

'Then I'm going to start fighting,' quipped Wilder, who won the Bronze Star for valour in the Korean War. Capitol employees filed up to the podium where Ali sat, flanked by the flags of the United States and the state of Virginia. He shadow-boxed, signed autographs and handed out a pamphlet called 'Religion on the Line', which distils Muslim philosophy for prisoners. When journalists questioned him about the current generation of boxers not being as good as him, he refused to take the bait. 'They always say that,' said Ali. 'They said that about Joe Louis when I was boxing.'

By that point in his life, Ali's property portfolio included a 47-acre horse farm near Afton Mountain, just outside Charlotttesville, where he spent a couple of months each year. Locals had grown used to the sight of him at the Downtown Mall in the town and he told the reporters how much he enjoyed the serene ambience of the surrounding area. 'I love it,' said Ali of life on the farm. 'It's peaceful, it's quiet, it's clean.'

However, the true nature of his drop-in at the Capitol was revealed by Richard Hirschfeld, his attorney, lurking as ever in the background. He boasted about Ali's financial good health, bizarrely mentioning he'd created 'a very nice trust at Sovran Bank yesterday', and that he now conducted a lot of business through a stockbroker in Charlottesville. Regarding Ali's recent divorce, Hirschfeld reckoned the superannuated fighter 'might like to marry a nice, quiet, dignified Charlottesville girl'.

That scuttlebutt was only to whet reporters' appetites. Then Hirschfeld gave them the real goods. Ali, he said, was interested in using a struggling Volvo plant in Chesapeake to make a customised sports car called the 'Ali 5000 3 WC' – the initials standing for three times world champion. Similar to the Vipre then being produced in Canada with a Pontiac Fiero engine, he wanted to make vehicles predominantly for the export market. That his photo op alongside Warner had been prefaced with a private audience with Governor Gerard L. Baliles was supposed to indicate this was a serious business venture.

* * *

Twenty-four hours later, the budding automobile tycoon was back in the ring in a makeshift affair hastily assembled outdoors at the Dade-Centre in Florida. Wearing a pinstripe suit and loafers, Muhammad Ali squared off with seven-year-old Thaddeus Ambrose. Dressed in full boxing gear and game for a fight, the little tyke was a blur of flailing fists and jabs as he went after the former champion. One photograph captured the boy seconds after missing with a wild right as Ali took evasive action.

Ali toured the three campuses of the Miami-Dade Community College as part of a push to promote 'health and fitness'. To those who turned out to glimpse their hero, that assignment appeared kind of ironic. When he spoke with a slur, more than one onlooker wondered aloud if he was 'wasted'. After he started to deliver a speech to students, many requested the microphone be turned up because his voice – that bombastic voice famous the world over – was so low they couldn't make out what he was saying. 'Though he looked wasted, he wasn't,' wrote Bob Rubin in the *Miami Herald*. 'It wasn't drugs or booze that have turned the former heavyweight champion into a slow-moving, dull-eyed figure with a bloated face and low, slurred speech. He spoke infrequently, the most telling evidence of the complete transformation from the Ali that was. The Ali shuffle was just that. He had to be helped up on to a poolside podium. He moved painfully slowly. He did everything painfully slowly.'

While younger spectators were taken aback at the slow-motion version of this man whom they'd heard so much about, he was still soundtracked by 'Ali! Ali! Ali!' as he moved through the Dade-Centre. The crowd surrounding him appeared determined to follow him, even on a visit to the men's room. During a question-and-answer session, he was asked about his conversion to Islam, a decision that owed much to his experiences at Temple No. 29, a mosque in Miami's Overtown neighbourhood. 'Angel's food cake is white, devil's food cake is black!' he said, launching into a familiar soliloquy. Except with one crucial difference this time around. 'He recited the spiel by rote,' observed Rubin. 'It was like listening to a record playing at the wrong speed.'

* * *

At the 12th annual 'Tribute to a Black American' ceremony in Atlantic City on 11 April, the National Conference of Black Mayors honoured Muhammad Ali with an award recognising his achievements in boxing. With Reverend Jesse Jackson and Marvellous Marvin Hagler among those paying homage, Dick Gregory, the comedian and activist, told Ali, 'You mean so much to so many people.'

* * *

On 28 May, Muhammad Ali was driving his Rolls-Royce in West Hollywood when he cut across traffic to make a left turn and hit Gregory Gray, a 26-year-old motorcyclist. Gray was taken to hospital and treated for bruises to a leg before being released. Unhurt, Ali was not cited for his part in the accident.

* * *

Four months after a company called Champion Brands launched a brand of Muhammad Ali shoe polish, replete with his smiling face on the cover, sales had surpassed $500,000 and prompted Sara Lee Corp, owner of Kiwi shoe polish, to file a lawsuit in Charlotte, North Carolina. Accusing the company of violating federal trade laws, the allegation was that Champion had produced a tin that brazenly copied Kiwi's distinctive red, black and gold colour scheme and directly lifted the instructions, word for word, from their cans. 'Anyone who can read can see my name's not Kiwi,' said Ali on 11 June. 'And I hope I don't look like no kiwi bird.'

Lawyers for Kiwi sought $1m in damages and for Champion to remove their copycat tins from sale. They also pointed out that one year previously, Arthur Morrison, a former record producer styling himself Ali's partner in the venture, met with Kiwi and showed them a sample can. When they saw the colours being used then, they warned him not to proceed with something so similar or face legal action.

Born in Tulsa, Oklahoma in 1947, Morrison had led a peripatetic life, living for spells in Colorado, New York, Jamaica, the Bahamas and England. He claimed to be a graduate of the University of the West Indies in Kingston, but the academic qualification was as invented as his story of how he first met Ali. He reckoned they shared a cell when Ali was briefly imprisoned in 1968 for a traffic offence but Ali had no recollection of that encounter.

Still, he carved out a corner in Ali's entourage and cropped up regularly in dispatches, most famously as producer of a bizarre piece of vinyl called *The Adventures of Ali and His Gang vs Mr Tooth Decay*. It was released in 1976 as part of a national dental hygiene campaign and featured guest appearances from Frank Sinatra (playing a shopkeeper trying to sell children ice-cream that will wreck their teeth), Richie Havens, Howard Cosell and Ossie Davis. Morrison is listed as both writer and producer of the record.

Ali claimed he had pulled out of a proposed deal with Kiwi when he learned they had a factory in South Africa, then a country still operating an apartheid regime. He further alleged that Kiwi had tried to use his name to regain access to Nigeria, having been banned from that country. 'Let the people decide if they're making a mistake in selecting our brand,' said Ali.

* * *

At a press conference in Hamilton, Ontario on 16 June, Protein Foods Group Inc. and Muhammad Ali signed a contract allowing them to produce chicken food products for the global market emblazoned with Ali's name and logo. 'We hope the most dramatic impact will be on the African continent,' said Joe Yarem, founder and chairman of Protein Foods. 'He'll get a royalty depending on how successful we are. If we're right, he'll be paid handsomely. Our marketing people say having him on the label will sell a lot of the product.' 'And you will pay!' said Ali, smiling alongside him.

* * *

Terence Moore, a columnist with the *Atlanta Constitution*, was granted an audience with Muhammad Ali in his suite at the downtown Marriott. When he arrived, Ali was still getting dressed, finally emerging in running gear and launching into a 15-minute magic show. The performance had gone on so long that it left little time for Moore to ask questions. So, the journalist did what every fan would have done, unfurling a poster of *The Thrilla in Manila* and asking him to sign. 'He reached for the pen, only to have it slip from his hand,' wrote Moore. 'He grabbed the pen again, smoothed out the poster with soft strokes and studied the scene of his jab settling against Joe Frazier's right cheek. Ali was motionless. I was speechless. Then I suggested that Ali address his message on the poster to me. He wrote, "To Terry, Love, Muhammad Ali – June 18 – 86." It seemed a century passed between Ali's scribbling of "To" and "86" and the closer he moved to "86" the shakier his hand became.'

* * *

Arthur Morrison, Ali's partner in Champion Brands shoe polish, was arrested on his way to Charlotte airport in North Carolina on 19 July, on an outstanding warrant from Washington, where he was facing a felony charge for snatching his daughter, Sunshine, from the home of his ex-wife in 1984. Over the previous weeks, Morrison had made headlines for delivering Bishop Desmond Tutu for phone interviews with newspapers such as the *Charlotte Observer* as part of his ongoing campaign against Kiwi shoe polish.

* * *

Three thousand people thronged the Sunrise Mall in Brownsville, the largest crowd the place had ever seen. They had come to this corner of the most southerly town in Texas on 24 July to see Muhammad Ali. Having spent 45 minutes signing autographs and posing for pictures, he embarked on a chaotic walk through the complex, his every step tracked by multitudes clapping him on his way. Over the next 36 hours, he traversed the Rio Grande Valley, appearing at Valle Vista Mall in Harlingen, El Centro Mall in Pharr and La Plaza Mall in McAllen.

There was also a luncheon with children from the Settlement Home charity and Ali was the star guest at a night of professional boxing at the Mercedes Livestock Showgrounds on 25 July. 'He was already showing signs of Parkinson's disease, and he would talk very low and slow,' said Sergeant David Wise, one of the off-duty officers from the Cameron County Sheriff's Department, assigned as his security. 'But he was such a character and genuinely liked everyone he met. The second you met him, it was like he had been your friend for years. He was just that kind of person.'

Ali already had a good friend in the area. Gil Martinez, a promising bantamweight out of Tennessee who'd been a team-mate of his on US amateur squads in the late-1950s, had settled in Brownsville. 'This man was the national, AAU and Golden Gloves champion,' said Ali, bigging up his old pal when the two climbed into the ring at Brownsville Boys' Club. 'He looks small but he's the world's best amateur. But I'm going to beat him. He won't stand a chance!'

As Ali spoke, Martinez wore the grin of a man being eulogised by the most loquacious boxer ever. The rules of their subsequent spar were simple. One round. No time limit. First man to stop moving lost. Then they went at it, like seasoned campaigners, the smaller man giving Ali enough room to be Ali. Even in a suit, he delighted the crowd with selections from his repertoire of theatrical staredowns and exaggerated windmill punches. For an encore, he allowed a local hopeful to whale on him.

At the more serious pro card the next night, Ali was invited into the ring and presented with the keys to the town of Mercedes and a pair of boxing gloves. His brief rendition of the 'Ali Shuffle' prompted spectators to break into, 'Ali! Ali! Ali!' The bouts went on so long that Ali was late getting back to Harlingen, where he was staying. But the locals were ready.

Sergeant Wise drove ahead to the Las Cazuelas Mexican restaurant, strode in the door shortly before 1am and announced, 'I know this might sound crazy and hard to believe, but in a few minutes, Muhammad Ali is about to come in here to eat.' The staff and remaining customers looked at him as if he had lost his mind until Ali arrived a few moments later. Even after eating, there was further drama when he went back to his hotel and remembered he'd left his key behind in Las Cazuelas.

Dispatching his limo back to the restaurant, he stayed in the parking lot with Sergeant Wise and other members of his security team, shadow-boxing with them. 'It was unreal, surreal, because you can imagine,' said Wise, 'Muhammad Ali, three-time world champion in the parking lot of a hotel in Harlingen at two o'clock in the morning. Unbelievable.'

When the limo returned, Wise escorted an exhausted Ali to his room, where he immediately threw himself on to the bed. 'It's been a long day, huh, champ?' asked Wise. 'It's been a long 20 years,' replied Ali.

* * *

On Monday, 27 October, the day before the Statue of Liberty's 100th birthday, 80 Americans from 42 ethnic groups were awarded the Ellis Island Medal of Honour by the National Ethnic Coalition of Organisations. Two dozen recipients, including John Denver, Arnold Palmer, Walter Cronkite, Gregory Peck and Martina Navratilova, didn't bother to turn up. Among those who did attend were Muhammad Ali, Rosa Parks, Victor Borge, Joe Di Maggio, Anita Bryant and Donald Trump.

Many present were unsure what they were being lauded for by interior secretary Donald Hodel as he draped medals around their necks. 'I've no idea what's happening,' said Di Maggio. 'I'm just here because I was invited here.' 'It's one of the biggest honours I've ever received,' said Ali. 'I'm happy to be part of it.'

* * *

Seven months after Muhammad Ali lit up the Capitol in Richmond, the proposed Ali Motors remained a live prospect in Virginia. On 30 October, the *Washington Post* carried a feature by Barbara Carton about South Boston, a depressed town two hours south of Chesapeake that was the proposed latest location for the factory.

In Dickerson's Pool Room there, Carton found jobless men hopeful Ali was really going to bring 410 new jobs to Halifax County. Unemployment was near enough nine per cent and the tobacco farming for which the area was once famous wasn't what it used to be. 'We need more industry that pays,' said 29-year-old Melvin Stephens, a seasonal worker earning $4 an hour picking tobacco. 'I think it would be a great boost to the county to have a famous person come in, especially a celebrity like Muhammad Ali.'

Everybody Carton spoke to sang from the same sheet. 'I think it would be great because it would open up a lot of jobs for people who need them,' said Reggie Briggs, a 25-year-old machine operator at a furniture plant. 'If Ali really does come.'

Carton's report delved into the precarious finances of the initiative and how those involved had already applied for $9.26m in industrial bonds from the Halifax County Development Authority. It concluded with Scott Eubanks of the Virginia economic development department warning that Ali Motors still had to find its own money to make the project viable. And, worryingly, despite the fact his name was the unique selling point, Carton included the ominous line, 'Ali was not available for comment'.

* * *

At the World Boxing Hall of Fame dinner at the Airport Marriott in Los Angeles on 8 November, 900 people saw Muhammad Ali accept his induction. He arrived through the back door of the hotel, and, unusually, was surrounded by six bodyguards as he moved through a crowd largely drawn from the sport he once bestrode. The audience included Aileen Eaton, impresario of combat sports in Southern California, often credited with playing a part in the young Clay's embrace of bombast and braggadocio as marketing tools.

In his speech, the tuxedo-clad Ali didn't cite Eaton but told the familiar tale of how seeing the wrestler 'Gorgeous George' sparked his personality makeover from humility to hubris. He also offered the audience and about 100 employees who had snuck into the banquet to hear him speak a reminder that a black athlete boasting in those days was an overtly political act. 'Remember, that was 25 years ago,' he said. 'A lot of people were saying, "That n***** ought to shut up." So did some n*****s!'

At the finish, he received a standing ovation and departed, again flanked by security, through the back door.

* * *

On 12 November, Ali told the Associated Press his lawyer had flown to Belize to explore the possibility of locating his car manufacturing plant there rather than in South Boston. 'I'm leaning to Virginia personally but I'm open-minded,' he said. 'We want the best industrial package.'

* * *

At a private ceremony in the Louisville home of Jefferson County judge-executive Harvey Sloane on 19 November, Muhammad Ali married 28-year-old Yolanda 'Lonnie' Williams. Ali and his fourth wife, who grew up on the same street as the Clay family, announced that they would make their home at his farm in Berrien Springs, Michigan. Among those in attendance were Ali's parents, Cash and Odessa, his brother Rahaman and Williams' parents. 'When I first met Muhammad, he was like a big brother,' said Lonnie. 'He didn't have any sisters and as I grew up he was my idol. And I think I was 17 when I fell in love with him. Muhammad and I are really like soul mates. I think I understand him pretty well and I know he understands me very well.'

* * *

On 22 November, the Las Vegas Hilton hosted a heavyweight title fight between WBC champion Trevor Berbick and young challenger Mike Tyson. With a record of 27 wins, including 25 by knockout, and no losses, 20-year-old Tyson had electrified the entire sport over the previous year and a half. Muhammad Ali was in town for the occasion, typically attracting huge crowds every time he walked through the Hilton lobby.

Before the bell, he visited the young pretender in his corner and whispered in Tyson's ear, 'Kick his ass for me!' Almost five full years had passed since Berbick defeated him in that baseball field in the Bahamas, but Ali hadn't forgotten. Two minutes and 35 seconds into the second round, referee Mills Lane ended Berbick's suffering after a left hook to the temple turned his legs to rubber, memorably causing him to topple three times before the fight was stopped.

* * *

Three days before Christmas, a dishevelled Muhammad Ali walked through the lobby of the Sheraton Hotel in Racine, his shirt hanging out, buttons in the wrong place. He went out to the car park and climbed into his camper van to gather up his prayer books before heading back to his room, stopping only to sign an autograph.

Ali had come to Wisconsin to announce that Ali Motors Inc. was to build a 77,000-square-foot manufacturing plant in Caledonia. There, 300 people would be employed hand-building the Ali – 3WC sports car, delivering 3,000 fibreglass vehicles a year, each boasting the chassis and drivetrain of the Pontiac Fiero. Already, pre-orders had been taken from celebrities like Bo Derek, Hank Aaron and a number of unnamed sheikhs in the Middle East.

The task of transporting Ali the ten miles from his hotel to Nielsen Building Systems (whose president, Clayton Nielsen, was an investor in Ali Motors Inc.) in Caledonia for the grand announcement fell to Tom Simons, a police officer, and Sam Beech, a postal inspector. A limousine had been laid on to deliver Ali in proper style but he wanted to drive his beloved Winnebago.

And, before the convoy kicked into gear, he entertained his escorts with some magic right there in the car park. 'He levitated himself off the ground,' said Simons. 'His body lifted off of the ground and it looked so real that I almost fell over.'

After posing for photographs and handing each of the men a copy of a Muslim prayer book, Ali decided to lead the way to Caledonia at top speed. The men charged with ensuring his safe delivery drove behind laughing at his utter disregard for the speed limit and the rules of the road. 'He asked for bodyguards,' said Beech. 'But what he wanted was really someone to talk to. He was one of the kindest people I've ever met in my life.'

At Nielsen Building Systems, the press heard how politicians and businessmen in Caledonia had lured Ali Motors Inc. to the state by offering them financial support of $10m in industrial revenue bonds to finance the construction. This, and the region's tradition in the auto industry, was enough to convince the putative car manufacturer to abandon South Boston and Belize. 'I was approached by Mr Nelson Boon [a Wisconsin businessman] and his friends and asked to put my name on a car,' Ali told the crowd. 'When I put my name on it, it's my car. I am the champion of the world. I don't know the salary of the workers. I don't know the colour of the bricks. But I do know it's named after me and I'm the boss. Mr Ford had a car and De Lorean has a car and they weren't as popular as me. I made boxing better than it ever was. I promoted it and I'm going to promote this car. It will be the greatest car of all time. I think it's a good venture for myself to get involved in 'cause right now I'm unemployed.'

The first four colours in which the car would be available were glove red, knockout black, ringside white and Olympic gold. The factory complex would include a 10,000-square-foot office block, including a permanent exhibition of Ali memorabilia. Like so many other manufacturing regions in America, this part of

Wisconsin suffered in the recession of the 1980s. Journalists were told the company looked forward to offering well-paid jobs to those who had previously worked in auto plants in Kenosha.

On the way back to the hotel, his entourage stopped at Serendipity Day Care, a building he'd spotted when driving along Six Mile Road. 'He visited the school, where we were having milk and cookies,' said Earlene Jornt-Girman, its owner. 'From his place on a small, child-size chair, he befriended the children. Soon, the delighted children responded to his charisma while he raised them in the air, listening to their giggles.'

* * *

On 30 December, the *Journal-Times* of Racine printed an artist's rendering of what the factory would look like and reported every vehicle would have Muhammad Ali's voice reminding drivers when they were running low on gas. However, the paper sounded a lot less sure of the entire enterprise, quoting an industry analyst about the difficulty of creating a viable car company and mentioning new obstacles in the way of accessing the proposed bond issue.

These included how Nelson Boon, one of the key movers in the project, remained under investigation by the Wisconsin Securities Commission for illegally selling securities worth $118,000 in the early 1980s and had forthcoming hearings dealing with that matter. For his part, Boon claimed everybody involved was aware of his case and bolstering his belief that Ali Motors would happen, he pointed out that the whole business was being underpinned by financial guarantees from the mysterious Sheikh Mohammed Al-Fassi, Ali's confrère from the early 1980s.

ROUND SIX

1987

I'm going to tell you something, brother. Some people
want to see the man come down. But they're not going
to see him come down. He paid the price if he has
bad health. But he's a three-time world champion.
And he'll always be a champion

Rahaman Ali, 17 September

ON 17 January, Arthur Morrison announced that Muhammad Ali
(celebrating his 45th birthday) was considering locating a distribution
centre for 'Champion' shoe polish in Benton Harbour, near his home
in Berrien Springs, Michigan. With a population of 14,800 and an
unemployment rate close to nine per cent, the economically depressed
town was badly in need of such a boost. 'I want to do something for
the people there,' said Ali, although nobody was quite sure that quote
came from him. There were growing suspicions about Morrison
forging Ali's signature on documents and pretending to be him in
phone interviews with journalists.

* * *

The *Philadelphia Daily News* reported four days later that recently
released FBI wiretap transcripts showed that Steve Traitz, boss

of the city's roofers' union, had planned to employ Jerry Blavat, a disc jockey, to impersonate Muhammad Ali to try to influence the previous year's election for district attorney. Traitz' idea was to have Blavat record a message as Ali in support of Democratic Party candidate Robert Williams and to have trucks blaring that audio drive through African-American neighbourhoods. 'I got Jerry Blavat,' said Traitz on tape. 'He talks like Muhammad Ali, better than Muhammad Ali. I drew up a skit for him to say, "Brothers and sisters, this is Muhammad Ali, I'm asking my Muslim brothers and sisters, please come out to vote!" Now I already told everybody I got Muhammad Ali, so don't tell nobody it's a fake.'

Traitz was also recorded explaining he would make the voice seem more authentic by having some black boxers from the Montgomery County gym he ran sit in the front of the truck as it blasted the fake Ali message.

Williams lost the election.

* * *

In an Orlando courtroom on 3 February, Muhammad Ali took a seat on the back benches alongside astronaut Tom Stafford. He had come to testify as a character witness for his friend Charles Bazarian, a 46-year-old venture capitalist on trial for bank fraud. Ali was not called to give evidence that day because Bazarian decided against it, telling reporters, 'We didn't want to embarrass the champion of the world.'

He spent much of the proceedings dozing behind sunglasses and, at one point, Judge G. Kendall Sharp called him back into chambers to sign an autograph. During recess, he was besieged by court workers and members of the public in the cafeteria. 'He's my friend and business associate,' said Ali of Bazarian, who had been involved in funding The Muhammad Ali Fan

Club International. 'I heard he was in trouble and had to come down to help. He's an honest man who's always helping others. He sure helped me.'

Bazarian was later found guilty, sentenced to two years in jail and fined $300,000.

* * *

Parco Foods Bakery in Michigan City, Indiana had contracted to make Muhammad Ali Champ Gourmet chocolate chip cookies. On 23 April, Ali caused havoc on the production line when, unannounced, he turned up to inspect how the confectionery bearing his name was made. He stirred the batter, watched the cookies come out of the ovens, hugged the women he met and shadow-boxed with the men.

* * *

On 26 April, *Folha de Sao Paulo* newspaper in Brazil reported that Muhammad Ali had formed Ali Vehicle Industry to produce sports cars in the South American country in a joint venture with a pair of existing Brazilian companies. 'The car will be as I was in the ring,' said Ali. 'It will flutter around like a butterfly and sting like a bee!'

Ali had been alerted to the opportunity in Brazil through a friend called Kevin Haines, a Texas-based businessman who had been involved with Araucaria Vehicles, a Brazilian outfit responsible for making the Puma GT sportscar until it ran into financial trouble in the mid-1980s. The new plan was to deliver three versions of the Ali Stinger for the Middle Eastern market, in association with Sheikh Mohammed Al-Fassi, making yet one more cameo in an Ali-related production.

And what of Wisconsin? 'The people in Racine were very earnest and worked very hard to see the deal go through,' said

Ali. 'But, unfortunately, difficulties that were beyond their control made it impossible to sign the final contract.'

* * *

A white limousine with American flags flying from the front bumper pulled up outside Wayne County Jail in Detroit on 25 May. Muhammad Ali climbed out and walked towards the gate, carrying a battered leather briefcase, stopping to pick up a little girl and kiss her on the cheek. It was a Memorial Day unlike any the facility had seen before. Evel Knievel, the daredevil rider, and the ubiquitous Arthur Morrison were among the entourage flanking Ali as he entered the prison.

Behind bars, he yukked it up with everybody. Here, he was hugging Deputy Alana Mack, there he was fake sparring with a prisoner as three other inmates looked on, wide-eyed, awed by his presence. At one point, a young man extended his hand to shake while wearing an almost beatific grin. Everywhere he went in the institution, he distributed religious pamphlets about Islam, performed some magic tricks to entertain and, perhaps most effortlessly of all, made them smile. 'Are you going to come back?' he asked a room of prisoners who were about to be released. 'No,' they responded. 'You're not as dumb as you look!' said Ali.

Vintage stuff, a veteran act reprising some of his greatest hits for a captive audience for whom his visit was the highlight of the year, maybe even of their lives. As they were leaving, Knievel told reporters that the pair would also be stopping at the Tried Stone Baptist Church in the city to distribute food to the needy.

* * *

Twenty-four hours later, shareholders gathered at K-Mart's headquarters in Troy, Michigan for the company's annual meeting. Executives and investors had come to hear Bernard M. Fauber, chairman and CEO, deliver an upbeat report on the company's financial situation – the usual stuff of these staid affairs.

However, this meeting was more memorable than most. That became apparent when the suits spotted a fleet of white limousines, replete with a police escort, suddenly rolling up in front of the building. Their eyes widened when Muhammad Ali stepped out of one of the limos, followed closely by Evel Knievel.

Behind the celebrity duo, exiting from the other vehicles in the convoy, came a gaggle of 25 bemused African-American boys and girls, not quite sure where they were or to what greater purpose. They didn't know they were extras in a geo-political business dispute that stretched all the way across the world from their home state to South Africa.

As this curious cavalcade marched into the packed auditorium, everybody stared. Some laughed. AGMs were not meant to be this dramatic but Ali, Knievel and their juvenile entourage had come to make a point about K-Mart stocking their Champion shoe polish.

As part of its minority purchasing programme designed to assist African-American businesses, K-Mart had ordered $500,000 worth of Ali's shoe polish – a considerable sum for a new and unproven product. When sales proved sluggish, however, there was no follow-up order. And that's when the trouble started.

Morrison, Ali and Knievel wanted K-Mart to place orders for $30m, a ridiculous demand the company couldn't or wouldn't ever meet. In retaliation, Morrison had taken the fight to the media. Desperate to drum up publicity for the cause, he had been phoning major newspapers across America claiming this was not just Ali's fight. Frank Sinatra was on board too and had bought shares, as had Jane Fonda and Marlon Brando. None of them had bought anything. Those were blatant lies.

This, then, was the man on Ali's arm as he walked into a room full of bemused shareholders. His self-styled business manager had brought him here to embarrass the K-Mart corporate big-wigs for failing to help this minority business get on its feet. That's why the children had been brought along too, their token presence intended to remind the corporation of their expressed responsibility to African-American communities. The message was clear. Not to order more Champion shoe polish was racist.

Ten years earlier, having Ali and Knievel, two K-Mart stockholders, at the annual meeting would have been a major coup for the company. On this day, however, the dynamic duo's celebrity wattage had dimmed. Ali hadn't been world champion for nearly a decade and his travelling companion was in even worse shape. After too many disastrous events, Knievel's retirement from stunt-riding was marred by his vicious assault on Shelly Saltman, a former promoter. He served time in jail, lost his final few remaining sponsors and bankruptcy inevitably followed soon after.

Far removed from the character who captured the imagination of audiences with his audacious jumps, Knievel was now an embittered, retired legend struggling to make a living, perhaps hoping his investment in Champion shoe polish and his association with Ali might revitalise his fortunes.

That Ali was hanging with Knievel, a washed-up novelty act, and Morrison, a recidivist liar, might explain why he never spoke at the meeting. Not a single word. When it came time for Champion to have its say, Knievel stepped forward and read a prepared statement, reiterating their demand that the store order $30m of their shoe polish. 'Muhammad Ali floated like a butterfly into K-Mart corp's annual meeting yesterday,' went a baffled report in the *Wall Street Journal* the next morning, 'but he let Evel Knievel do the stinging for him.'

Those who knew Ali struggled to remember a high-profile event where he didn't utter a single word. Stranger still because this was his kind of fight. Supposedly. This was his company. Allegedly. It was his name and image on the front of the tin. Certainly. For once, once more than any reporter present could recall, he kept his counsel. The Louisville Lip tongue-tied.

When reporters hurled questions, he remained mute. Worse, he stared back at them. Some present wondered whether this was one of the down days of his illness, an occasion when failure to take his medication thieved him of his charisma and wit. Others reckoned he might just have been embarrassed by the entire debacle.

* * *

On 14 June, the *Chicago Tribune* published a lengthy investigation into Arthur Morrison, his ongoing association with Muhammad Ali and the shoe polish controversy. It included evidence of Morrison passing himself off as Ali in phone interviews with both the *Tribune* and the *Detroit Free Press*. In one incident, a reporter called 'Ali' back and discovered the number given was a pay phone in Lindy's restaurant at 42nd Street and Eighth Avenue in New York. Spokespersons for Jane Fonda, Frank Sinatra, Marlon Brando and Robert Mugabe all issued statements reiterating their denials of Morrison's repeated assertions they had any interest, financial or otherwise, in Champion shoe polish. 'I know of no formal deal between Ali and Morrison,' said Charles Lomax, a long-time attorney and business adviser for Ali. 'Ali may have signed something, but I don't know anything about it. But he will sign anything, and sometimes he refers it to me, and sometimes he doesn't.'

* * *

The World Boxing Council's annual medical symposium took place in Mexico City in the second week of July. Muhammad Ali was an invited guest whose presence caused headlines when it emerged he was flirting with undergoing an especially controversial procedure to alleviate his health problems. Ali had visited Dr Ignacio Madrazo at the Universidad Nacional Autonoma de Mexico to discuss his suitability for having cells extracted from one of his adrenal glands and then implanted in the part of the brain that regulates body movement.

It was an operation so new that Madrazo had performed it on just 18 patients up to that point and two of those had died soon after.

The prospect of Ali becoming the 19th person to go under the knife in this way caused consternation. 'Don't be a guinea pig!' said Lonnie Ali.

His personal physician was equally forceful. 'I had advised him not to have it done,' said Ali's primary physician Dr Dennis Cope, director of the training programme in internal medicine at UCLA Medical Centre in Los Angeles. 'I think Ali's condition is not severe enough to warrant the risk of the procedure.'

While Cope and others argued against the procedure, Jose Sulaiman, president of the WBC, used the heightened media interest to offer his non-medical opinion that Ali seemed to be in improved shape. 'I'm very surprised to see him better,' said Sulaiman. 'I invited him myself because I think he's the most important personality in boxing. His presence and opinions are important. He was very kind, very nice. I was very surprised to see that he's very bright in the mind. He congratulated the whole group of doctors, saying he deeply appreciated the doctors helping and protecting the boxers. He said he hoped in the future that boxers would be better protected.'

Ali, of course, downplayed the kerfuffle. 'I see doctors everywhere I go,' he said to reporters in a barely audible voice. 'I feel fine. Don't worry about me.'

* * *

The Hyatt hotel in downtown Tampa, Florida was hosting the Ice Cream and Chocolate Lovers HyattFest. On Friday, 24 July, Muhammad Ali arrived to sell his gourmet cookies but the size of the media contingent awaiting him required a press conference to be held. Reporters were warned beforehand that questions about his health were off limits. When one breached that embargo and asked how he felt, he responded, 'Pretty good.'

Other inquiries were less combative. 'Anyone you didn't fight that you wished you had?' 'Yeah, Rocky [Balboa],' replied Ali.

After the obligatory magic trick, making his handkerchief disappear, Ali departed the stage and stopped in the lobby at the shoeshine stand of Chandler Cato Jr. A crowd gathered around to see his black leather shoes get worked over. 'I feel like I'm in a zoo, in a cage with all these people watching me,' said Ali.

When a journalist asked if he'd miss all the attention and adulation, he shook his head. 'I pray for the day when it happens,' he said. 'Can't go shopping. Can't take my kids anywhere. New York's the worst place. Can't walk a block without a crowd of 100, 150, following me, yellin' at me.'

When Cato Jr finished working his magic, Ali paid him the $2 fee and left him a $20 tip.

* * *

On a sweltering June day along Jefferson Avenue in Detroit back in 1976, Tom Thibodeaux, a former cut man for Thomas Hearns and an artist, unveiled an 11-foot-high sculpture of Muhammad

Ali made from car bumpers. 'Am I not that ugly?' asked Ali when he saw it.

The two men met again in a corridor at the Las Vegas Hilton, where Ali had come to see Mike Tyson defeat Tony Tucker for the WBC, WBA and IBF heavyweight belts on 1 August. 'I know I know you from somewhere,' said Ali as they shook hands. 'I did that sculpture of you in Detroit, remember?'

It took Ali a few seconds to make the connection. Once he did, he placed an arm around Thibodeaux and whispered in his ear, 'You are a great man!'

While in Vegas, Ali addressed questions about his health with the *Chicago Sun-Times*. 'I know I'm sick and I know it's getting worse,' he said. 'I can't talk when I want to. Can't talk as fast and as often as I like. My body just moves slow and feels drained a lot. I know that sooner or later I will have to have surgery if my condition keeps getting worse. I was about to have that operation in Mexico but some members of my family and my doctor persuaded me to wait Basically, I feel great except for fatigue. I do get tired a lot, but I feel no pain. I don't feel any pain. Sometimes I look down and see my hands shaking and I don't even know why they are shaking. The feeling around my mouth isn't there like it used to be. I'm now aware when there's food left on my lips.'

* * *

There were ten boxers and trainers knocking around the TKO gym on Market Street in Louisville on 17 September when a brown Rolls-Royce pulled up. Minutes later, Muhammad Ali, clad in his old workout gear, climbed through the ropes and started shadow-boxing. Word filtered out that he was in the house and by the time he'd finished in the ring, another 50 people had made their way inside to watch. 'I looked up and there he was,' said Tim Tipton, a super-lightweight with a professional record of 3–0. 'It's like an inspiration to see somebody like him. Seeing him hit the heavy bag, right now, he looks like he can beat half the heavyweights in the world.'

Tipton was looking with a fan's eye rather than a boxer's judgement. And that was the mood all around. 'The man looks good,' said LeRoy Edmerson, former trainer of Greg Page and somebody who knew Ali from back in his amateur days. 'A lot of guys fighting now don't look as good as he does. Ain't nothin' wrong with Ali. And, like he told me, he still looks pretty.'

Ali claimed he'd been working out for the previous six weeks back in Michigan, and the famous jab looked intact. His well-worn schtick, that was in fine fettle too. 'You're as ugly as Joe Frazier!' Ali shouted at one young fighter. 'I want you!'

The bombast of the theatrics contrasted with the low voice in which he responded to a reporter's questions. 'How do you feel?' asked J.C. Clemons of the *Louisville Courier-Journal*.

'I feel good,' said Ali.

'Does it bother you that people make an issue of your health?'

'I'm glad they are so concerned.'

'What about your condition?'

'It's under control.'

* * *

At the Fourth Chocolate Festival and Fair in the Fontainebleau Hilton Hotel in Miami on 19 September, Muhammad Ali was asked, in between kissing babies, why he had chosen to launch his own brand of cookies. 'Because it's clean,' he answered, 'not like alcohol or cigarettes.'

When Felicia R. Lee from the *Miami Herald* inquired as to what he was up to these days, aside from promoting confectionery, Ali pressed an eight-page pamphlet called 'A Message from Muhammad Ali' into her hands. The tract asserted that peace between the races would never happen as long as 'Caucasian images of Jesus predominate'. Ali was accompanied to the event by an entourage that included his wife Lonnie. 'He's fine, he's great,' she said. 'He just got back from the doctor and he's okay.' When asked about how quiet he seemed, she explained, 'People don't know it, but Muhammad is very shy.'

* * *

Drew 'Bundini' Brown died at the Good Samaritan Hospital in Los Angeles on 24 September, three weeks after being found unconscious at the bottom of a staircase leading to his second-storey room at a motel. One week before he succumbed to injuries that had left him paralysed, Muhammad Ali came to his room to say a final goodbye to a character with a remarkable biography of his own.

In post-war New York, Brown's ability as a smooth-talking street hustler earned him instant notoriety and a job as a gofer in Sugar Ray Robinson's sizable entourage. That role later led to an introduction to an up-and-comer then known as Cassius Clay, and by the time of the first Sonny Liston clash, Bundini was in the future heavyweight champion's corner, usually racing Angelo Dundee, the actual trainer, to be first to tend the fighter at the bell. It was the start of a beautiful friendship and a tumultuous relationship.

Few people were closer to Ali over the next two decades yet nobody was fired by him more often. Profligate with money and fighting a lifelong battle with alcohol and other demons, his official title was cornerman. His place in history is as the most famous carnival barker in all of sport. The illiterate son of an alligator hunter from the Florida swamplands, he coined 'Float like a butterfly, sting like a bee'.

For the most important fights he was on Ali's shoulder, a constant in his ear, providing the freeform soundtrack to so many weigh-ins and epic encounters. 'Rumble, young man, rumble!' was another timeless improvisation from his back catalogue.

Ali sat by the bed, asked a nurse for a damp towel and dabbed the forehead of his friend, whispering, 'My turn to wipe your sweat off.' He repeated the motion several times, and when it came to leave, he stood up and leaned into Bundini's ear. 'Drew, can you hear me?'

Brown tilted his head ever so slightly. 'Float like a butterfly,' said Ali. 'Sting like a bee. Rumble, young man, rumble.'

After that final goodbye, a doctor urged Ali to visit a teenage boy in the room next door who was suffering from a skin condition. Having composed himself anew, Ali opened the door, shouting, 'Where's this boy wants to box me? You have to get better. That's my order. And when you do, me and you have to fight. You get better and I'm going to get back in shape!' The boy smiled.

* * *

Twenty-four hours after Bundini's death, children at St Jude's Research Hospital in Memphis, Tennessee lined the corridors for the visit of Muhammad Ali. He picked some of them up to kiss, play-fought with others and flirted with every nurse. One little girl asked him to marry her and Charlie Harmon, a nine-year-old battling Hodgkin's Disease, was singled out for an extended spar. 'I'm going to wait 'til you're well,' said Ali. 'You stay in shape.' 'He looks mean in his eyes,' the boy told reporters who asked him about the showdown.

* * *

Muhammad Ali attended the reopening of The Main Post Commissary at Fort Bragg in North Carolina after a renovation in September. The presence of the most famous conscientious objector to the Selective Service draft for the Vietnam War was a measure of how that act was by then perceived very differently than it was back in the 1960s. 'Times change,' said George Vasalei, a Vietnam veteran from Hope Mills. 'He stood up for what he believed in.'

Pamela Castro teared up as she waited in line for Ali's autograph. When he saw her distress, he got up from the table and hugged her. 'I grew up with you,' said Castro through tears. 'I love you!'

Afterwards, Michael Futch from the *Fayetteville Observer* asked her about the encounter. 'To see him – he's so slow and the other times he was so fast,' said Castro. 'I just hope he gets better.'

* * *

On 10 October, Muhammad Ali stood in a tent full of Afghan refugees near the Khyber Pass in Pakistan. Not far from the border with Afghanistan, he assured the assembly of men, tribal elders and mujahideen, displaced by the conflict between their nation and the Soviet Union, that he knew the scale of what they were doing. 'You are much greater than I because you are fighting a much bigger power than all my boxing matches combined. You are fighting the greatest power in the world and giving them all the hell they want.'

There was more where that came from. 'Your cause is a great cause,' he said. 'Your war is a just war. Your jihad is my jihad. And if you give me a gun and permit me to participate in the war in Afghanistan, I will take part wholeheartedly!'

At which point, guns and rifles of every calibre were produced from inside jackets and pants by the men and boys gathered in front of him, showing him they had weaponry on hand in case he was ready to do battle. While some in his entourage, most notably Larry Kolb, were taken aback by the presence of so much firepower, Ali just kept talking. Eventually, the residents of the Nasir Bagh Camp, 30 miles outside Peshawar, responded to his praise by chanting, 'Muhammad Ali zinzabad!' which translates as 'Long live Muhammad Ali.'

He and Lonnie had come bearing gifts, four tonnes of Primo powdered milk with his face emblazoned on every tin. The latest business venture, under the umbrella of Gulf & Pacific Holdings, involved backers such as Kolb and Tony Guccione, son of *Penthouse* magazine publisher Bob. If they all believed Ali's name was enough to guarantee a portion of the lucrative Middle Eastern and South-East Asian market for their product, he spoke about loftier matters on visits to mosques and schools and to government offices. 'Many people in America know nothing about Muslims,' he told a gathering in an auditorium in Peshawar. 'Many people in America know nothing about Prophet Muhammad. America is a big country. America is a beautiful country. All peoples, all races, religions are in America, but the power structure and the news media present a bad picture of Muslims. Whenever Muslims are mentioned, people think about Palestinian guerrillas. Whenever Muslims are mentioned, they think about [Ayatollah] Khomeini, they think about Col. Gadhafi, and whatever he may do that they consider rebellious.'

Kolb videotaped that particular speech and noted a tall, slender Arabian gentleman in the front row, wearing a white crocheted skull cap. It was only years later when he rewatched the footage that he recognised the face. 'There he sits,' wrote Kolb, 'listening politely, not eight feet in front of me, younger, yes, and not quite ready to set the world on fire, but all the same his name is Osama Bin Laden.'

With stops in Lahore, Islamabad and Peshawar, Ali's itinerary was so extensive that he found the schedule too punishing and had to cancel a number of appearances, once even sending Lonnie to speak in his stead at the Liaquat Gymnasium in Islamabad. He was fit enough to fulfil an appointment with the acting president Ghulam Ishaq Khan, who reportedly briefed him about the country's politics, geography and history, and asked if he'd be interested in training Pakistani boxers.

Whenever he was up to it, he performed magic tricks, in between speaking about his devotion to Islam and determination to do everything possible to promote the faith. 'Islam gives us lessons of equality and justice which play an important role in the welfare of masses,' said Ali at Liaquat Gardens in Rawalpindi City. 'That is why I am striving hard to eliminate poverty, injustice and racism from society.'

Among those travelling with Ali on the trip was Lindsey Clennell, an English film-maker who was working on a documentary about him. It was a job that offered him a unique insight into his subject's punishing travel schedule. 'When we went to Pakistan,' said Clennell, 'he'd flown from Chicago, via New York, to Cairo via Paris, stopped over in Cairo, gone to Karachi, changed planes – we're talking about a flight of 20-something-odd hours – he got off the plane, went to the hotel, washed up, went out, drove through a screaming crowd 15 miles to a new town outside Lahore, waving at everybody, people, dust, heat – serious dust, serious heat – did the opening of this new town and then back to the hotel. This is one strong, strong man.'

His time in Lahore overlapped with the visit of the English cricket team. A journalist covering that trip was taken by Ali's performance under duress. 'Broken but not bent, he has not retreated from the limelight to live in decent obscurity, hiding his decline from adoring fans,' wrote Peter Roebuck. 'Certain of his faith, hugging his public, possibly needing the money and aware that he is dying, Ali has nevertheless insisted on facing his public. He continues to shuffle. In his way, he is still majestic. A big man undone by sickness. You can be a temporarily great sportsman, but you cannot be temporarily a great man.'

* * *

On 9 November, Carol Beck was working the Monday night shift at the drive-in window at a Wendy's in the small town of Chesterton, Indiana (pop. 8,500) when a brown Rolls-Royce pulled up and ordered take-out. At first, she didn't notice the driver until a man in the car behind got out of his own vehicle and approached the Rolls in a great hurry. 'Somebody ran up to his car with a notebook and I thought there was an accident,' said Alan Mills, restaurant manager. 'I asked Carol if there was an accident and she said, "No, that's Muhammad Ali!"'

* * *

The Olympic flame arrived in Halifax, Nova Scotia shortly after 8.30am on 23 November, the latest stop on its way to Calgary for the opening of the Winter Games in February 1988. A crowd of just over 2,000 gathered in sub-zero temperatures in the downtown square, fortifying themselves on free coffee and doughnuts. Muhammad Ali sat in a sleek, maroon Cadillac until he was invited on to the stage by Premier John Buchanan. 'One hundred thousand welcomes to Nova Scotia, particularly to Muhammad Ali, 1960 Olympic champ and world champ,' said Buchanan. 'Here in Halifax this morning, we have caught the spirit of the 1988 Olympics.'

Ali took possession of the torch and held it aloft briefly while maintaining what one newspaper described as 'a vacant stare'. He never spoke. 'I'm down here to see Muhammad Ali,' said Brenda Webster, an architecture student. 'I was wondering whether or not I would bear the elements this early, but I heard he would be here and that's what made up my mind to come down. He looks very sweet, adorable. And he's a wonderful representative of achievement in sport.'

After Ali departed the stage and returned to the Cadillac, employees of a local grocery chain moved around the square, handing out free samples of Champ Gourmet Chocolate Chip Cookies bearing his face, and allegedly his words too.

'My cookies are like stars in a crown
They should go one round.
My cookies measure up
They were trained to be!
Why buy less than the best?
Don't be afraid! Be my guest!'

Jack Todd of the *Montreal Gazette* shadowed Ali on his visit to Halifax, spending time alone with him in his hotel room, close enough to see here was a changed man. 'Now, at age 45, Ali has become more Marcel Marceau than the Mouth that Roared, substituting magic tricks for speech,' wrote Todd. 'Since he can no longer perform magic with his quicksilver tongue, he has turned to a kind of magic mime, letting his hands talk for him. In Halifax, he does the same trick over and over again, offering it as a silent pantomime instead of speech, tacking a handkerchief down into his hand and making it disappear, slipping it deftly into a false thumb, repeating it over and over for audiences who either don't see through it or don't want to see through it.'

After performing the sleight of hand for the umpteenth time, Ali turned to Todd and whispered with a smile, 'I feel like an animal in a zoo.'

1988

Now, Muhammad is a brain-damaged, incoherent ex-boxer, a sad sight to all of us who remember the grace and power and beauty of this remarkable boxer. But he is an even sadder sight to those of us who admire him even more for his courage outside the ring, for the legal and moral stand he took that used up the best years of his professional life.

Howard Cosell, *Miami Herald*, 25 February

With an estimated 15 million flowers, 22 bands and 275 horses, the 99th annual New Year's Day Rose Parade filed down Colorado Avenue in Pasadena, where it was reviewed by grand marshal Gregory Peck. The pick of the 60 floats on view was the one containing Mickey Mouse, former astronaut Buzz Aldrin and Muhammad Ali.

* * *

Moments before Mike Tyson and Larry Holmes did battle at the Convention Hall in Atlantic City, New Jersey on 22 January, Muhammad Ali, wearing dark sunglasses and seeming unsteady on his feet, was introduced to the crowd. Don King raised Ali's right arm aloft and, when he let go, it fell immediately to his side again.

'Ali looked as though he were receiving the night on a tape delay,' wrote Phil Berger. 'His movements, his reactions, had the dreamy self-absorption of the underwater swimmer; once the boy beauty of movement and ring wit, Ali was now the haunting man.'

The day after Tyson's fourth-round knockout of Holmes, Ali was in his hotel room promising his old friend Budd Schulberg, the novelist and the screenwriter of *On the Waterfront*, that he was going to make a perfume bottle levitate. With everybody in the room focusing on the bottle, Ali wiggled his fingers in front of it as if about to make it go airborne. 'April fool!' he shouted when it didn't.

Dave Kindred, then a journalist with the *Atlanta Journal-Constitution*, was also in the room. 'Muhammad Ali was once a butterfly on the wing,' wrote Kindred. 'Now, 46 years old, six years past his last fight, he moves with a shuffling gait. He speaks slowly and only occasionally above a gurgled whisper. His face is mask-like. When Ali takes medication daily, he is alert and articulate, friends say. But he is inconsistent with the medication because he dislikes its side effects.'

That night, Donald Trump hosted Ali's 46th birthday party, where 500 people gathered to watch a retrospective of his career, replete with fistic highlights and witty one-liners. A cake was eventually produced and, on his way to cut it, he bowed to the guests and announced with a grin, 'I wish I could make a comeback!'

Sugar Ray Leonard was on hand to help him with the formalities and to explain what the birthday boy meant to him. 'I loved only two men in my lifetime,' said Leonard. 'My father and Muhammad Ali.'

* * *

In Los Angeles on 14 February, Arthur Morrison was shot in the back when driving away from a group of men who had just robbed him. With one newspaper describing the wound he suffered as 'near-fatal', Morrison spent the next two weeks in hospital before continuing his recuperation at home.

* * *

The Bengal Bouts were a Notre Dame University tradition dating back to Knute Rockne initiating boxing on campus in 1920. They really took off as part of college culture under coach Dominic Napolitano, who devised a competition to raise funds for the Holy Cross Missions in Bangladesh in 1931. Fifty-seven years later, 3,136 filed into the Stepan Centre on 4 March to watch the annual event, the motto of which was 'Strong bodies fight that weak bodies may be nourished'. Muhammad Ali joined them for the evening, posing for photographs with undergraduates and, on the most Catholic campus in America, handing out pamphlets promoting Islam that were titled 'Is Jesus really God?'

* * *

On 25 April, Kentucky Governor Wallace Wilkinson welcomed a contingent to his office at the Capitol Building in Frankfort to discuss finding a new home for an expanded version of the ten-year-old World Boxing Hall of Fame in Louisville. Among the group were Wolf Cowen, curator of the museum, former Governor A.B. 'Happy' Chandler and Muhammad Ali.

At a meeting of the University of Kentucky board of trustees three weeks earlier, where the divesting of financial holdings in apartheid South Africa was being discussed, the 89-year-old Chandler had commented, 'You know Zimbabwe is all n***** now? There aren't any whites.' He apologised for the remark but refused to resign. Now back in the office he once held, he used his presence alongside Ali (who gifted Wilkinson a pair of red gloves) to rehabilitate his fallen reputation.

After confessing to reporters that he didn't know Chandler well at all, and refusing to describe him as a friend, despite the former governor claiming they were old pals, Ali then offered his own unique take on the controversy. 'I hear the word every day, n*****,' said Ali, slurring his words slightly. 'Every day I say n*****. My friends say n*****. All blacks I know say n*****. Plenty of you white people say n*****. So what's the big thing?'

* * *

Muhammad Ali and Abuwi Mahdi, his business manager, checked into the Clift Hotel in San Francisco in the early hours of the morning on 1 May. Not long after that, Ali walked through the lobby and left again. The night clerk on duty was a little startled at the manner of his departure and, concerned about his safety due to his well-reported health problems, decided to call the police. It was not a move that impressed Mahdi, who'd travelled the globe with him. 'I wasn't worried about him,' said Mahdi. 'I didn't even get out of bed when the hotel staff called me. I told them Ali can take care of himself.'

He returned from his walk shortly after the alarm was raised.

* * *

On Friday morning, 20 May, Tony Mendenhall skipped out of his job as assistant principal at Indian Valley Middle School to pick up Muhammad Ali at Dayton International Airport. He had booked Ali as a special guest at a sports card and collectibles show at the Winterland Arena that weekend. As they drove along, Ali asked his driver what he did for a living.

'Let's go,' he said, once he heard the answer. 'I want to meet the kids.'

'Are you sure?' asked Mendenhall. 'Take me to your school!' said Ali.

At one point in the 20-mile spin to the town of Enon, just east of Dayton, Mendenhall pulled over to use a pay phone, to give his boss, the school principal Jeffery Lewis, a heads-up about the imminent arrival. A decision was made to assemble 700 students in two sessions in the gymnasium, so nobody got to miss out on the opportunity of an audience with Ali. 'I didn't know who Muhammad Ali was at first, but some of the students told me that he was one of the greatest boxing champions of all times,' said Erica Tipton, then a fourth-grader. 'I walked over to him and asked if I could shake his hand. Before I knew what was happening, he picked me up and gave me a big hug. I went home that afternoon and told my parents that Muhammad Ali visited my school and gave me hug!'

Ali had the students rapt with a speech about effort and reward, speckled with magic tricks and the inevitable impromptu spar. A delighted Jason McKinney, the tallest student in the gym, was invited up on stage to go toe to toe.

At the convention the next day Ali cut a subdued figure for the first hour, not really engaging with fans. One man handed him a copy of *LIFE* magazine from 6 March 1964, with his younger self on the cover, and asked, 'Can you sign both Cassius Clay and Muhammad Ali.' He nodded and he wrote.

Another student proffered an old boxing glove and asked him to endorse it with Cassius Clay. Ali wrote, 'Cassius Clay, Feb 26, 1964', the date after his defeat of Sonny Liston when he announced his conversion to Islam. Over the course of the afternoon he grew more animated, mugging for cameras and putting his fist up to the faces of delighted punters.

Dave Schumann brought a wooden sculpture on which, as a 12-year-old in seventh grade, he had carved a version of the famous photograph of the then Cassius Clay standing over the prostrate Sonny Liston. 'I made this in woodshop in 1969,' he explained. 'I never thought you'd hold it. I got an 'A' on it. I've had it on my dresser ever since.'

Ali examined the artwork and added his signature. 'People like him are why I do this,' he told the *Dayton Daily News*. 'I know they're out there. I just never know how many.'

* * *

K-Mart's annual meeting took place at its headquarters in Troy, Michigan on 24 May. For the second year in a row, Muhammad Ali was part of a group, now including singer Eartha Kitt and former Miss America Suzette Charles, and led by his associate Arthur Morrison, that gatecrashed the affair. Sat near the front of a crowd of about 1,000 people, Morrison asked questions from the floor of K-Mart's new chairman, Joseph Antonini, about the company's orders of Champion Brand shoe polish.

Accused of reneging on its contract to take $700,000 of liquid shoe polish as well as $500,000 of regular shoe polish, Antonini assured Morrison and Ali the product was being tested in various stores. 'If K-Mart rejects Muhammad Ali,' said Morrison, 'then no black businessman can do business in America.'

Throughout the back and forth between the men, Ali sat silently. He signed autographs but never spoke.

* * *

On 7 June, Muhammad Ali gave an odd press conference on Capitol Hill endorsing the proposed appointment of Stephen A. Saltzburg as deputy attorney general in the Justice Department. An unlikely topic, he described Saltzburg as a friend, claiming their relationship dated back to 1967 when the then University of Virginia law professor invited Ali to address one of his classes.

Reading from a prepared script, Ali described Saltzburg as 'a brilliant and compassionate man' and mentioned his expertise in criminal law. But his speech was faltering, weak and uncertain, a fact noted by several reporters present.

Within hours of that shambling display, Ali, or somebody sounding very like him, phoned the *Washington Post* and gave an hour-long interview, holding forth so flawlessly in the style of old that the journalist struggled to take notes fast enough to keep up. The struggling character from earlier suddenly riffed about Ronald Reagan and Mikhail Gorbachev, evaluated the presidential ambitions of Reverend Jesse Jackson and even considered the transformation in his own view of Strom Thurmond.

The then Republican senator from South Carolina, Thurmond was a politician whose entire career had been about trying to keep the south segregated. Through a mutual association with Ali's lawyer Richard Hirschfeld, he had somehow befriended the boxer. 'He's not the same man who ran as the presidential candidate on the States' Rights ticket in 1948,' said Ali of Thurmond, betraying a sudden knowledge of political history nobody close to him ever knew he had. 'He's learned through exposure. He believes in equity. He believes in justice, that you rule by right and not by might.'

As if conscious of how different he sounded from his earlier display on Capitol Hill, Ali explained himself. 'I bet you're surprised I'm talking this good,' said Ali. 'See, I'm not stupid. I'm not brain-damaged. The mind is good. I just sometimes have trouble articulating. When it's crowded, I just feel pressure and I can't project. The difference now is that I don't feel so crowded.'

As explanations went, nobody who had ever spent time in Ali's orbit could possibly believe it.

* * *

As he bounced around the ring moments before fighting Mike Tyson at the Convention Hall in Atlantic City, New Jersey on 27 June, Michael Spinks bowed to three gentlemen sitting together at ringside: Reverend Jesse Jackson, Donald Trump and Muhammad Ali. Asked about the undefeated Spinks' chances of defeating Tyson, Ali reckoned Spinks had 'the speed of hand and foot to pile up points, keep out of danger and win a decision.' Tyson destroyed him in 91 seconds.

* * *

On 5 July, Muhammad Ali had an appointment in Hilton Head, South Carolina, where Dr Rajko D. Medenica was gaining a following for his use of a blood-cleansing technique called plasmapheresis. Medenica had some rather radical ideas about his new patient, believing Ali had been misdiagnosed.

According to this physician, Ali's physical deterioration was unrelated to two decades of shipping percussive blows to his head. His difficulties were all down to household pesticides. Apparently, his supercharged athlete's metabolism made his body unable to excrete toxins from those products fast enough. Once that issue was dealt with, Ali's symptoms would immediately alleviate. 'My goal is to remove the circulating toxins,' said Dr Medenica, ahead of an initial eight-hour procedure in which he replaced Ali's plasma with a mixture he had prepared. 'By the end of the year, he should be much better.'

Ali had been advised to visit the supposedly wondrous Dr Medenica by his new pal, Strom Thurmond, a big fan of a medic who came trailing quite the resume. After studying medicine in his native Yugoslavia, Medenica spent years in Geneva before arriving in America in 1981. During his sojourn in Switzerland, his patients had included Marshall Josip Tito, president of his home country, and the former Soviet leader Leonid Brezhnev.

While his medical peers were sceptical of his often-bizarre methods, he had supposedly successfully treated the daughter-in-law of South Carolina's Governor John West for cancer. That case had been his entrée into the US, West even stepping in when Yugoslavia tried to extradite him for financial crimes.

'I feel like I can fight Mike Tyson!' said Ali after his first treatment by Medenica.

* * *

Most famous for his novel *The Sunshine Soldiers*, Peter Tauber was commissioned by Lorimar-TelePictures to write a screenplay for a new television movie about Muhammad Ali. To this end, he had been granted access to the inner sanctum, visiting Ali at the farm in Berrien Springs, Michigan and accompanying him to events on the road. At a certain point in the relationship, however, the Writers' Guild of America went on strike and Tauber's project was put on ice.

With so much work done, he asked Ali for permission to use the material to write a 3,500-word profile for the *New York Times Magazine*. Published on 17 July, 'Ali: Still Magic' offered some new insights about the man (Ali admitted to dying his hair to look younger) he'd observed at such close quarters over the first quarter of 1988. 'A curious and delightful paradox is how much he enjoys playing cat-and-mouse and putting people on, yet how disarmingly direct and honest he can be,' wrote Tauber. 'He tests others' honesty and distrusts their flattery. Having heard it all, he doesn't need to hear it all the time. He tests to see if he is being condescended to. For 30 minutes he will mumble and exaggerate his palsy, then look up and smile, speak more clearly and show almost no tremor, while talking about it.'

Whether trailing Ali around the Tyson-Holmes fight in Atlantic City or journeying through Chicago's South Side with him in his beige Winnebago, Tauber gained unique access but didn't shy away from more difficult topics such as Ali's financial situation. He touched upon the growing number of bad deals he'd been involved in while discovering that a casino in Las Vegas had offered him $100,000 a week to be a greeter and a television station many multiples of that to work as boxing analyst. Ali and his wife Lonnie asserted they were doing just fine for money. And everything Tauber glimpsed seemed to affirm that.

His health was discussed too, and the profile contained accounts of Ali on good days and bad, one minute cycling around his farm, the next napping in the middle of the day. Although Tauber's time in Ali's world predated the new relationship with Dr Medenica, he did speak to his longer-established personal physician Dr Dennis Cope at UCLA. Predictably, Ali was open as well about the extent of his issues. 'I've got Parkinson's syndrome,' said Ali. 'I'm in no pain. A slight slurring of my speech, a little tremor. Nothing critical. If I was in perfect health – if I had won my last two fights – if I had no problem, people would be afraid of me. Now they feel sorry for me. They thought I was Superman. Now they can go, "He's human, like us. He has problems."'

Even though the pair had wide-ranging discussions about race and religion and the place of Islam in Ali's life and ongoing mission, the one topic he and Tauber never touched upon, not a single time, was American politics.

* * *

The Fair Housing Amendments Act was passed by a vote of 94 to 3 in the United States Senate on 2 August. Just over a week later, a voice purporting to be Muhammad Ali called up Nancy Lewis at the *Washington Post* to outline his role in its passage. He claimed that after Senator Ted Kennedy briefed him about opposition to the bill on the Republican side, he phoned Senator Orrin Hatch, whom he now considered a friend, and Hatch then became a co-sponsor of the bill. 'It was Muhammad Ali that [sic] really turned that bill around for me,' said Hatch through a spokesman. 'We compromised and passed a good bill, all because of Ali.'

No doubt the senator from Utah was being sincere in his account of events but it seemed odd that Ali, somebody with no previous recorded interest in the inner workings of parliamentary process, told Lewis he had researched the costs of the bill and its potential impact on housing before getting Hatch involved.

At a time when just about every public appearance Ali made led to people pondering his diminished speech, the character speaking to Lewis sounded in rude health. He admitted to just realising the growing power he had in Washington, offered unsolicited opinions on wider political matters and even unveiled some of the rhyming for which he'd once been so famous.

'The Post had called it even between Reagan and Carter
But when the polls closed in '80, it was a slaughter
So follow the polls for amusement and fun
but remember they're just an opinion and everybody's got one.'

There was more where that awful stuff came from.

'Bush and Dukakis, they're both fine and dandy
But Bush has experience and that's mighty handy.'

* * *

On 18 August, George H.W. Bush accepted the party's nomination at the Republican National Convention in New Orleans. Muhammad Ali was among the guests featured as the cameras panned the cheering crowd. His presence for the week of festivities caused quite a stir, especially given his almost constant proximity to Senator Orrin Hatch.

Ali arrived at reception for the Utah delegation at the Marriott Hotel, wearing a badge that read 'Bush in 88, Hatch in 96!' Bob Bernick Jr and Lee Davidson, a pair of reporters from the *Deseret News* in Salt Lake City, tried to interview him there but were turned away. They observed him struggling to talk to those pressing him for photographs and autographs but Richard Hirschfeld, his omnipresent lawyer, told the journalists Ali would do a phone interview with them later and gave them a number to call.

The Ali who answered that call spoke as he did in his heyday, and again this improbably mouthy version of his old self was in the mood to talk politics. 'I want to tell black people that Republicanism doesn't equate to racism,' said this suddenly rejuvenated Ali. 'When Orrin Hatch speaks, he speaks for all Americans, for truth and justice. I believe that with all my heart. I'll do anything for him. I'm coming to Salt Lake City [to campaign for Hatch] because I asked to. I invited myself to come and help him in his election. I predict Orrin Hatch will be president before the year 2000.'

At a breakfast hosted by the Pennsylvania delegation, Ali was presented with a 'Win One for the Gipper!' Ronald Reagan T-shirt. Although Lonnie Ali told reporters her husband, swamped by the party faithful throughout that week, was not a Republican, just somebody who supported politicians of either party whose style he liked, many fans were not happy to see him at the convention. 'There were previous Republican conventions where Ali would have been more than welcome, of course,' wrote Ron Rapoport in the *Los Angeles Daily News*. 'If he were riding a rail. Or had been dressed in tar and feathers. Or had been wearing a target around his neck. That was back when people like Orrin Hatch, Strom

Thurmond and George Bush would use the spectre of Ali to give nightmares to little children who hadn't been behaving properly and needed a good scare at bedtime.'

* * *

Gomeo Brennan was a game middleweight out of Miami's fabled Fifth Street gym who put together a professional ledger of 84 wins, 21 defeats and seven draws over the course of a 16-year career. In the 1960s, he often sparred with Muhammad Ali, a lighter opponent chosen to improve his speed. After he hung them up, Brennan became a deputy in the Broward County Sheriff's Office, a role that included looking after the department's new boxing gym in Lauderhill.

On 27 August, Ali was invited to perform the ribbon-cutting ceremony at the facility where the police department hosted boxing and other sports for neighbourhood youngsters. A decade since they'd last seen each other, Brennan had been reading newspaper reports about Ali's physical decline. So, when he picked Ali up at the airport, he was thrilled that he asked him about his daughter, then 21, who'd posed for a photo with Ali back in the day.

However, at the gym, Ali's interaction with the crowd of 200 who turned up for the event was mostly silent. He posed for photographs, kissed some babies and, with a disturbingly blank stare on his face, handed out religious pamphlets. 'There is a difference,' said Brennan. 'Back then, when I saw him, he was yelling, talking, carrying on. It slowed him up. You know if Ali from years ago was here, he'd be yelling all over the place and there'd be more people here because they'd hear him from over on 19th Street and say, "What was that? That's Ali!" But he's the greatest, he is the greatest.'

After the dedication ceremony, there was a picnic at Snyder Park where Ali sparred with teenage boys yet remained silent. 'He should have said at least one word,' said 17-year-old Christopher Wellington.

* * *

Directors International Productions announced on 4 October that Muhammad Ali had signed a deal for exclusive rights to a six-hour documentary series about his life. With a budget of $7m, *The Muhammad Ali Story*, directed by Lindsey Clennell, who had been filming Ali on and off for much of the previous year, was slated for release in early 1990.

* * *

Almost four months after beginning Dr Medenica's initial treatment, Muhammad Ali was invited to the World Boxing Council's annual convention in Mexico City. Sitting on the dais, an esteemed guest at the opening ceremony on 31 October, he looked smart in a black pinstriped suit but his eyes were closed for a long time.

'We have with us the man who became for a time the most important and best recognised person on earth,' said Jose Sulaiman, the WBC president, announcing a special recognition bauble for Ali. 'We honour ourselves by giving him this award.'

The delegates reacted with rapturous applause, but Ali's eyes didn't open. His face betrayed no flicker of recognition. An audience full of boxers, trainers and promoters from 129 countries were aghast. When reporters mingled with the boxing fraternity that day, they were honest about what they had witnessed, a man far removed from the hopeful prognosis of Dr Medenica.

'Ali is now very much a sad personality and a shadow of his former self,' said Dr Adrian Whiteson, co-chairman of the WBC medical committee. 'Towards the end of his career, he took probably more punches than I would have wanted him to take. I think we have to learn from this.'

In what might be perceived as an attempt at damage control, Ali invited a trusted journalist to his hotel suite later in the week.

'What changes would you like to see made in boxing?' asked the writer.

'They should [pause] stop [pause] the fights [pause] sooner,' replied Ali.

After five minutes of halting conversation during which the most loquacious athlete of all struggled to put his thoughts into words, the tape recorder was turned off. By way of explaining his sorry state, Ali said, 'I don't take [pause] my medication like I should. I don't [pause] feel [pause] no pain. But I have a slight [pause] tremor in my hand. And slurred [pause] speech.'

* * *

Seven days before the presidential election, Paul Harvey, the right-wing talk radio show host, dedicated his nationally syndicated column to the potential impact of Muhammad Ali's public support of George H.W. Bush on the race. Moreover, he reckoned Ali's growing political power stood in contrast to the waning influence of Reverend Jesse Jackson on the Democratic Party.

'Muhammad Ali can't be bought,' wrote Harvey. 'He's too smart and too rich. In the years since retirement from the ring, he has immersed himself in politics. He is genuinely concerned about the safety of the planet's people and about our nation's oppression of blacks by a white-dominated welfare system. He wants fervently "to improve the lot of all brothers and sisters of all races".'

* * *

On 4 November, Muhammad Ali turned up, unannounced, for Friday prayer service at the Mosque on V Street in Sacramento,

California. Afterwards, he briefly addressed 200 or so worshippers, many of whom had trouble hearing his barely audible voice as he explained his continuing efforts to proselytise on behalf of Islam. Then he signed autographs and posed for photographs.

His next stop was the office of Mayor Anne Rudin. A gaggle of civil servants gathered outside the door in City Hall to hear her eulogise him before handing over the key to Sacramento. 'Will it fit the bank?' asked Ali when he took it in his hand.

Councilman David Shore wondered aloud if it was true the champ was coming out of retirement. 'How did you know?' responded Ali. 'You're not as dumb as you look.'

Faizah Alim, a reporter with the *Sacramento Bee*, trailed Ali throughout his visit and noticed a change in him over the course of the day. Slow-moving, whispering and sometimes appearing almost lost during earlier engagements, he was much more animated during a luncheon at the house of Jay King, a Grammy-winning producer. There, he ate barbeque chicken and did a version of the Ali shuffle while guests watched a tape of his first victory over Sonny Liston. 'He sings old 50s songs and then claims he wrote them,' wrote Alim. 'He performs magic tricks for anyone who will watch; self-levitation, the disappearing scarf, the detachable thumb. He hugs and kisses babies and personalises each autograph he signs. He jokes and raps and shadow-boxes with each young man who challenges him. And he teasingly calls people ugly and old-looking.'

* * *

Dave Kindred had first met Muhammad Ali when he started working at the *Louisville Courier-Journal* in 1966. Over the next 22 years, he interviewed him around 300 times and visited his homes in Chicago, Louisville, Los Angeles and New Jersey. He'd covered the glory years, the exile, the second coming, and even the bitter end. After a distinguished spell with the *Washington Post*, Kindred joined the *Atlanta Journal-Constitution*, where he remained one of the most respected sportswriters in the country.

On 11 December, Kindred published the first article in an explosive three-part series titled 'The Man and the Voice', forensically exposing how somebody had been phoning up politicians and journalists pretending to be Ali. 'Talkative Ali Imposter Deceived Senators With Phone Calls' went the headline on page one. A dogged reporter who had put months of research into the project, Kindred conducted a face-to-face interview with Ali on 7 November in which he denied ever making any of the calls to 51 different individuals to talk politics. 'Why would a black Muslim mess with politicians?' he said. 'I don't care!'

Between March and September, a man purporting to be Ali had called up influential characters in Washington, including seven United States senators, to lobby them. He had campaigned for the appointment of Stephen A. Saltzburg to deputy attorney-general, requested an investigation into Susan Watt, a federal prosecutor in Virginia, and asked for legislation to allow somebody whose conviction had been overturned by the US Supreme Court to seek damages if the government admitted an error.

Kindred discovered all three enterprises had something in common. Ali was not a long-standing friend of Saltzburg, contrary to the story peddled earlier in the year; he'd only met him once, back in January when he sat in on one of his lectures. The law professor, however, was a long-time friend and occasional legal associate of Richard Hirschfeld, Ali's lawyer.

And Watt, the federal prosecutor in Virginia, well, she happened to be centrally involved in a case against Hirschfeld. And, of course, it was also Hirschfeld who had filed a lawsuit on Ali's behalf in 1984, seeking $50m from the federal government for his wrongful conviction in the 1967 Draft Evasion Case. A judge had dismissed the case but Orrin Hatch and others had talked about introducing 'concession of remedy' legislation and had a draft of it compiled. Some of that legal work was done by Stephen Saltzburg.

Over the course of three days, Kindred stitched together a compelling case that Hirschfeld, known to do a very convincing impression of Ali, made most of the phone calls. 'To longtime students of the Ali legend, Ali's emergence as a political insider was so bizarre as to invite disbelief,' wrote Kindred. 'They characterised him as a man not given to thoughtful analysis of politics.'

Not to mention the dichotomy between the loud phone actor and the reality of the 46-year-old retired fighter in a diminished state, silent for long stretches, slurring words regularly and often speaking in the faintest whisper.

Among those interviewed by Kindred was Ruth G. Carroll, who worked in Senator Orrin Hatch's office. She had hilarious, lengthy conversations with 'Ali' on the phone but when he came by the office, she couldn't reconcile the contrast between the voice and the palsied man struggling to speak in front of her. 'I cried,' said Carroll. 'Ali wanted to articulate but couldn't.'

* * *

Muhammad Ali held a press conference on the steps of the Capitol Building in Washington on 14 December denouncing the *Atlanta Journal-Constitution* story, claiming he told Kindred he didn't make the calls just so the reporter would leave him alone. 'He followed me so much,' he said. 'I just said, "No, I haven't made no calls". So, he wasn't writing and didn't have no pen. I looked up and a week or two later I read in the paper that Ali didn't make those calls. I'm here to tell you it was me. I did make the calls.'

Ali then went on to describe Richard Hirschfeld as 'the best friend a man can have'.

In response, Glenn McCutcheon, the managing editor of the newspaper said, 'We absolutely believe that everything we published was on the money and nothing Mr Ali said today changes my mind about that. Muhammad Ali, on more than one occasion, has said that he did not make the phone calls to politicians.'

ROUND EIGHT

1989

I got a time machine. I'm coming back to beat Tyson.
Everyone I fought I had names for. Sonny Liston was
'The Bear'. Floyd Patterson was 'The Rabbit'. George
Foreman was 'The Mummy'. Tyson will be 'Kong' and
the true king will beat the tyrant

Muhammad Ali – *Boxing Illustrated*, 18 January

THE JUNIOR varsity basketballers of Michigan Lutheran
and Eau Claire high schools were startled by the appearance of
Muhammad Ali and his wife Lonnie at their game on Saturday,
7 January. The couple arrived at the gym, ten miles north of
Berrien Springs, just after half time and a long line of people
wanting autographs immediately formed. Ali handed each one a
pamphlet about Islam, explaining he liked to distribute at least
2,000 of them every week. 'Some of the kids were nervous,' said
Ali. 'But I don't blame them with a big guy like me.'

* * *

The next morning, the *Louisville Courier-Journal*'s magazine
carried a lengthy feature by Davis Miller called 'My Dinner with
Ali'. A lifelong fan, he'd been driving past Odessa Clay's house

in Louisville when he noticed an enormous Winnebago with Virginia numberplates parked outside. Knowing that was Ali's preferred mode of transport, Miller knocked on the door and was invited to spend time with a man he'd been worshipping since the age of 11.

The revealing article Miller wrote about hanging with his hero contained many poignant and telling encounters between the pair, the funniest perhaps when the visitor excused himself to go to the bathroom. At which point, Ali decided to lock the door from the outside. 'When I unlocked the door to leave, it wouldn't budge,' wrote Miller. 'I couldn't even turn the handle. After trying several times, I tentatively knocked. There was laughter from the other room. I distinctly heard Mrs Clay's and Rahaman's voices. I yanked fairly hard on the door a few times. Nothing. Just when I was beginning to think I was stuck in Odessa Clay's bathroom for the millennium, the door easily opened. I caught a glimpse of Ali bounding into a side room to the right, laughing and high-stepping like some oversized, out-of-shape Nubian leprechaun.'

* * *

Muhammad Ali told reporters in Dakar he was considering spending six months of every year in an African country and that Senegal might be just the place because 'the people are warm and, above all, religious'. During a six-day trip that began on 15 January, he met with government officials and invited them to use his name to attract foreign investment. There were reports he wanted to buy into a mineral water company and was looking to purchase a hotel on Goree, the island that was once the departure point for slaves being transported across the Atlantic Ocean. 'I feel good in Senegal,' he said. 'More at home than in the US. Here the people are more civilised. You see it in their eyes and faces.'

Following reports in the American press that he was visiting the Grand Mosque in Touba to meet local marabouts (holy men) who could help cure his health problems, he denounced those claiming he was sick. 'The American press portrays me like a dying man,' he said. 'Behind this campaign are the enemies of Islam. Allah made me famous and is not going to destroy me. There is nothing serious about my health.'

* * *

Muhammad Ali Champion Brand Co. filed a lawsuit in the US District Court on 31 January seeking $550m from K-Mart Corporation and Melville Corporation for failing to fulfil contracts to order big batches of the shoe polish with Ali's face on it. 'They promised they would put the shoe polish in 500 stores and they didn't do it,' said Evel Knievel, senior vice-president of Muhammad Ali Champion Brand. 'They only put it in about 60 stores.'

Ali did not comment on the case.

* * *

When he first arrived in Miami in 1960 to train at the fabled Fifth Street Gym, the still-teenage Cassius Clay was given $5 a day walking around money by his sponsors, the Louisville Group. Responsibility for doling out the cash to the fledgling pro each morning fell to Chris Dundee, Angelo's brother. Twenty-nine years later, on 1 February, Dundee found a letter in his mail from Berrien Springs, containing a $5 bill on which Muhammad Ali had signed his name and drawn an enormous love heart.

* * *

'ALI: They used me!' blared the back page of the *New York Daily News* on 2 February. In the article beneath, reporter Bob Raissman recounted a tale of Arthur Morrison calling the sports desk to announce Muhammad Ali Champion Brand's lawsuit against K-Mart. During that conversation, Morrison claimed Ali couldn't speak personally about the case because he was on a flight to Paris from Nigeria, where he had just been receiving medical treatment. Once Raissman made calls to clarify the information, he discovered Ali had been in Berrien Springs that day, not Africa.

Sensing a much bigger story, Raissman spoke to Thomas Hauser, then working on his official biography of Ali, and to Howard Bingham, Ali's best friend, and discovered alarm in the camp about Morrison's continuing misrepresentations, exaggerations and lies. With growing allegations Morrison was often passing himself off as Ali and/or his attorney, Raissman eventually spoke to Ali himself. 'No, I didn't know about it [the case against K-Mart] and wasn't given a chance to even approve of it,' said Ali, speaking in a tone that fluctuated between sadness and anger at a close friend exploiting his reputation. 'He [Morrison] just took my name and used it for publicity. I don't even know who he's suing. He did this without my permission. He had no permission. He's just using me, he's just using my name. They all want my name.'

* * *

As he left the Geneva courtroom, Muhammad Ali was coralled by reporters. 'Are you still the greatest?' asked one journalist. 'Used to be,' he answered.

His mood was sombre, the delivery flat. He exited the building as he'd entered it hours earlier, slowly, shuffling, his gait almost uncertain. It was 16 May and he had flown to Switzerland to testify on behalf of Dr Rajko Medenica. The Yugoslav physician was being tried in absentia for a $3m fraud and his most famous patient agreed to traverse the globe to offer a character reference.

In trying to exalt Medenica's medical prowess, Ali's shambolic performance unintentionally weakened his defence.

On the stand, the interpreter had to remind him repeatedly to speak up, his voice so weak that Lonnie intervened to speak on his behalf more than once. It was F. Lee Bailey, the defence lawyer, who wanted Ali to appear as a living, breathing example of Dr Medenica's alleged ability to miraculously heal the sick.

'He improved my physical condition,' said Ali, unconvincingly.

'Muhammad had a low image of himself,' said Lonnie, backing up that assertion. 'After this treatment, he was full of life.'

Unfortunately, neither answer tallied with the reality of the paltry figure in the room. He didn't look full of life. Far from it. For somebody there ostensibly to bolster claims of his doctor's genius, Ali's physical condition was parlous and he uttered just seven laboured sentences under cross-examination.

Almost exactly 12 months since Dr Medenica pronounced all previous diagnoses of Ali incorrect and promised to cure him using plasmapheresis, Ali was trying his best, and mostly failing, to appear in any way improved.

'How do you feel?' asked the prosecuting attorney.

'I've never felt better,' Ali replied.

Pressed about exactly how his quality of life had improved under Dr Medenica, Ali extended his arms in front of him and said, 'When I held my hands like this they shook. Also, he cleaned my blood.'

Ali repeated the doctor's strange assertion that boxing hadn't caused his problems by pointing out, 'Joe Frazier has no problem. He's taken more blows than me.'

When the prosecutor pointed out the obvious, that he couldn't possibly claim to have had his speech improved by Dr Medenica, Ali said, 'I talk when I feel like it. Sometimes I don't feel like it. I'm tired of press conferences.' Then, he pretended to snore. The type of gag that always yielded laughs except the joke wasn't funny any more.

Dr Medenica was found guilty.

* * *

Over the course of 90 minutes at San Jose Convention Centre on Saturday, 27 May, one reporter estimated Muhammad Ali signed 600 autographs at $22 a pop. When it was put to him that it was odd for somebody so charitable to charge for his signature, Ali pointed out he did just three memorabilia shows per year and the demand was such, he could do a hundred if he was so inclined. 'They pay me money to come here but I'd do this for free,' he said. 'I would pay $5,000 just to do it.'

As if to prove his point, he later spent nearly as long again outside the building signing autographs for free. A quartet of local journalists had turned up to try to interview Ali. The company running the show declared him off-limits but Ali, being Ali, noticed the reporters tracking his elongated departure from the building and invited them for lunch. His treat and their luck to pick up the usual selection of eclectic and entertaining quotes. 'If I didn't believe in Allah, I would have been dead a long time ago. Some white cracker would have shot me! When I grew up, Charlton Heston and Elvis were my heroes. Now God has made me more popular than any of them. The reason I like kids so much is that they are pure. They don't know racism. They are not conniving. They want no money. Kids, as far as I'm concerned, are on exile from heaven.'

The journalists all noticed that the longer you spent in Ali's company, the easier it became to pick up on every word he was saying. 'After a while, you grow accustomed to the hushed rhythm of his speech,' wrote Mark Purdy. 'It is as if you are listening to a 45 rpm Ali being played at 33 rpm. You get the impression that inside, he is the same old Ali but he can't make it happen on the outside. It is some lunch. You expected the worst. But you got a guy who obviously still enjoys life, who enjoys meeting people. It must frustrate him terribly that he can no longer make his body do what it once did, but he is handling the situation with amazing dignity.'

* * *

In 1983, storied journalist Mark Kram interviewed Ali and discovered a man with a tremor in his hands, struggling with his post-boxing career, who confessed, 'Everybody git [sic] lost in life. I just git [sic] lost, that's all.' Six years later, Kram spent time with Ali again throughout the spring and the subsequent feature, 'Great Men Die Twice', published in the June edition of *Esquire*, would be regarded as magazine writing at its very finest. For the profile, he had tagged along with Ali on a visit to one of his blood-cleansing appointments. 'I find absolutely no brain damage,' said Dr Medenica. 'The magnetic resonator tests show no damage. Before I took him as a patient, I watched many of his fight films. He did not take many head blows.'

Kram was incredulous at this nonsense. He'd covered all of Ali's toughest bouts from ringside. He'd heard every concussive thwack of leather against his head.

'Are you kidding?' he asked. 'No, I do not see any head blows,' said Dr Medenica, claiming to have watched 16 different fights from the Ali canon before reaching that conclusion. 'When he came this summer, he was in bad shape. Poor gait. Difficult speech. Vocal cord syndrome, extended and inflamed. He is much better. His problem is he misses taking his medicine, and he travels too much. He should be here once a month.'

* * *

Muhammad Ali paid a surprise visit to the St Louis Cardinals' locker room before their game against the Pittsburgh Pirates at

Busch Stadium on 18 June. He shook hands, signed autographs and even performed a couple of magic tricks. 'You heard about me floatin' like a butterfly?' asked Ali. 'Watch this.'

Then he appeared to levitate for a second.

In town to promote a fight night involving Lavell and Terrell Finger, a couple of promising local welterweight brothers, at Whitey Herzog's Restaurant and Powerhouse Nightclub, Ali was introduced to the cheering crowd, wearing a Cardinals' baseball cap.

The Pirates went on to trounce the Cardinals 12-4 and the *St Louis Post-Dispatch* wrote that the home team 'floated like bricks and stung like Junebugs'.

* * *

On 21 June, Senator Orrin Hatch brought Muhammad Ali to the West Wing of the White House to meet Chase Untermeyer, President Bush's director of personnel, to talk about a possible gig in the administration. The senator wanted the new man in the White House to give his friend an ambassadorial role, perhaps fronting a campaign to help urban America. Untermeyer listened to the pitch but was greatly troubled by how silent Ali remained throughout the encounter. 'As his handlers talked on and on, Ali sat still, a model of handsomeness in repose, perhaps screaming internally for them to shut up and to express himself as vividly as he once could,' wrote Untermeyer. 'Sensitive to the way he was being treated, I frequently turned to Ali to draw him into the conversation. At one point, I said, "I'd like to know what the champ wants to do". Ali said he isn't sure other than working with kids and helping the homeless.'

After the meeting ended, Untermeyer asked Ali for an autograph, and he produced one of his pre-signed tracts denying the divinity of Christ and handed it over. Nothing further came of an encounter Untermeyer described in his diary as, 'at once captivating, amusing and sad'.

* * *

On 13 July, the *New York Daily News* published a letter that Muhammad Ali wrote to Arthur Morrison, expressing concerns about how his name was being used in business deals. Following the K-Mart shoe polish case, Ali and those close to him were reportedly growing worried about new plans to sell Original Old Kentucky Syrup and Barbecue sauce with his face on every bottle. 'I am in question of your use of my name and likeness with the firm Muhammad Ali Champion Brand,' wrote Ali. 'As of this date, I have not been assured or convinced that business conducted by this firm has been in an ethical and proper fashion. All rights and privileges granted heretofore to you by me are hereby terminated and your contract(s) are voided.'

Lloyd Robinson, Morrison's lawyer, responded with a letter pointing out his client had behaved perfectly within the bounds of a 1986 contract with Ali allowing him to market his likeness. He also requested Ali sit down with Morrison in Chicago to clear the air. That offer was rejected. Instead, Lonnie Ali sent a 'cease and desist' letter to Peter Young and The Young Market Co., a California-based outfit reputedly involved with Morrison and the Ali brands of syrup and barbecue sauce.

Not long after that, Young received another letter, purportedly from Muhammad Ali, assuring him that 'Mr Morrison and the above-named companies are in good standing, and do have valid contracts with me to use my name, voice and likeness for food products, and health and beauty side [sic]'. The signature on the letter was a forgery. Even Morrison's lawyer went public with that information.

After years of Morrison profiting off his association, those around Ali were finally moving to stop his various schemes and to dissuade others from trying to wring easy money from their friendship with him. Laughably, one of those speaking out was Richard Hirschfeld, still somehow unblemished from the revelations he'd impersonated Ali to twist the arms of influential figures in Washington. 'Muhammad is one of the most trusting and forgiving people I've ever met,' Thomas Hauser told Bob Raissman. 'He's such a decent, honest person that he finds it difficult to question other people's motives. There have been many instances in the past where people have taken advantage of his good qualities, but Muhammad has come to understand that when he allows someone to misuse his name, other people get hurt as well.'

* * *

Four days after that story broke, Arthur Morrison phoned Raissman at the *Daily News*, denying all allegations except the forging of the signature. He claimed Ali was not involved in the attempt to end their business relationship. The whole episode, he believed, was the nefarious handiwork of his enemies in the Ali camp. 'I've known Muhammad Ali for 25 years,' said Morrison, breaking down in tears. 'Until he tells me, what others say about me have no relevance and no significance. I am not in search of justice, for I don't feel there is justice to be given. I am prepared to endure and suffer the persecution that may be bestowed on me. I have survived before and certainly shall try and survive again.'

* * *

The advertising copy for the latest Muhammad Ali cologne promised to deliver 'style, elegance, and a touch of daring: the very essence of a winner ... the legend continues.' Produced by Crystal Fragrances of New York, promotional photographs showed an Ali who was much younger than 47 years and slimmer than 260lbs, wearing a white tuxedo, alongside a slogan proclaiming 'a cologne for the man who lives to win'.

'Ali is *the* most well-known person in the world today,' said J. Arthur Worth, president of Crystal Fragrances. 'We wanted to do something, so we came upon the idea of a cologne. It's a clean product. Because of his religious beliefs, he couldn't promote any alcoholic beverages, or underwear, or anything too sexually explicit. You know, Michael Jordan is doing underwear now.'

On 2 August, Ali appeared on *The Arsenio Hall Show* on CBS, the first stop in a national campaign to launch the fragrance. 'Do you actually wear this?' asked Hall, brandishing a bottle of the cologne in his hand. 'Why you ask me such a dumb question?' answered Ali.

When Hall told a story about only recently learning that Sylvester Stallone was inspired to write *Rocky* after watching Chuck Wepner fight Ali, he leaned across towards to the host and said, 'They owe me.' The voice was faint, barely discernible. As dapper and handsome as Ali looked in a black tuxedo, his movements were slow and stiff.

Smartly, the producers lined up a couple of guests to share the couch with him. Enter Sugar Ray Leonard and Mike Tyson. Both boxers enveloped him in extended embraces, and when Hall posed the bar-stool question as to who would have won in a fight between the then heavyweight champion and his predecessor, Ali pointed at Tyson and said, 'I was a dancing master. I wasn't that powerful. I was so fast, but if he hit me ...' Then he slumped in the chair pretending he had just taken a punch.

At that sight, the audience broke into 'Ali! Ali! Ali!', and Tyson reacted by ridiculing the very idea of him ever defeating the three-time champion. 'I'm vain,' said Tyson. 'I know I'm great. But I've got to tell you something. In this situation, every head must bow, every tongue must confess, he's the greatest. I've seen him in the ring with killers who hit much harder than me.'

Tyson then spun a yarn about how, when he was in a juvenile facility in the Bronx, a visit from Ali made his ten-year-old self think that he could and should make something of his life. 'I remember you,' said Ali. 'You were the one in the brown pants and the yellow shirt.'

'Oh wow,' said Hall, impressed with his recall.

'Everybody had brown pants and yellow shirts,' said Tyson. 'It was the uniform.'

Cue laughter.

Pairing Ali with Leonard and Tyson was a masterstroke by Hall and his team. Aside from three true greats chatting it up being box office gold, truth is there was no way Hall could have filled the airtime doing a one-on-one with Ali. Hall's own difficulty even hearing Ali's voice was illustrated by the fact he got out of his usual chair to sit on a footstool right next to him throughout so he could better decipher his speech.

* * *

Forty-eight hours later, the promotional cavalcade pulled into Detroit, where Muhammad Ali made three appearances in the area over two days. At Hudson's-Fairlane Store in Dearborn, several hundred turned up for an audience and a free autograph, his name signed across a card promoting the cologne. 'I shook his hand in 1968,' said Ron Samarian. 'He was here for an exhibition against "Blue" Lewis [who he later fought in Dublin]. And when I shook his hand, he said, "You shook the hand that shook the world!"'

When his turn came to meet Ali, Samarian told the tale of the previous encounter and the line that stuck with him. Ali responded by looking up, eyeing the man in front of him and saying, 'White T-shirt and blue jeans?' Which is exactly what Samarian had worn that first day. But, of course, as he walked away he realised that's what everybody else was wearing back then too and smiled. 'He was an incredible man,' said Michael Schroeder, who had taken time off work to come. 'It's sad to see people in a condition like that.'

Charlie Vincent, a columnist with the *Detroit Free Press*, asked Ali if he actually used the cologne, retailing for $25 a bottle, himself. The answer he got was a dismissive, 'Hrmpft!' 'I'm not sure why these hundreds of people were here,' wrote Vincent. 'Maybe some came to recapture the past. Maybe some came just to say they shared a few moments with a man who once upon a time was the greatest boxer on Earth. Mostly, I think, they came to say, "Thanks for the memories".'

As Ali left Hudson's, the store sound system blared George Benson singing 'The Greatest'.

* * *

Champions Forever was a video chronicling the glory years of heavyweight boxing through footage and interviews with Muhammad Ali, Joe Frazier, George Foreman, Ken Norton and Larry Holmes. To promote the film, Ali, Foreman and Joe Frazier flew to England. 'The days of wine, women and press conferences are over,' said Ali at a press conference in London on 17 October. 'I've had all that. This is boring now. I don't wish I could turn back the clock. I've learned so much. I wouldn't change anything.'

Two days later, the trio appeared on Terry Wogan's television show on BBC One, the actress Joanna Lumley sitting in for the absent host. Foreman and Frazier spoke first and most often, cutting a lively, animated pair as they regaled her with tales of the damage they suffered in the ring.

Eventually, Lumley turned to Ali, who had yet to say a word, and asked, 'How did you keep that face pretty as a picture?'

'Praying to God,' he humbled, the voice faint, the slightest grin on his face.

Later, she tried another tack. 'How are you the greatest, the greatest champion in the world,' she asked.

'That was only publicity to build the fight,' he whispered. 'I never really believed that.'

Midway through an appearance dominated by his peers and Harry Carpenter, the BBC's voice of boxing, Ali offered a glimpse of the character who lit up so many cameos on British television in previous decades. As Lumley tried to remember who beat who in the various fights between the triumvirate, Ali mockingly clenched his right fist and declared, 'She's trying to make me mad!'

Aside from offering brief advice on how to defeat Tyson – 'Stick and move!' – there were long spells in the show when Ali barely spoke, apart from the odd funny one-liner. When Frazier proudly showcased his singing voice, Ali leaned over and urged, 'Please go back boxing.'

Near the finish, Lumley asked him if he still recited poetry. He told her he had written something especially for the appearance. Off he went.

> *'I love your show*
> *I admire your style*
> *But your pay is so cheap*
> *Don't call for a while!'*

A stanza he'd been offering up for decades, the delivery wasn't a patch on his vivacious prime. That mattered not a jot. Lumley and her audience lapped it up.

* * *

Jeff Share grew up in a Jewish household in a small town in Pennsylvania in the 1960s with a father who was a boxing fanatic. Work in the oil business brought Share to live in Texas, and when he read about Ali's tour stopping off at Foley's on South Main Street in Houston on 2 November, he went along carrying an Effanbee doll of Ali. An 18-inch model of the fighter in his pomp, wearing a robe with his name stencilled across the back, and white and red shorts, it was a hugely popular collectible. 'As I approached Ali's table, I pulled the doll out of the bag, and though I tried to be discreet, it caught everyone's attention, including Ali's,' said Share. 'His hands were shaking slightly and I'm trying to figure out where he's going to sign the thing. He took it in his hands, posed [with] it in a boxing pose for a few seconds and then asked me my name, which he carefully inscribed on the white robe along with his name and date. He shook hands with me as I was leaving and said, "Thank you".'

* * *

In a scheduled detour from the relentless commercial itinerary, Muhammad Ali made his way east to the small Georgian town of Fort Valley State for the local college's annual homecoming parade on 4 November. An estimated 15,000 people thronged the streets, nearly twice the normal population, lured to the self-styled peach capital by the celebrity grand marshal of the whole affair.

This had all been Brenda Bender's idea. A Fort Valley alumnus and wife of one of Ali's childhood friends from Louisville, she beseeched her husband to invite his old pal. He only had to be asked. There was no appearance fee. No fuss. He looked at his schedule and made space for a day being driven down main street in a convertible and attending a football match at one of the south's many historically black universities.

Of course, his visit caused utter havoc. The town had never seen traffic like it. The only person unperturbed by the chaos en route to Wildcat Stadium was the guest of honour. 'He's been excited this whole weekend,' said Victor Bender. 'He was up at six o'clock this morning, ready to go. He has been in so many cities and states, and this kind of college atmosphere is something he wanted to experience. He's been surrounded by people everywhere he's gone. Some people in his position might veer from it, but he enjoys it. He was the people's champion when he was boxing. And he's still the people's champion.'

Ali joshed with onlookers who tried to goad him into impromptu sparring and appeared buoyed by youngsters who'd never seen him fight chanting his name. When he sat to be interviewed by children for a local television show, one local reporter noticed the ex-boxer's physical decline. He wrote, 'His movements are slow and deliberate, his eyes often appeared sunken and vacant, his voice thin and raspy. That famous voice has been reduced to almost a whisper.'

When people in Fort Valley asked him where he was headed next, Ali told them he was on his way to his now regular three-monthly appointment with Dr Medenica in Hilton Head, South Carolina.

* * *

The 35th anniversary issue of *Sports Illustrated* magazine was published on 15 November. To celebrate three and a half decades, the cover photograph showed Muhammad Ali holding a copy of the edition from 10 June 1963 in which his younger self featured, with a backdrop of Big Ben and the headline, 'Cassius Invades Britain.' The strap explained, very simply, 'The Champ Ali graces our cover for a record 31st time!' 'Before the big fights these days, when he is introduced in the ring, I see all the pity and pain on people's faces when he gives that little wave, that glazed look across the audience and makes that exit through the ring ropes that seems to last forever,' wrote Gary Smith in a typically insightful and poignant essay about the subject of the cover. 'I see all the people who wanted him to be a symbol of something wonderful and liberating for all of his life, for all of their lives. Look once more, look harder, I want to nudge them and say, "He is".'

* * *

During a 20 November appearance to promote his cologne at Dillard's in Fort Worth, Texas, Muhammad Ali was approached by Major Bill Smith, a record promoter. He handed over a photograph from September 1984 showing Ali, Reverend Jesse Jackson and a couple of other men in the lobby of Columbia Presbyterian Medical Centre in New York City. Smith remained convinced, like plenty of other conspiracy theorists, that Larry Kolb, one of those in the picture, was actually Elvis. 'I handed him the picture and I wish somebody had been videotaping this,' said Smith. 'And he took the picture, held it up, pointed to the man in the middle [Kolb] and said, "That's Elvis!"'

The *Fort Worth Star-Telegram* put the story on the front page, replete with a doctored version of the photograph on to which Smith had added open eyes because Kolb's were shut.

* * *

Muhammad Ali prefaced his arrival at Gayfers Store in the Eastdale Mall in Montgomery, Alabama on 1 December with a press conference at the Madison Hotel. The media noted the sluggish physical movements and weakened voice. Still, they got the gist of what he was saying. And selling. 'We're whippin' all of them,' he said, sitting on a sofa. 'Whippin' Calvin Klein, Liz Taylor. We're not going to stop. We're going to Ghana, Nigeria, Egypt. I've got the world. We're going to other nations, where Liz Taylor and Calvin Klein aren't known. I predict I'll sell more cologne than anyone else in the world. Women love it. Makes 'em chase men they don't even know.'

Ali doused himself in the cologne, then sprayed it at reporters in the front row. He performed the obligatory disappearing handkerchief magic trick and answered a question about what products he would not endorse by saying, 'No jockey shorts! Nothing the pope wouldn't do!' Everywhere he went that day, J. Arthur Worth, president of Crystal Fragrances, was by his side, making grand claims for how well the enterprise – Ali drew 3,000 people to the mall – was going. 'Most colognes have a life expectancy of two to three years,' said Worth. 'We feel like we'll be around a very long time with the Ali name and product. He transcends race, colour and creed. Ali loves everyone.'

* * *

On New Year's Eve, Muhammad Ali and Lonnie flew to the south Indian coastal city of Kozhikode to participate in the jubilee celebrations of the Muslim Education Society. The invitation had come about due to a friendship struck up between Ali and KP Hassan Haji, treasurer of the school. The men met when both performed Hajj in Mecca the previous year. During a four-day visit to the subcontinent, he spent most of his time with the children living in the JDT Islam Orphanage, and 25,000 people turned up to see him appear in Mananchira Grounds alongside the Hindi actor Dilip Kumar at the jubilee party. 'Since I am a neurologist, I could easily distinguish his disease when I shook hands with him,' said P.A. Fazal Gafoor, MES president. 'He did not speak much and was generally quiet. But he still came across as a strikingly handsome man. Ali was invited for the function of the MES, not because he was a Muslim but because of his fight against racism.'

ROUND NINE

1990

*In his silence, induced by his weakened health, he
is deceptively aware of far more than people give
him credit. His words hang in his throat longer
and come out softly. It takes a patient and attentive
ear to hear him. But to hear him is to decipher a
miraculous code. To hear him is to discover the real
Ali. He is still there.*

Hugo Kugiya, *Seattle Times*, 17 July

THE INAUGURATION of Doug Wilder as the nation's first
black governor on 13 January drew a star-studded line-up of
politicos, grandees and celebrities to the Richmond Coliseum
in Virginia. When Muhammad Ali arrived, however, the crowd
parted ways as if the real guest of honour walked among them
and Wilder later joked that he'd been upstaged at his own party.
Somebody asked Ali what had brought him to the event, and he
replied, 'Wilder's my older brother.'

Two months earlier, the day after his historic victory in the
gubernatorial election, Wilder had received a package in the
mail containing a large onyx and gold ring commemorating Ali's
second victory over Liston.

On it had been inscribed the message, 'To Doug Wilder with respect.'

* * *

Police in South Bend, Indiana received a call about teenagers causing a disturbance on 6 February. When officers arrived, they discovered Muhammad Ali at the centre of the good-humoured mayhem. Driving along, Ali had spotted a group of juveniles hanging around and decided to get out and talk to them. Soon, he was running through the full panoply of his repertoire, sparring one minute, performing magic tricks the next.

Earlier in the day, he'd arrived in the city to make a surprise call on Edie Smorse, a 19-year-old who had been battling brain cancer. He'd heard her story through the Make-A-Wish Foundation and arrived at her West Side home unannounced. She wasn't a boxing fan but she knew exactly who he was. 'I was amazed and a little taken aback that someone of his celebrity would come to my house,' she said. 'He was very kind and humble. He was very giving and sincere.'

Having pretended to levitate for Smorse and her family, he posed for the obligatory picture with his fist up to her smiling face. It was when Ali left to return to Berrien Springs that he saw the teens in the street and recognised the opportunity for more mischief.

The police who answered the call-out were as excited as everybody else and Corporal John Collins asked Ali if he would play his part in a prank. He agreed. So, having bade farewell to the youngsters, Ali was mock arrested, put in handcuffs and brought to Central Police Station, where Collins announced he'd made the arrest of his career.

Until everybody in the house started laughing and lined up for photographs and autographs. 'He likes to surprise people,' said

Floyd Bass, groundskeeper at Ali's home in Berrien Springs, his travelling companion that night.

* * *

Cassius Marcellus Clay Sr suffered a massive heart attack when leaving a Louisville department store and was pronounced dead at Humana Hospital-Suburban on 8 February. The 77-year-old known affectionately as Cash was survived by his wife Odessa, two sons, a sister, four brothers and 12 grandchildren. Muhammad Ali was in Berrien Springs when he heard the news of his father's death and immediately flew to Kentucky to be with his mother. Gene Kilroy, Ali's long-time confidante, conveyed a brief statement to the media. 'This is the saddest moment of my life,' said Ali. 'My father was my friend, my first trainer in boxing, my pal. There isn't a day in my life I won't be thinking of him.'

A self-taught commercial artist who made his living painting signs, Clay Sr also contributed murals to churches. Visitors to Ali's training camp at Deer Lake in Pennsylvania recalled him regularly working on his art there. A gregarious character by reputation, he liked to talk as much as his most famous son. 'When Cassius is working on a sign, he has to stop a hundred times a day to talk to people he knows who are just passing by,' said Mel Davis, who hired him to paint the sign over his pawnbroker's shop on Louisville's Market Street. 'You don't want anyone else doing your sign painting for you but you sure don't want to pay Cassius by the hour.'

Greg Simms of the *Dayton Daily News* was friends with Ali and called in at the Clay home to pay his respects. He found Ali on a couch with Kilroy, Lloyd Wells (the former Kansas City Chiefs scout) and Howard Bingham, talking boxing. Later, Simms stood with Ali on the back porch and asked him how he felt about his father's passing. The delivery was slow and laboured, the message clear. 'He lived a good life,' he said. 'We are all gonna die. He's gone to meet God and he's a sensitive man. I'm sure there's a heaven. I know there's a heaven. He's gone there. God made us. You got to return to him. A true believer in God neither fears nor does he grieve. So, I believe in God, Allah. He takes lives and brings lives. It's just another part of life. One of the highest things.'

* * *

Almost one month after his shock victory over Mike Tyson in Tokyo, Buster Douglas arrived in Huntington, West Virginia to appear at the state's Golden Gloves tournament at the Civic Centre on 9 March. The hottest property in boxing, Douglas reverted to the role of fanboy when he found himself in a hotel suite meeting Muhammad Ali. Five years earlier, he had asked for a photograph when Ali turned up at a public workout before Douglas' fight with Greg Page in Atlanta. Now he was granted a private audience and a bear hug from his hero. 'Being around him, I was looking at him and listening to him with a straight face,' said Douglas. 'But inside my mouth was open. "Wow, he is actually sitting here talking to me".' And it was on a level of *mano a mano*. He was sharing the emotions he had as he was watching the fight between Tyson and me. And it was pretty cool to know that I moved a man like him. That was an awesome experience.'

At a press conference, somebody mentioned the previous meeting between the two, and Ali quipped, 'He was wearing blue jeans and a red shirt and had a snotty nose.'

Then he plotted out a path for himself to become champion for the fourth time because, he speculated, if Douglas beat Evander Holyfield and George Foreman beat Douglas, he'd come back to defeat Foreman. Beyond the joking, he gave Douglas his due. 'It's an honour being with him because what he did shows that he's a true champion,' said Ali. 'He took a great fighter, a knockout artist and beat him to show he was the real knockout artist.'

Inevitably, a reporter asked him to identify the greatest boxer of them all. *'He's* the greatest now,' Ali said, and Douglas smiled. *'I'm* the greatest of all time.'

* * *

An estimated 70,000 people gathered at Istiqlal Mosque in Jakarta to hear Muhammad Ali speak after Friday prayers on 16 March. Chanting 'We love you, Ali!', the crowd was so large that afterwards security kept Ali in the building for an hour until they figured out a way to navigate the throng. He had arrived in Indonesia three days earlier to participate in a music and boxing extravaganza at the Bung Karno Sports Stadium, the arena where he defeated Rudy Lubbers in 1973.

Ali was guest of honour at the Super Show, where ringside seats cost $1,000 (US) and the headline match-up was an exhibition between 40-year-old Larry Holmes and James 'Quick' Tillis in which both fighters wore large gloves and headgear.

* * *

Five hundred people lined up at the Holiday Inn Expo-Centre in Harvey, Illinois on 24 March to pay $20 each for a Muhammad Ali autograph. Wearing a black silk suit with white pinstripes, he declared, 'I am the greatest and I'm getting back in the game.' He claimed to be surprised at the size of the crowds he still drew. 'This is an honour,' he said. 'I'm so surprised that they remember me, people five years old, seven years old, weren't even born when I fought.'

Some asked him to sign Muhammad Ali, others Cassius Clay and a few even wondered if he'd do both signatures. No request was turned down. When somebody asked about what he'd been up to lately, he pointed out that he'd just returned from a trip to Indonesia and Australia was on his upcoming schedule. 'The aborigines are having a celebration,' he said, 'and they want me there.'

* * *

Bob Greene, a columnist with the *Chicago Tribune*, was assigned to spend 3 April hanging out with Buster Douglas as the new heavyweight champion visited the city. When Greene fetched up outside the Fairmont Hotel on Columbus Drive, he came across Muhammad Ali on the sidewalk, looking slightly bemused, searching for a taxi. 'Ali,' said Greene, who had interviewed him for *Esquire* in 1983. 'What are you doing?'

'I have to get to the airport,' said Ali.

'Do you know Buster Douglas is staying in this hotel?' asked Greene.

'I just went up to call on him,' answered Ali, who had just returned from the Douglas suite on the 37th floor.

'A scene from a bad novel,' wrote Greene. 'But here Ali was, alone, and looking for a ride.'

* * *

Muhammad Ali's tour of May Company department stores across California began in Baldwin Hills on 9 April and finished in Northridge four days later. Dianne Klein of the *Los Angeles Times* caught the roadshow when it swung through the outlet at South Coast Plaza, where hundreds lined up for hours to purchase some of his eponymous cologne and to get Ali's autograph.

Joe Kasper, a car salesman from Huntington Beach, brought a baseball, wanting to add Ali to a collection of signed balls that already boasted Richard Nixon, Oliver North, Joe DiMaggio,

Mickey Mantle and George Bush. Eleven-year-old Ara Akoubian came because just the week before he'd completed a sixth-grade project on the man now selling cologne. From time to time security walked up and down the line, making sure those waiting had bought a bottle, otherwise they were not entitled to an audience. 'Ali is sitting behind a table, an armed bodyguard standing on either side,' wrote Klein. 'He is wearing a very dark suit and a very red tie. He isn't saying much, although he is smiling a lot. His voice is barely above a whisper. He is shaking hands and kissing women and babies. He is signing colour glossies [free with purchase] very, very slowly, with quivering hands. Nobody is talking too much about the quivering. That wouldn't be nice. They are noticing, however.'

* * *

A gaggle of the greatest fighters of all time gathered in Graziano's restaurant in the little upstate New York town of Canastota on 10 June for the inaugural induction class to the newly opened International Boxing Hall of Fame. Kid Gavilan, Archie Moore, Jersey Joe Walcott, Jake LaMotta, Bob Foster, Billy Conn, Emile Griffith and Willie Pep were names that evoked entire eras in the sport. 'Then, there were a few whispers,' wrote George Owens in the *Ithaca Journal*. 'Heads began to turn. All attention was focused on the back entrance. The Greatest had arrived. Muhammad Ali walked slowly into the room, and suddenly the rest of the Hall of Famers were, well, just a few boxers.'

Fans inside Graziano's surrounded Ali and the relentless autograph signing began. Even after he sat in a booth with a bowl of spaghetti, they continued to press gloves, posters and pictures into his hand. And he continued to write and to give out a brochure on Islam, which he personalised with his name and the date.

During the induction ceremony, the announcer called the names of deceased fighters first and when he got to Jack Johnson, he quoted Nat Fleischer, the famed boxing writer and long-time editor of *The Ring* magazine, describing Johnson as 'the greatest heavyweight of all time'. At which point, Ali raised his eyebrows in mock shock and looked around as if wondering whether he'd been pranked. The crowd loved it, immediately breaking into 'Ali! Ali! Ali!' He responded by conducting the chorus with his hands.

Knowing his audience, the master of ceremonies waited to induct Ali last of the 13 living fighters present. He approached the microphone with a brief 'Ali shuffle' and then spoke about his life and, of course, his transformation from Cassius Clay to Muhammad Ali. But not everybody could hear him. The voice was so faint, the delivery sometimes so slurred that many remarked later that much of his ten-minute monologue was unintelligible. 'I did things other fighters wouldn't do,' he said at one point. 'I was controversial!'

* * *

At G. Fox & Co. in Hartford, Connecticut on 13 June, Joe Camposeo bought the cologne, waited in line and, when he reached Muhammad Ali, produced a photograph that had originally appeared on the front of the *Louisville Courier-Journal* in February 1964. It captured the then Cassius Clay's arrival back at Standiford Field following his wresting of the world heavyweight title from Sonny Liston in Miami.

Ali began to tear up, then turned to his wife Lonnie and whispered something in her ear. It was the sight of his mother Odessa in the crowd shot that moved him so. Camposeo told them he too was in the picture. He pointed out his younger self – then a graduate student at Bellarmine University – to Ali, who responded again by muttering to his wife. 'He said that you are just as pretty as he is after all these years,' said Lonnie.

Evelyn Thomas came trailing a connection to Louisville too, having attended the city's Central High with the teenage Cassius Clay in the 1950s.

'Do you remember Miss Porter [the vice-principal]?' asked Thomas.

'She was tough,' said Ali, before kissing his fellow alumnus on the cheek.

Afterwards, as the Ali entourage made their way to a local restaurant, 22-year-old John Scully tracked their every move then slipped in the door behind them. A light heavyweight out of nearby Windsor, with a pro record of 19–1, he was well known enough for somebody to mention to Ali that a local prospect was in the room. At which point, Ali rose from his chair. 'He came around the table and started shadow-boxing with me,' said Scully. 'Then he took my scrapbook from my hands and looked at every page.'

* * *

Nelson Mandela arrived in Los Angeles on the last leg of an exhausting eight-city tour of the United States. Having spoken at City Hall, there was a star-studded event at the Museum of Sciences and Industry, attended by, among others, Quincy Jones, Jane Fonda, Lionel Richie, Harry Bellafonte, Sidney Poitier, Kris Kristofferson and the Reverend Jesse Jackson. By that point in his visit to America, tour co-ordinator Roger Wilkins bristled a little at the relentless celebrity clamour to get close to Mandela, warning that a man recently released after 27 years in prison was not 'a movable photo opportunity'. Yet, the leader of the African National Congress remained a fan at heart too.

'We were walking together and, all of a sudden, I saw his face light up as I'd never seen it light up before,' said Wilkins. 'He looked past me with a radiant smile. I felt his entire body straighten up and, almost reverentially, he whispered to me, "Champ". And, of course, walking towards us was Muhammad Ali.'

* * *

Shortly after 2pm on the afternoon of Friday, 13 July, a Rolls-Royce convertible with Muhammad Ali in the back pulled up outside Talbot's Drug Store on Pipestone Street in Benton Harbor, Michigan. Soon, the vehicle was surrounded by men, women and children, and the object of their attention was loving every traffic-stopping interaction. Eventually, he climbed out of the car to stand on the sidewalk posing for pictures, kissing babies, signing autographs and throwing playful jabs. 'I came to see the small people,' he answered, when somebody asked why he had driven the 15 miles or so from his farm in Berrien Springs. 'His speech was slurred and his movements were sluggish but his fans didn't seem to mind,' wrote Craig Swanson, editor of the local newspaper. 'Far more important to them was the ever-present twinkle in his eyes and the mischievous grin he exhibited when trading jibes with his young admirers.'

* * *

Seventy-two hours later, Muhammad Ali arrived in Seattle for a three-day visit designed to drum up interest in the first ever professional boxing promotion at the city's Kingdome Stadium. Heavyweights Tim Witherspoon and Tony Tucker were among the names on the card for the 'Seattle Showdown' but promoter Bill Wheeler was hopeful Ali's presence would help him recoup his $1m investment in the event.

The way people swarmed around him at the airport was promising. Those requesting autographs were handed a pre-signed religious pamphlet entitled *The Real Cause of Man's*

Distress, an essay based on the writings of the Islamic thinker Maulana Maududi. As Ali navigated the sea of adulation, Howard Bingham was by his side, a man who'd seen it all before. 'He always draws a crowd,' said Bingham. 'I don't know how the word gets out sometimes, but people come running. Sometimes I wonder how and why. He always gives an autograph to anyone that wants one.'

Governor Booth Gardner and Mayor Norm Rice jointly declared 17 July to be Muhammad Ali Day in Washington State and Seattle. Also honoured as 'Fighter of the Century' at an awards dinner, Ali announced, 'I am making a comeback ...' then, waiting a crucial beat to finish the sentence, 'in my dreams tonight.'

In the locker room at the Kingdome on fight night, Ali went to pay his respects to the combatants. 'Mr Ali, I just want you to know when I'm going to the ring for a fight, I get real nervous,' said one of the undercard fighters. 'So, I say to myself, "I'm Muhammad Ali. I'm the greatest fighter of all time, and no one can beat me."'

'When I was boxing and got nervous before a fight,' whispered Ali, 'I said the same thing.'

* * *

Broadcaster Marv Albert arrived in Berrien Springs on 29 July with a crew from NBC to interview Muhammad Ali for the Greatest Fights Ever series. His initial impressions were not good. 'We're in trouble,' whispered Albert to David Neal, his producer, when he witnessed Ali's gait as he shuffled around the living room. 'This is not going to work.'

But it did. First, they all sat down to watch a tape of the fight and Ali seemed enthralled by his old self, declaring, 'Boy, I was crazy!' During the 15-minute conversation between himself and

Albert that was recorded for the show, he admitted old footage often made him feel like he was watching somebody else. 'Most of it, I've forgotten,' he said. 'I've said so much and did so much in my prime that I look back and say, "Was that me? Was I that fast? Show that over!" At that time, I was so wrapped up in promoting and boxing and fighting. I return and I'm really surprised to see the things that I've done – like watching a movie.'

Albert didn't shy away from raising the elephant in the room. 'Some people will watch this interview and say, "What a shame", when they compare Muhammad Ali of today to the Ali they remember.'

'Things change,' said Ali.

'Does that bother you at all?' pressed Albert.

'No, it doesn't bother me. I'm fatter now. I move slower. I get tired quicker. I can't go like I used to. I can't fight. And when I come back when I'm 90 years old, I'll look different. Twenty years from today, there will be a lot of changes. Mainly my mind is still on top. Ask me a tough question.'

'What do you do every day?' Albert asked.

'Breathe,' responded Ali.

* * *

On 12 September, Phil Berger, boxing correspondent of the *New York Times*, wrote about how Muhammad Ali had shed 42lbs from his frame, going from 266 in January down to 224 in August. The weight loss was the result of a fitness regimen that included walking up to 25 miles per day and putting in rounds on the speed bag.

Ali had been so enthused by his improved physical condition that, after receiving a special tribute from the people of Berrien Springs back in August, he invited 20 youngsters from the local boxing club to come with him to the farm to spar. There, under the glow of the streetlight by his garage, he took off his shirt and offered every boy their shot.

'Ali still moves well, and he would drop his hands and expose his chin,' wrote Davis Miller, who was present that evening. 'And talk to them between his teeth, "Don't you know I'm the greatest of all time?" They laughed. They were having a good time. One of the kids was good enough to hit Ali. And you could see it turned Ali on. He hit the kid back with a straight right and buckled his knees. But when he saw that, he backed right off. He didn't want to hurt any of them.'

* * *

On 19 September, the *Sunday Correspondent* in Britain ran a lengthy profile of Muhammad Ali by Dudley Doust, a veteran American-born sportswriter whose personal history with Ali went back to the 1960s. Invited to Berrien Springs, Doust became the latest visitor to gain a close-up of Ali in the homestead. 'I like the loneliness of the country,' said Ali. 'I like the peace and quiet. I don't enjoy talking about fights any more. It's boring.'

And how did he spend his days?

'I get up and pray at four o'clock in the morning,' said Ali. 'I pray five times, five times a day. Billions of people in the whole wide world pray five times a day.' He punctuated the answer by mimicking the cry, 'Ahhlaaaa, Ahhlaaaa.'

They talked in the coach house where Ali boasted about being thrown out of the Magicians' Society for exposing trade secrets then showed Doust photographs of his children. Together, they watched the *Champions Forever* video he made with Frazier, Foreman and Norton. Eventually, his visitor posed a question about his Parkinson's syndrome. 'Joe Frazier took more beatings – and he's all right,' said Ali in the slow, soft cadence that was now the norm. 'Ken Norton took more punches than me and he's all right. Twenty million people in America have Parkinson's and they don't box. Their hands don't shake like this [he held up his trembling fist to illustrate his point]. If I concentrate, sometimes I don't shake.'

Doust enquired after the blood-cleansing techniques of Dr Rajko D. Medenica, the South Carolina-based physician. 'I don't do that no more,' said Ali. 'I stopped that not long ago.'

In the years since their last interview, much had happened, and Doust remained bothered by Dave Kindred's exposé of somebody impersonating Ali's voice when lobbying in Washington. 'Lots of people can copy my voice,' Ali whispered. 'It's the most famous voice in the world. It wasn't me making those phone calls. I got better things to do.'

* * *

Muhammad Ali walked through the grounds of Thy Kingdom Come's Children's Home in Deer Lake, Pennsylvania, introducing himself to the unwed mothers living there by saying, 'I'm Joe Frazier.' He knew every inch of this secluded corner of Sculps Hill because he had ordered these log cabins built when he first purchased the property in 1970 to become his training camp. With a mess hall, a mosque and a gym, once famous around the world as 'Fighter's Heaven', it was now occupied by a Christian charity assisting pregnant women with no family support.

Ali visited on 6 October with a film crew, wanting footage of him revisiting the place where he honed his skills. Boulders painted with the names of Jack Johnson, Rocky Marciano, Joe Louis, Joe Frazier and Gene Tunney still manned the perimeter, although Jack Dempsey's had faded over time to just 'Jack Demp'.

The compound where the likes of Frank Sinatra, Elvis Presley and Dizzy Gillespie came to pay homage was now full of Ali's favourite people – babies.

Some who had passed through the home over the previous six years had returned to give thanks to the man who charged the Christian charity $1 a year to lease the property. He had words and affection for every infant pressed into his arms, although he stared into one unsmiling face and told the oblivious toddler, 'You bad!'

Troubled teens who also lived in the complex sparred with Ali, wearing a suit and tie, and he asked one in a threatening voice, 'Did you call me a name?' He shot hoops with others and performed magic tricks, after which he declared, 'I am the greatest!' to an audience most of whom weren't born when that boast was true. Then, he did a brief question-and-answer session.

'What was your greatest fight?' he was asked.

'My first wife!' he answered, pausing for laughter. 'Oh, you mean in the ring? That was the thrilla' and the chilla' when I met the gorilla in Manila!'

* * *

On 2 August 1990, Saddam Hussein, then President of Iraq, ordered 100,000 troops to invade Kuwait, a neighbouring country he claimed had been stealing from the Rumaila oil field. Amid widespread condemnation, Hussein responded by taking foreign nationals living in Iraq and Kuwait as hostages, sometimes deploying them as human shields near security installations, even as countries like the USA, Britain and France deployed huge numbers of soldiers to Saudi Arabia in preparation for 'Operation Desert Storm'.

A stream of international envoys flew to Baghdad to plead for the release of hostages. These included the then president of Austria, Kurt Waldheim, and several members of the British and Canadian Parliaments. Former Prime Minister Yasuhiro Nakasone of Japan won the release of 74 Japanese citizens. One-time West German Chancellor Willy Brandt took home nearly 120 of his countrymen. Meanwhile, President George Bush condemned any such attempts to liberate the people Hussein called his 'foreign guests'.

Muhammad Ali touched down in Baghdad on 21 November, accompanied by Arthur Morrison, once more back in the fold, and two representatives of The Coalition to Stop U.S. Intervention in the Middle East. They had organised Ali's 'Goodwill Tour'. He didn't speak at the airport, but a statement was issued on his behalf, announcing his intention to negotiate the release of the 900 Americans being held throughout Iraq and Kuwait. 'He will meet President Saddam and discuss the crisis,' said Gavrielle Gemma, a spokesperson for The Coalition. 'He is on a mission of peace and love.'

The delegation was brought directly to the city's famed Al-Rashid hotel, where in the dining area they met groups of western hostages, mostly medical workers – including Irish nurses – sitting down for dinner. In the bar that night, Ali performed magic tricks for their benefit. 'The Champ, Muhammad Ali, rose slowly from his table in the Scheherazade Lounge and feinted a one-two combination at the 5ft 2in Indian barman,' wrote Nick Williams for the *Los Angeles Times*. 'The little fellow never flinched. He stood stolidly, proudly, as the big American wrapped an arm around his shoulder, eased a small smile and faced the Al-Rashid hotel photographer. Flash. One more memory for the Al-Rashid staff, which lined up one by one Wednesday night for the honour of posing with the Champ.'

For the next week, Ali waited for his audience with Hussein. The prevarication by the president created a problem because Ali had planned for a short stay and, eventually, ran out of his Parkinson's medication, something that seriously impinged on his well-being. Indeed, the *New York Times* speculated about his ability to dialogue at all. 'Surely the strangest hostage-release campaign of recent days has been the "goodwill" tour of Muhammad Ali, the former heavyweight boxing champion,' wrote Philip Shenon on 27 November. 'Mr Ali suffers from the impaired muscular control of Parkinson's syndrome, and he has attended meeting after meeting in Baghdad despite his frequent inability to speak clearly.'

As the *Times*' readers digested that paragraph, Ali was on his way to meet Hussein, bolstered by doctors at the city's Irish hospital getting him the prescription he needed. After a productive 50-minute discussion, during which Hussein spent a lot of time talking about the region's ancient history, the Iraqi leader announced, 'I'm not going to let Muhammad Ali return to the US without having a number of American citizens accompanying him.'

For his part, Ali told Hussein, 'a man of conviction', that freeing some Americans would be 'good for maintaining peace in the area and good for the image of Iraq in the United States'.

Ali and 15 newly released American hostages departed Baghdad on 2 December aboard a chartered Iraqi Airways plane to Amman, Jordan. Upon landing there, they were met by officials of the United States State Department. With President Bush having been firmly against Ali's trip throughout, his representatives weren't in the mood to offer congratulations. Indeed, their purpose was to diminish the impact of his achievement. 'U.S. government representatives huddled with the hostages and tried to convince them that they leave Ali's delegation and return on a plane provided by the State Department,' wrote Brian Becker of The Coalition. 'One of the men told me they felt pressure from the U.S. government to abandon Ali even though they were immensely grateful for his effort.'

The government flight was also offering to get them home a lot quicker to their loved ones. Yet, six of them opted to stay to make the final leg of the journey with Ali. 'I was anxious to get home,' said Harry Brill Edwards, an engineer from Fort Lee, New Jersey, who had been in Kuwait on business when taken hostage by the Iraqis. 'I was ready to leave. I went to thank him and say goodbye. So, I went to him. I looked in his face and how can I say this? He'd made such a torturous trip; he'd secured our release. And I said to myself, "I can't do this. We should be in Muhammad Ali's presence when we go home." We did it out of sheer gratitude and respect for the man. And it's the best decision I made in a long time. I told my family when I got home, "I've always known that Muhammad Ali was a super sportsman, but during those hours that we were together, inside that enormous body, I saw an angel."'

* * *

Having just spent two years writing *Muhammad Ali: His Life and Times*, the definitive biography, for which he'd interviewed every significant character in Ali's story, Thomas Hauser leapt to his defence as criticism was heaped upon him for his trip to Baghdad. In an editorial for the *New York Times*, he put Ali's efforts in proper context, adding nuance to the more simplistic portraits of him as just a retired athlete. 'Ali knows what many of us sometimes seem to forget, that people are killed in wars,' wrote Hauser. 'Every life is precious to him. He understands that each of us has only one life to live. Many Americans now favour war with Iraq, although I'm not sure how many would feel that way if they personally had to fight. Ali, plainly and simply, values every other person's life as dearly as his own, regardless of nationality, religion or race. He is a man who finds it impossible to go hunting, let alone tolerate the horrors of war. It may be that war with Iraq will become inevitable. If so, it will be fought. But that shouldn't cause us to lose sight of what Muhammad Ali tried to accomplish last month.'

ROUND TEN

1991

The ring used to speak to me in a thrilling way. It stopped for good on a cold morning not too long ago in a Michigan farmhouse when I looked into the eyes of Muhammad Ali, and all that was left within me was a dead pool of old, mocking and now obscene rationales

Mark Kram, *New York Times*, 14 April

ON ST Valentine's Day, Muhammad Ali walked, coatless, through the doors of River Rouge High School, just south of Detroit. He barely spoke, offered perfunctory handshakes to the principal and teachers, and had a faraway look in his eyes. Until he spotted some pupils staring at him and was suddenly throwing jabs, glaring menacingly, and for the next hour he had the whole building in the palm of his hand.

He posed for pictures, shook hands, offered hugs and kisses, and when the mood took him pretended to chase miscreants around the lunchroom. Teachers were as in awe of his presence as teenagers too young to have any memory of his heyday. A classic Ali school visit, aside for one thing. He barely spoke at all and when he did it was in whispers. 'Every now and then his face would explode in this wonderfully expansive smile,' wrote Susan Watson in the *Detroit Free Press*. 'His eyes would dance with merriment and mischief. When someone said that a school official should be thanked for arranging Ali's visit, the champ shot back, "Don't thank him! Thank me!" Those were the only words I heard him say but they were enough. They were more than enough. Despite the years, he was still brash and bold, fast and funny.'

* * *

Jacquelyne Frazier-Lyde, an attorney, and Marvis Frazier, a one-time heavyweight prospect, organised a dinner to commemorate the 20th anniversary of their father's epic 1971 victory over Muhammad Ali. On 13 March, Ali walked into Joe Frazier's gym in North Philadelphia and the pair of them were engulfed by hundreds of children. 'This is for the kids,' shouted Frazier above the din. 'I love them,' said Ali.

As the man he fought three times worked his usual magic with the little ones, Frazier assured reporters, 'We were always friends. We just pretended to be angry so we could take the white folks' money.'

At a press conference before a black-tie event the next night, both men sat framed by posters of a *LIFE* magazine cover of 'The Fight of the Century'. Asked what he remembered most about that first fight with Frazier, Ali responded, 'Third round. He hit me so hard it shook up my kinfolks in Africa.'

An old line recycled for a fresh laugh, Frazier raised a pantomime fist and warned, 'Watch it, Muhammad! Don't get started!'

A reporter asked Ali if he thought he had won that night. 'No,' he replied, smiling. 'Do you think I won?'

Once the laughter subsided, he said, 'My jaw told me he won!'

After the press conference, the *New York Daily News*'s Vic Ziegel tried to speak to Ali as he walked towards an elevator. 'I cut around a few people and was almost at his side, anxious to say something, "Ali! Ali!"' wrote Ziegel. 'He didn't turn around. A space was being saved for him on the crowded elevator and he was taking the smallest steps. I put my hand on his elbow. He stared straight ahead, a vacant look on his face. The doctors call it a facial mask, Ali's legacy after catching and ignoring punches for more than 20 years.'

Hours later, as the dinner wound down, Ziegel was deep in conversation with Thomas Hauser about Ali, when the man himself appeared. 'You look the same,' whispered Ali. 'Bald guys always look the same.'

Ziegel shook his hand and said, 'I wanted to thank you for all the good times.'

Ali responded by leaning forward and whispering in his ear. All Ziegel heard was a buzzing sound.

* * *

Before Evander Holyfield's unanimous decision over George Foreman to retain three different versions of the heavyweight crown at the Convention Centre in Atlantic City on 19 April, Muhammad Ali and Joe Frazier were introduced to the crowd. Their presence was a reminder of how hard the challenger was working to turn back the clock. Ali watched his old foe put on a brave performance in defeat from a ringside seat next to Donald Trump and Kevin Costner.

* * *

Muhammad Ali's flight to Fayetteville, North Carolina touched down earlier than scheduled on 2 May and nobody was at the airport to meet him. When his ride, Adam Beyah, the local imam, finally arrived, he found Ali posing for pictures, signing autographs and kissing babies. The purpose of his trip was to mark the fourth anniversary of the dedication of the Masjid Obmar Ibn Sayyid mosque on Southern Avenue, and to help raise funds to finance relocating the facility.

During a dinner in Chicago earlier that year with Imam Warith Deen Mohammed, by then regarded as 'the spiritual leader of American Muslims', Ali had asked what he could do to help advance Islam in the country. Mohammed advised him he could help in the Fayetteville community's search for a new home. 'I got a call from a lady who said she was his wife,' said Beyah. 'Being the natural sceptic that I am, I thought it was a joke. She convinced me it wasn't.'

Ali dropped in at Westover High and Middle Schools, where he spoke to packed gyms and inevitably sparred with delighted teens. Fifteen-year-old Hector Ruiz-Smith, an immigrant from Panama, was pressed forward by his track and field coach Ray McGee. Wearing a T-shirt that read 'Florida Beach Bum' and garishly coloured shorts suited for a day on the sand, Ruiz-Smith struggled to throw even fake punches because he was grinning so much at being so close to Ali.

On Saturday morning, a group that included Beyah and Mitch Capel (a well-known local celebrity) took Ali on a two-mile jaunt down Southern Avenue to Gillespie Street and on to the Market House, where slave auctions were held in the decades before the Civil War. The location was specifically chosen because several speeches given at the venue touched upon the theme 'From Slavery to Freedom'. Ali rode the route in a burgundy Chrysler convertible but did participate in a shorter walk down Person Street following the speeches. 'It was surreal to be walking with Muhammad Ali and listening to his comments,' said Capel. 'The whole time we were walking, he was hilarious. He was just funny and kind and open to everybody who wanted to come up and touch and shake his hand and hand him babies.'

* * *

Bryant Gumbel was 17 years old, playing hoops in the backyard of a friend's house in New Hyde Park, Chicago when Muhammad Ali arrived to visit Elijah Muhammad, who lived next door. The starstruck teen who shook the champ's hand that day was now the host of NBC's *Today* show, charged with interviewing Ali to promote Thomas Hauser's new book *Muhammad Ali: His Life and Times*. As Michael Katz put it in the *New York Daily News*, Gumbel asked 'the hard questions softly'. Only one person watching Ali's performance was particularly appalled. The man himself. 'I'm shaking too much,' he said, watching a tape of the appearance at Hauser's apartment in New York on 3 June, two days before the rest of America got to see it. 'You're doing fine, Muhammad,' said Hauser. 'You're talking very clearly and well about the subjects that are close to you.'

'If I were a fan, I'd be embarrassed,' said Ali.

'Oh, stop,' said his wife, Lonnie. 'You're your own worst critic!'

The tape continued to play and Ali muttered the word 'embarrassing'. Then his 19-year-old daughter Miya climbed on to his lap and started reassuring him with kisses. 'This is why I don't like to do television,' said Ali, still unnerved by how he looked on screen. 'I'd like to see a sportswriter follow him around for a week, do the things he does and see how he looks,' said Lonnie, conscious perhaps of the presence of Katz, the *New York Times'* Robert Lipsyte and Jerry Izenberg of the *Newark Star-Ledger* in the room. 'I know I can't keep up.' 'Made 147 trips by plane last year,' said Ali, seeking to bolster that argument.

These were all reporters Ali knew well and for a long time. Men he trusted enough that Howard Bingham counselled the journalists that the 11-week-old baby boy named Asaad in the room that day, recently adopted by Ali and Lonnie, was 'off the record'.

Later, on the corner of West 74th Street, Miya, then working as a phlebotomist in New Jersey, showed him her new car, a Honda, and pushed the driver's seat back so he could try it on for size. A normal daddy-daughter interaction except every passing motorist stared, wondering if that was really who they thought it was getting behind the wheel. A lady walking past on the street stared a little too long, then smiled and said, 'You're cuter in person!'

The *Today* show was the start of a week of book promotion in and around New York that included a bus ferrying Ali and 50 members of the media down to Deer Lake, Pennsylvania to visit his old training camp. Some of the journalists had not been around him for years and, as he made his way down the aisle to greet them, walking slow, his posture stooped; they were a little shocked. Then, three rows from the back, he stopped, turned around smartly and shouted, 'I don't have to ride back here no more!'

Suddenly, they all remembered the reason he had been such a compelling figure for so long and why they were heading for the hills with him one more time. Dick Schaap, the veteran reporter, was aboard filming the trip with his own video camera. Not for broadcast. For posterity. At the other end of the time frame, Ralph Wiley, a 20-something most recently of *Sports Illustrated*, reminded Ali he was 'everybody's champion'. 'There's little kids who weren't born when I was champ,' said Ali, as the bus trundled along Interstate 78 through Pennsylvania. 'They see me, they say, "Ali! Ali! Ali!"'

When he had last visited Deer Lake just nine months earlier, the camp was home to Thy Kingdom Come's Children's Home. That enterprise had failed so the facility was about to be taken over by a Washington Muslim group called Muhammad Ali Saving Our Future Foundation Inc. for teenage black males. Their representatives swarmed around him when he got off the bus. Sensing a story, one reporter wondered aloud how the local, mostly white community, might respond to the new tenants. Ali didn't answer because he was distracted by somebody handing him Muhammad Ali Potato Chips in a variety of flavours.

Earnie Shavers had come along for the ride. Once an opponent, always a friend. 'He's a shell of the man he used to be,' said Shavers. 'Over a long period of time, we all had a little to do with his condition today. Everybody who fought him added a little to it. I feel sorry for him. You almost ask, "Why Ali? Why not somebody who deserved it?" Not that anybody deserved this. But he's not down and out. He's cheerful and happy. He doesn't resent his condition or regret it. He says, "If it's Allah's will, so be it".'

Ali led a walkthrough of his old stomping ground, each log cabin sparking a reminiscence about the glory days when he put the work in there, far from the bright lights.

'For a few moments, the years rolled away,' wrote George Vecsey in the *New York Times*. 'Photographers led Ali to the large boulders with names like Louis and Frazier painted on them. They posed him atop the boulder with the name Sonny Liston painted on it. Instinctively, he cocked his fists and crouched menacingly over the boulder, the way he did that night when Liston refused to fight, and the young champion shouted, "Get up, you chump". The boulder, too, stayed down, and Ali raised his fists triumphantly, still champion of his own world.'

On the bus ride back to the city, Lonnie handed Ali a bottle of water. Ron Borges of the *Boston Globe* was sitting nearby. 'He looks at it and begins to remove the top,' wrote Borges. 'His hands shake. Thirty seconds go by, 40, 50. His eyes never leave the top of the bottle as he works to free the lid with the same hands that once rapped opposing fighters' heads before they saw a single punch coming. Finally, he frees the top but now is faced with the aluminum lining. He picks at it until a piece comes loose. Ever so slowly, he works the aluminum foil free from the lip of the bottle. Piece by piece, he works it off, his eyes never leaving his task. Finally, nearly five minutes after receiving the bottle, he takes the first sip. He smiles with satisfaction.'

Once back in New York, many of the journalists disembarked the bus. For Ali, however, after 13 hours on the go, there was more work to be done. He headed to Our Children's Foundation community centre at the junction of 125th Street and Amsterdam Avenue in Harlem. His visit to a group that ran after-school education programmes throughout the city's five boroughs had been arranged by Tom Hoover, a one-time New York Knicks basketball player.

The reception he received there was predictably rapturous, the venue packed. Ali took a seat on the floor in among the hundreds of children, the same ones who had been primed to perform African dances in his honour. 'Back in 1974, I went to Africa and saw these same dances you're performing now,' he said. 'I dreamed one day the people of America – the black people – would learn these dances to do them themselves. Twenty-five years ago, these dances were not performed in Harlem or anywhere in America. I'm proud to know you know and recognise them.'

Ali was given a tour of the building, laying his hands on every child who crossed his path. When he strolled to the limo waiting outside, there was a reprise of the lusty chorus of 'Ali! Ali! Ali!' that had greeted his arrival hours earlier. A carload of black teenagers pulled alongside and nearly clambered out of their own vehicle once they saw who was next to them. Even when he and his entourage finally reached the Omni-Berskhire hotel, his progress was checked by a young black man, approaching with a smile.

His name was Raghib Ramadian 'Rocket' Ismail, a wide receiver out of Wilkes-Barre, Pennsylvania who two months earlier had eschewed the NFL to sign a record-breaking contract with the Toronto Argonauts of the Canadian Football League. The 21-year-old had hung around the lobby in the hopes of meeting his hero. Ali stopped, hugged him and chatted. It was near enough 16 hours since he'd left the hotel that morning.

* * *

The next day, the book promotion train pulled into Gracie Mansion for the ninth annual Joe Louis Memorial Scholarship award ceremony. David Dinkins, mayor of New York, had invited Muhammad Ali to his official residence but failed to inform his caterers about his religion. 'Leave it to a politician to invite the world's most famous Muslim,' said *Boston Herald* columnist George Kimball, 'and then serve ham and cheese sandwiches for lunch.'

Chuck Wepner, the real-life inspiration for Rocky Balboa, was also present. The Bayonne Bleeder had famously scored a knockdown against Ali in their 1975 clash even though it was generally agreed he'd tripped him with his foot. When Wepner jockeyed for position on the mansion lawn so his old rival could see him, Ali feigned to ignore him. Just as it appeared as if he was going to walk on by, Ali's foot suddenly landed on Wepner's. The crowd laughed, the two former fighters embraced.

* * *

A celebrated columnist with the *Chicago Tribune*, Joan Beck's work was syndicated in hundreds of newspapers across America each week. When she wrote an article on 20 June calling for the abolition of boxing in recognition of the damage it had wrought on Muhammad Ali, the piece subsequently appeared in just about every state in the union over the following days.

Apparently, Beck was motivated by the publication of Hauser's biography and the plight of Kid Akeem Anifowoshe, a Nigerian super-flyweight who had collapsed in the ring after suffering a blood clot on the brain following an IBF title fight against Robert Quiroga in San Antonio the previous week. She reckoned Ali represented 'one of the best arguments why boxing should no longer be tolerated as a spectator sport or an athletic competition' and accused Hauser's book of trying to put the best face on the subject's condition. 'It can also be argued that what boxing gave Ali was well worth what it is costing him now,' wrote Beck. 'He may feel that is so. Certainly, most of the people who profited one way or another from his efforts were willing to let him go on, even after brain damage became obvious. Boxing as an organised amateur and professional sport should be halted in loving memory of the Muhammad Ali who used to be and as a cry of rage about what it can intentionally do to vulnerable and irreplaceable human brains.'

* * *

In Boone County Superior Court One in Indiana on 25 June, Judge Ora A. Kincaid ordered Muhammad Ali to pay $12,907 to a Zionsville sports promoter for failing to sign photographs and posters at a memorabilia show in Cincinnati in 1988. Ali was not present and not represented by a lawyer at the hearing, where William E. Daniels claimed he had breached a personal services contract by failing to sign some items presented to him on the day.

After Ali autographed all sorts of stuff for hours for fans paying $35 a pop, Daniels testified that he asked if it was possible to get him to privately sign 150 posters and 250 photographs for a particular customer. Ali signed 106 of those posters before he grew too fatigued to continue. Daniels complained the remaining posters and photographs had never been returned to him and he'd begun legal action seeking redress in 1989.

While Daniels wanted compensation worth $75 per autograph – what he claimed Ali's signature on a photograph was worth by that point – Judge Kincaid based his judgement on the $35 valuation in the original agreement. He ordered Ali to pay court costs, plus $9,750 for the unsigned posters and photos, $2,442 in interest, and $660 to recompense the original owner of the items which hadn't been returned.

* * *

During a four-hour appearance at Cody's Bookstore in Berkeley, California on 9 July, Muhammad Ali broke Hank Aaron's record for most books signed at a single event. Earlier in the year, Aaron had managed to autograph 796 copies of his autobiography *I Had a Hammer!* when he swung through town. Ali blew past that number and Charles Browning, of Cody's, reckoned he surpassed 1,000 books by the time he left the building.

* * *

Muhammad Ali arrived two hours early for his appearance at Stacey's Bookstore on Market Street in San Francisco on 27 July. Accompanied by Howard Bingham, he repaired to the manager's office, where he performed magic tricks for the staff. Then he took his seat at a table between the stacks and applied pre-signed stickers of his autograph to the first page of Thomas Hauser's book for three hours. When he finally rose to leave, his face was besmirched with lipstick marks from hundreds of kisses on his cheeks. 'Thank you for staying,' said an older man, holding close his copy of the biography. 'Thank. You. For. Waiting!' said Ali.

The voice was weak, sometimes a whisper, but when they listened hard enough, the crowd could make out the mischief.

'What. Color. Is. The. Sky?' he asked, slowly.

'Blue!' a few of them replied.

'What. Colour. Is. Grass?' Another question. Another stilted delivery.

'Green!' came the answer from the chorus.

'Spell silk,' he requested.

'SILK,' they responded.

'What. Do. Cows. Drink?' One more riddle.

'Milk,' shouted the crowd. And then Ali smiled before correcting them. 'Cows. Drink. Water. They. Give. Milk!'

And everybody in the room had fallen for his ruse, the wit a reminder to those invariably concerned by his physical deterioration that the heart and soul of the man remained the same.

'Still, there's a mystique about him, something special, something spiritual,' wrote Joan Ryan in the *San Francisco Examiner*. 'And his debility has somehow enhanced all that. It has made him even more beloved. The brash, braggadocious, showy champion with the ferocious punch is not the most gentle of men. But he isn't docile. He isn't to be pitied; to see Ali is to see a man who seems to be at peace. As Ali made his way out the door, someone shouted after him, "You're still the greatest, you're still the champ!" Ali stopped and turned towards the voice. "I. Was. The. Champ!" But he was smiling. Surely he knows whatever he has now – whatever it is that makes a grown man kneel and kiss his hand and a child too young to know who he is bury his head in Ali's arms – is far greater than a belt.'

* * *

At the Miami Convention Centre on 29 July, Hall C, the place where the then Cassius Clay dethroned Sonny Liston in 1964, was renamed 'Muhammad Ali Hall of Champions'. Among the 600 people gathered for the luncheon and ceremony were heavyweight champion Evander Holyfield, Ali's former trainer Angelo Dundee, his former physician Ferdie Pacheco and his best friend Howard Bingham. A slew of ex-boxers including Jimmy Ellis, Pinklon Thomas, Earnie Shavers and Beau Jack were also on hand, along with three of Ali's children, twin 21-year-old daughters Jamillah and Rasheda, and son Muhammad Ali Jr, 19.

During the ceremony, Alex Daoud, mayor of Miami Beach, invited Holyfield to speak and introduced him as 'the heavyweight champion of the world'. At which point Ali rose from his own seat on the dais, half smiling, half aghast at the very notion of somebody else carrying that description. The crowd laughed then clapped. 'I love Ali from the bottom of my heart because of the stands he's taken and the things he believes in,' Holyfield said. 'I look back to when he was fighting Liston, and people said he was too small, too young, too inexperienced. People said I was too small, but Ali gave me inspiration to go ahead. There is only one Ali. There will never be another Ali.'

After numerous paeans to his greatness from the likes of Dundee, it came time for Ali to talk. The speech was far removed from the fluent patter of the young man who took on Liston (when they showed footage from 1964, that point was hammered home) but sparks remained. 'I've been telling people for years that I was pretty good,' he said. 'I've never been the type to brag.'

Then he offered Holyfield advice about his forthcoming clash with Mike Tyson. 'Please watch Tyson's left hook,' said Ali, 'keep your distance and listen to him [he pointed at Holyfield's trainer Lou Duva]. Stick and move.' He paused then before delivering the punchline, 'Tyson told me to tell you that!'

He also recited a parable about a slave who was saved from the auction block by a generous king. He went on to lead a successful life but eventually gave up all his riches and donned the robe he wore the day he was supposed to be sold into bondage and told himself, 'Never forget the day you wore this garment. Never look down at the people who look up to you.'

After the event, Ali visited the Miami Beach Theatre of the Performing Arts' Walk of Fame, where he was invited to press his hands and fists into wet concrete to leave a lasting impression there. Later, he was guest of honour at an evening of boxing. Throughout a day in the public eye when he was constantly besieged, one of his daughters observed the way young and old idolised her father at every turn. 'It takes things like this to make me realise his impact on others because I just look at him as a father,' said Jamillah Ali. 'Actually, he's more like a brother, he's so playful. He's so kind-hearted, down-to-earth and wise. In real life, he's the opposite of what he was like in the ring. He's very sensitive, with a heart the size of this state. Let him see a child cry and he'll cry. He's such a tease with us. He'll always say he has two sons and seven mistakes but he's just kidding. He's always kidding with us. We have to help him with his mail. He gets boxes.'

During his visit to south Florida, Ali also promoted Hauser's book. Three weeks after he left town, the *Miami Herald* published a letter from Carol Green, who had attended his signing at Bookworks. 'Let me tell you that Ali's charm, grace, sense of humour, intellect and the twinkle in his eye when he saw a child were intact and an inspiration to those who had the pleasure of speaking with him,' wrote Green. 'I've met many public figures. None would extend an autograph session four hours and miss a plane to avoid disappointing one single person. Our community has done well to honour him. He is world class and all class.'

* * *

The denizens of Berrien County Courthouse were surprised on Thursday, 15 August when Muhammad Ali turned up. Not to testify or to stand trial. He just wanted to watch his friend and sometime attorney Paul Jancha in action. Inevitably, his presence interfered with legal business as lawyers, plaintiffs and witnesses all lined up for autographs and photographs. Even Circuit Court Judge Casper Grathwohl posed for a picture in which a smiling Ali hoisted a right jab towards his chin.

* * *

To mark the 25th anniversary of his clash with Englishman Henry Cooper at Highbury, Muhammad Ali was to be guest of honour at a £100-per-plate dinner at London's Grosvenor House Hotel on Sunday, 22 September. In aid of the Boxers' Benevolent Fund, the event was part of a ten-day tour of England to promote Robson Books' British edition of Thomas Hauser's book. Forty-eight hours before his appointment with Cooper, when Ali failed to arrive on his scheduled flight, it was discovered he had decamped to Abu Dhabi with Herbert Muhammad, his former manager, instead. 'None of Ali's friends and associates in England, including myself, know precisely why he is absent at the moment,' wrote Hauser, who found himself turning up alone to a book signing at Manchester's Sherratt & Hughes, where police had been laid on to cope with the crowd expected to swarm the place for Ali. 'And I suspect that the personal motives of the two men currently travelling with him have a great deal to do with the situation. But no clear answer will be available until he returns safely home and has a chance to rest a bit and reflect upon what has happened with his wife and others who care about him.'

The English press expressed grave concerns about his welfare, using the word 'kidnapping' to describe his absence, and speculating about whether he was being held against his will. In an explanatory essay for *The Observer*, Hauser recounted how he had painstakingly read every word of his book aloud to Ali over ten days in Berrien Springs before it was published in order to verify accuracy and to add any supplementary material he believed necessary. Even though the criticisms of Herbert Muhammad contained in the manuscript had been approved by Ali, his former manager had, upon publication, immediately tried to get him to disavow the book. 'There have been certain people close to Ali who have never liked the book, primarily because it included some criticism of them personally,' said Lonnie Ali, speaking from Michigan on 25 September. 'Before the start of the book tour in America, they were able to convince Muhammad that his endorsing the book was a sin against Allah and all of his blessing would be taken away for every book he signed. I can only pray to Allah that Ali makes it home safely and in good health.'

A reporter from *The Guardian* tracked Ali down to the Inter-Continental Hotel in Abu Dhabi, where he was supposedly working on behalf of a foundation linked to Herbert Muhammad. 'He will not come to London,' said Rashad Musawi, styling himself a spokesman for Ali. 'He does not support the book any more. He is very well and in good health. He has all his medicine, everything he needs.'

* * *

Three weeks after arriving in Damascus, Muhammad Ali gave a press conference on 13 November. After a strict fasting and prayer regime, eating only honey and drinking only water and herbal tea under the supervision of the Grand Mufti of Syria, Sheikh Ahmed Kuftaro, at the city's Al-Asad Institute for Learning Qur'an, he said his symptoms had greatly improved. 'I feel a lot better,' said

Sports Illustrated *magazine cover*

Muhammad Ali cologne

Muhammad Ali in a restaurant in England, August 1983

Muhammad Ali hushing the crowd in Dudley, Birmingham, August 1983

Muhammad Ali working as a referee at Wrestlemania 1 in March 1985

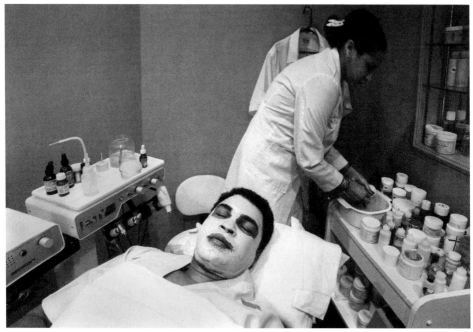

Ali getting a facial in a Louisville beauty parlour, Christmas Eve, 1985

Muhammad Ali shoe polish

Paul Howard with Ali, New Jersey, 1992

Muhammad Ali in a Baghdad hotel as he works for release of POWs in May, 1993

Ali walking across mural saying 'Bush is Criminal' outside a Baghdad hotel, May 1993

Ali with Liberace and Hulk Hogan, promoting Wrestlemania 1

Muhammad Ali lights the flame at the Olympics in Atlanta, July 1996

Ali with Joe Frazier, George Foreman and Joanna Lumley on the set of BBC's Wogan, *October 1989*

Ali with Max Clifford and fans, in a cafeteria in London, 1992

Ali. 'I have lost 37lbs. My speech is a little better. My trembling is a little better.'

With a week left in his regimen, he announced plans to return within six months to repeat the process. While Ali spent much of the press conference with his head bowed, fingering his prayer beads, bolder claims were made on his behalf. 'He had been up to 30 tablets a day,' said Rashad Musawi, by then calling himself vice-president of the Muhammad Ali Islamic Foundation. 'He has stopped all medication. His blood pressure and heart are better. He is walking much better.'

* * *

Art Tinajero was flying back to Los Angeles from Las Vegas on 3 December and his reading material for the flight was Thomas Hauser's book, a gift from his children back on Father's Day. A passenger across the aisle asked him if he'd ever met Ali. Tinajero said, 'no' and left it at that.

When they reached LAX, the mystery man approached him again at baggage claim and repeated the question, 'So you've never met Ali, huh?'

'Nope, never.'

'Would you like to? I'm having lunch with him at a hotel nearby this afternoon. If you'd like to stop by, I'm sure he wouldn't mind signing your book.'

Having stopped at a gift shop to buy a disposable camera, Tinajero made his way to Loews Hotel in Santa Monica, where the stranger told him he was dining with Ali at 3pm. The restaurant was deserted and, just as Tinajero wondered whether he'd been pranked, he saw Ali sitting with a group in a corner near the back. It was a group that included the passenger from earlier. Hoping to get his book autographed, Tinajero happened upon a whole lot more.

'Have you had lunch?' whispered Ali and, before an answer even came, told him, 'Sit down.'

Tinajero spent the next 90 minutes with Ali, Lonnie, Howard Bingham and the stranger who'd invited him there. Flicking through his copy of the Hauser book, Ali smiled when he saw where Tinajero's children had inscribed in childish handwriting, 'To our Dad, we love you, Happy Father's Day, 1991! Erik and Philip.' Then he added his own signature, with a message that read, 'To Art from Muhammad Ali. Love is the net, where hearts are caught like fish.'

One of the bus boys asked Tinajero in Spanish about getting an autograph. Within minutes, Ali was in the kitchen hanging with the waiting staff and chefs. 'Although he said very little, and when he did speak it was low and slow,' wrote Tinajero, 'he was still every bit the legend.'

1992

*I remember one night my late wife, at a party at
promoter Aileen Eaton's house, took one look at Ali and
his next opponent, Alejandro Lavorante, resplendent
in white dinner jackets, and she moaned. 'Who in the
world would put two such beautiful specimens as you
two in a ring to knock each other bloody? Two years
later, Alejandro Lavorante would be in a coma, dying
a lingering death from the effects of beatings in the ring.
Two decades later, Ali, the quick-witted, quick-tongued
artist of the squared circle, would be a shambling,
stumbling, stuttering, mumbling replica of himself.*

Jim Murray, *Los Angeles Times*, 21 July

ON 13 January, *Sports Illustrated* put Muhammad Ali on its cover
for the 32nd time. The headline read 'Once and Forever' and the
photograph showed a smiling Ali in a tuxedo with a cake in the
shape of a boxing ring alight with candles. William Nack, one of
the greatest writers in the history of the magazine, visited Ali in
Berrien Springs two months earlier to write the accompanying
feature, devoting much of the space to a retrospective about the
formative years of young Cassius Clay.

An intrepid reporter, Nack wrung some telling quotes, including one that put Ali's remarkable journey into some perspective. 'As a kid in Louisville, the city seemed so big to me,' said Ali. 'New York seemed so big. Chicago seemed big. And London, England seemed far away. Africa was far away. I was Cassius Clay then. I was a Negro. I ate pork. I had no confidence. I thought white people were superior. I was a Christian Baptist named Cassius Clay.'

The interview was conducted in the office behind Ali's house on the farm and for the occasion he, of course, delivered some good-natured braggadocio. 'I'll win the heavyweight championship back when I'm 50 years old!' he said, shadow-boxing back and forth across the room in front of Nack. 'Isn't that something? Is that powerful? They can pay $20m or $50m to whoever I fight, Holyfield or Tyson? This is gonna shake 'em up. It's like a miracle. A dream. Muhammad Ali is back! Can you picture this? Can you believe it? Dancing at 50! Ooooohhh. Dancin' at 50. Maaannn. It'll be bigger than the moon shot! I'm dedicatin' the fight to the baby boomers, the people who were six years old when I beat Sonny Liston. Now they're 34. I'll do the Ali shuffle!'

By the time he'd finished sparring, his left hand was pressed against his chest, trembling. But there was a smile on his face.

* * *

A belated celebration to mark Muhammad Ali's 50th birthday was held at the Chiltern Theatre in Los Angeles, where musicians, singers, comedians and actors performed a two-hour extravaganza before a packed house. The whole thing was filmed and shown two weeks later on a Sunday evening by ABC. The party started with Dustin Hoffman introducing Ali and featured performances by The Four Tops, Diana Ross, Whitney Houston, Billy Crystal, Little Richard, MC Hammer, Tony Danza, Sinbad, and the

Pointer Sisters. Ella Fitzgerald walked on to the stage, flanked by Ken Norton and Joe Frazier, and then sang 'Too Close for Comfort'.

'We have all just enjoyed a wonderful tribute to you, my good friend,' said Mandela in a video link from South Africa towards the end of the night. 'Your courage and determination have made you an outstanding champion. You are also a man who not only took a stand against the war but are opposed to bigotry, inequality and injustice among all people throughout the world. It is only fitting that the proceeds from this event are going to the United Negro College Fund and that memories of this event will live with us forever. Congratulations and happy birthday. From one boxer to another, you are a knockout expert. As far as life is concerned, you will always remain the undefeated heavyweight champion of the whole world.'

* * *

Tunney Hunsaker retired as the police chief of Fayetteville, West Virginia in February after 38 years of service. A pillar of the local community, a decorated lawman, he taught Sunday School at the Oak Hill Church of the Nazarene, and local children didn't talk of growing up to become a police officer but to become a 'Tunney'.

Named for Gene Tunney by a boxing fan father, the genial chief had been a Golden Gloves boxing champion when serving in the United States Air Force in Lakeland, Texas and in 1959 won the heavyweight title in his home state. After a fine career in and out of the ring, his footnote in history was being Muhammad Ali's first professional opponent at Freedom Hall in Louisville in 1960. 'I want to come to your hometown,' said Ali when he called to congratulate Hunsaker on his retirement.

So, 32 years after a bout that earned Ali $2,000 and the part-time boxer/full-time police officer $300, Hunsaker and his wife

Patricia hurriedly booked a conference room at the Comfort Inn for an impromptu retirement party now featuring a very special guest of honour. Ali worked the room the way he always did, signing everything, posing for each camera and constantly throwing jabs in the direction of his old foe.

As a 30-year-old journeyman, Hunsaker sustained a bloodied nose going six rounds with the highly touted teen debutant on the night that bound them together forever. 'I gave him a hard time,' said Hunsaker. 'Later, he said he almost lost the hamburger he'd eaten for dinner when I gave him some good chops to the stomach in the second and third rounds. But I was too old to be fighting an 18-year-old fella. He had these long arms and he could hit you from anywhere and from any angle.'

At 50, Ali had lost his speed but not his charisma. After the party, he toured the town. In a flower shop, a woman pinned a bud to his jacket. When a school bus carrying special needs students came along, Ali insisted Hunsaker flag it down so he could climb aboard and play with the young passengers. Then the pair visited the spectacular New River Gorge Bridge, a dramatic span in the Appalachian Mountains only open to pedestrians on one day a year. When Ali expressed interest in walking across it, Hunsaker stopped the traffic and allowed his old foe that privilege.

* * *

On 28 September 1979, a time of heightened racial tension in Boston's busing crisis, moments before Jamaica Plain began the second half of a high school grid-iron game at Charlestown High, three white teenagers clambered on to a nearby roof with a sniper's rifle and started firing. One of their shots hit Darryl Williams, a 15-year-old black sophomore on the visiting team. He suffered injuries that confined him to a wheelchair for the rest of his life.

By 1992, Williams was working in the office of Joe Malone, Massachusetts state treasurer, who was fundraising to purchase a vehicle specially customised for use by a quadriplegic. At Boston's Visa Waltham Hotel on 30 March, Malone sold out a $500-a-ticket dinner where the star guest was Muhammad Ali. Before the event, Ali met Williams and described this extraordinary character as 'the second greatest of all time'.

* * *

Ireland's Steve Collins fought Reggie Johnson for the WBA world middleweight title at the Meadowlands Arena in New Jersey on 22 April. Paul Howard, a young sportswriter from Dublin, was in town to cover the bout and staying at the Meadowlands Hilton. Suffering from terrible jet lag one evening, he was in the lobby talking to the bellman when a limousine pulled up and Muhammad Ali got out. 'You never met The Champ before?' asked the bellman.

Howard shook his head. 'You want to take the luggage up?'

Scarcely believing his luck, he pushed the trolley, now loaded with cases, towards the elevator as Ali and his minder walked alongside. Nobody spoke.

Once the doors opened, the minder pushed the button then remembered he'd forgotten something, leaving the boxing writer and Ali devotee all alone with his hero as the lift ascended. 'After a few seconds, I noticed that he was staring at me, his top teeth hanging over his bottom in a display of mock aggression, then slowly, out of nowhere, he started throwing punches at me, jabs and uppercuts, calibrated to stop within an inch of my face,' wrote Howard. 'Then he laughed, so I laughed too. We reached the floor and I pushed the cart into his room. As I took the bags off it, I sensed him behind me, silently demanding my attention. When I turned around, he was performing a magic trick for me, pushing a handkerchief into his balled-up fist, then opening his hand to reveal it gone. I applauded and he smiled and nodded appreciatively. Then he handed me a $20 bill and 30 seconds later I was back in the lift, reflecting on the fact that, in five minutes in the company of a man I had worshipped from childhood, I didn't manage to say anything.'

Ali was in New Jersey to be guest of honour at the Newark Boys and Girls Club's Brightest Star Awards. Attending an event to raise money for the charity, he had paid his own expenses from Michigan and waived any appearance fee. 'Another group, Project Pride, will also share in the evening,' wrote Jerry Izenberg of the *Star-Ledger*. 'Ali knows about both organisations. He knows who they are and the magnificent results they achieve. More important, he knows about the kind of children who need them and he worries about what can happen to them on the mean streets if these institutions should disappear. There never has been an athlete who cared more.'

* * *

During Muhammad Ali's visit to the Boys Home in Tulsa, Oklahoma on 7 May, a 16-year-old boy read a verse that ended,

> *'Float like a butterfly*
> *Sting like a bee*
> *The man, the legend*
> *Muhammad Ali.'*

When the teen had finished, Ali asked him if he'd really wrote it himself. He replied, 'Yes!' 'Well, you're not as stupid as you look,' said Ali, smiling.

Earlier in the day, Ali was approached by a 51-year-old businessman from Broken Arrow who whipped out his driver's license to show Ali that his name was Cassius Clay. 'You have to come along with me,' said Ali.

And Clay did. He spent most of the day as part of the entourage. 'What you see is what he's like everywhere,' said Clay of the experience. 'The man just doesn't stop giving.'

Later, Ali attended a black-tie 'Fight Night' at the Westin Hotel, where patrons paid $250 each to watch six bouts. The proceeds for the evening, in excess of $40,000, were shared between Catholic charities and the boys' home. The loudest cheer of the night was the inevitable, sustained rendition of 'Ali! Ali! Ali!'

* * *

In Charlotte, North Carolina, 450 junior high school students boarded buses for the fifth annual Beach Blast on Saturday, 16 May. Underprivileged, they were being ferried across state lines for a day at Huntington Beach State Park in South Carolina. Only when they boarded the bus did somebody tell them that Muhammad Ali was going to be joining them at the seaside.

Hours later, Ali sat on a picnic bench as the boys and girls lined up to shake his hand and receive an autographed copy of his pamphlet *Introducing Islam*.

As was always the way, Ali decided one 15-year-old, Amauris Gabot, a ninth-grader from Hawthorne Traditional Junior High School, reminded him of an old foe. 'You look like Joe Frazier!' he told the boy, confronting him as if about to fight.

Gabot decided to try his luck and threw a jab. Ali slipped the punch but now the game was afoot. 'Ali takes a long step towards the boy, who immediately takes off running,' wrote Davis Miller, who was in Ali's entourage that day. 'Ali falls in behind. It takes him a couple of steps to get going, then he's churning his legs so hard that his knees are almost waist high. They race around the concrete shelter, through a field of grass and a stand of oaks, then out on to the beach.

'Part of the time, Ali is making comically mean faces; at other moments, he's smiling and chuckling. They run probably 200 yards down the beach at a dead sprint, this high-strung adolescent in cutoffs and the tired old giant dressed in a custom-tailored suit and shiny leather uppers.'

Ali was in the area to sign autographs at Sports Mania, a memorabilia store at the Inlet Mall in Myrtle Beach. The version of him that turned up there, just hours after he'd made merry in the dunes, was very different, seriously reduced. He was still handing out *Introducing Islam* pamphlets but appeared tired and sluggish. 'At the Sports Mania store, Ali was drooling,' wrote Christie Blatchford, a columnist with Canada's *National Post*. 'A long stream of spittle fell from his mouth as a man was pumping his hand and saying, "We love you, man, we love you!" People who saw it and saw that Ali was completely unaware, turned away from him and wept. But that was the first reaction. Ali might call it the easy one. Ali's mind is working just fine.'

There was plenty of evidence of that as the afternoon wore on and Ali worked his usual schtick. When a baby was pressed into his arms, his face lit up and he kissed it on the cheek three times. After a pretty young woman named Ayesha stepped forward to kiss him on the cheek, he pretended to fall backwards, blown away by the impact. Blatchford departed the mall that day figuring she'd seen a very different kind of courage and a man embroiled in 'the toughest fight' of his life. 'Why should anyone be surprised,' she wrote, 'that even now, as Parkinson's has him firmly in its humbling grasp, Muhammad Ali is still on the road, making about 100 public appearances a year, almost all of them for charity, willingly subjecting himself to the stares and whispers and tears of strangers.'

* * *

Nine months after her husband failed to turn up to promote Thomas Hauser's book in England, Lonnie Ali phoned Jeremy Robson, publisher of the British edition, and told him that Muhammad Ali was coming to London to make amends. He touched down at Heathrow on 26 May, checked into the Cumberland Hotel and before embarking on a nationwide tour visited Homerton Hospital, where Michael Watson was recovering from brain injuries suffered during his world title fight with Chris Eubank at White Hart Lane eight months earlier. Watson had not yet recovered the power of speech but was aware enough of his surroundings that night to realise there was a kerfuffle of some sort. 'I could sense that something was happening,' said Watson. 'There was noise coming from the hall leading into my ward. Then I saw him at the end of my bed. Muhammad Ali. My idol. A friend of mine said it was the first time I smiled since before the fight. Ali was smiling too. He leant over and whispered in my ear, "Boy, you're pretty. But I'm prettier than you." I raised my right hand and we touched fists, still smiling. Ali's visit was a breakthrough for me, an overwhelming moment, a tremendous boost that undoubtedly helped me in my subsequent recovery.'

In Leeds on 1 June, fans began lining up outside Austicks Bookstore at 7am. Police were called to organise the throng and at 1.30pm a decision was made to close the shop. While nobody else was being allowed in to meet him, Ali remained for another hour signing the books of those who were still inside. 'This must be a freak situation in a recession,' said John Lauder, Austicks' manager, 'to actually have police stopping people getting into a shop.'

A couple of customers that day were devout Muslims who invited Ali to pray with them at the Bilal Masjid mosque in nearby Harehills. The packed timetable of his book tour called for him to move straight on to Nottingham for his next engagement but, as usual, the schedule-setters didn't allow for Ali's ability to be waylaid by well-meaning strangers – especially those coming in the name of Islam. 'My mam, bless her, would not let me go to Austicks to get to the book signing,' said Buster Scanlon. 'I was meant to be revising for my GCSEs [secondary school exams]. That afternoon, my mam let me out for an hour; I went to Banstead Park, Harehills, a street away from where we lived, to play football with friends. Then a friend of a friend came over to us and said, "You'll never guess who is in the Mosque up the road? MUHAMMAD ALI!" I was off. I sprinted up and stood in the crowd. I was out of breath and shaking with shock. He was getting into a car, got in, looked over and waved and noticed me in the state I was in!'

While Scanlon and plenty of other residents of Harehills thrilled at glimpsing Ali in their neighbourhood, those organising the trip were in a bit of a tizzy.

'He suddenly disappeared with a group of people,' wrote Robson. 'Nobody knew where he had been taken and we eventually drove on to Nottingham, hoping that someone with him had details of where he was supposed to be. We'd only been at the shop there for a few minutes when a smart Mercedes drew up and out stepped a smiling Ali, as cool as anything as he greeted crowds so dense that after the signing we needed a police escort out of town.'

By Hauser's estimate, Ali had signed 900 books that morning in Leeds, as well as shaking the same number of hands, posing for umpteen photographs and kissing babies. There were 500 people waiting at Dillon's Bookstore in Nottingham and Ali cut a tired figure, his day having started at 5am with morning prayer.

Inevitably, the voice was flagging and some were saddened by the sight of how diminished he had become. 'Most of the people in line were joyful,' wrote Hauser. 'But one of them, a middle-aged woman with a kind face, wasn't. Muhammad's condition grieved her. As she approached him, she burst into tears. Ali leaned over, kissed her on the cheek, and told her, "Don't feel bad. God has blessed me. I've had a good life, and it's still good. I'm having fun now." The woman walked away smiling.'

Next day, Ali had other business to conduct, making good on the previous year's promise to meet up with Henry Cooper. The one-time rivals posed for photographs before a charity dinner in London, Cooper raising his famous 'Enry's 'Ammer as if about to strike Ali's chin. After that engagement, Max Clifford, then Britain's leading publicity guru, asked Ali to drop into the cancer ward at the Royal Marsden Hospital in Surrey, where patients were being treated in strict isolation.

'His visit was extraordinary,' said Professor Ray Powles, the doctor in charge of one of the most innovative treatment centres in the world. 'He went to each room and communicated through the glass to each of my 16 desperately ill patients. It was amazing to watch their reaction. Initially, each one looked startled to see him, but somehow through his simple gestures and words, he managed to communicate with them at a profound level and the change in their demeanour and morale was visible. Princess Diana had previously visited my unit. She had made a good impression, but Ali's impact was far greater. I could tell that in some indefinable way he'd given each patient hope and encouragement in their personal fight for life.'

The visit was supposed to last an hour and a half. Ali stayed for four. Once he had seen the most gravely ill patients, he spent time with the staff, talking with everybody from Powles to the cleaning ladies.

Two days later the caravan pulled into Oxford, where hundreds were waiting at Blackwell's on Broad Street.

'Suddenly, bedlam breaks loose,' wrote Michael Tanner. 'A white Rover 827 has drawn up outside. Traffic grinds to a halt; tourists forget the Sheldonian Theatre opposite and cross the road for a better view. Inside the shop, a hundred necks crane for that first, confirmatory glimpse of The Man. The spotlights surrounding the table intended for Ali are switched on and an unsightly scrum promptly develops as a posse of photographers, TV cameramen and radio reporters fight for a prime position.'

Among those jostling in the queue was Adrian McKinty, an undergraduate from Carrickfergus, who should have been studying for his final exams. But he was also a sports fan and couldn't resist the opportunity to get close to one of his heroes.

'Many of the hard-bitten hacks in the British tabloids hadn't seen him for over a decade, not since he was the lippy, skinny, sarky promoter of his own fights, always by far the wittiest man in the room,' wrote McKinty. 'He looked old, gaunt, grey. Some of the hacks in the front row were even starting to well up as Ali stood there holding his book, shaking and saying nothing. "You're the greatest, champ!" one reporter said as tears rolled down his face. Ali smiled and started fumbling in his tracksuit pocket. He took out a £10 note, reached across the stage and gave it to the man. Then he winked and said into the microphone, "I told him to say that." Everyone laughed. The Champ, brought low by disease and time, still bloody had it.'

Afterwards, Ali was brought upstairs for lunch. Eschewing the canapes and sandwiches on offer, he requested a burger and fries so somebody was immediately dispatched to McDonald's. When the food arrived, he offered to share it with Rodney Smith and James Blackburn, a pair of Blackwell's employees. After Smith took some fries, Ali curled his lip in mock anger and delivered a fake punch to his solar plexus. Mostly, though, he sat in silence for the duration until right at the end, when he declared, 'Man, I'm going back in the ring.'

During his time in Oxford, somebody pressed a note into Ali's hand from Paddy Monaghan. president of his British fan club, a resident of nearby Abingdon and somebody with whom he'd been good friends for decades. Monaghan wanted Ali to know he couldn't make the signing because his mother had just died. 'Where is this?' asked Ali, showing the address on the page.

Jeremy Robson told him it was about eight miles away. 'We'll go there when we finish here,' Ali announced.

But Robson started to complain. They were due in Birmingham immediately after this signing had ended. 'We'll go there then we go to Birmingham,' insisted Ali.

Monaghan had written letters of support to him during his period of exile from the ring in the late 1960s, once collecting a petition calling for his reinstatement containing 22,000 signatures. He'd also worked his corner the night he fought Al 'Blue' Lewis in Dublin in 1972. Book promotion would have to wait. Ali never neglected those who were by his side in their darkest hours. The convoy took a detour to a tiny council house on Saxton Road, where Ali was soon sitting down with Monaghan, telling him about plans for a movie about his life and speculating whether Paul Hogan was the man to play the part of his most devoted supporter.

* * *

Nutmeg Mills, a Tampa-based clothing manufacturer, announced the signing of a licensing deal with Muhammad Ali on 27 May to produce a line of T-shirts, sweat shirts, caps, jackets and sweaters, all featuring Ali and his slogan, 'I Am The Greatest!' The company hoped to debut the Ali Collection by the end of the year, and George Derhofer, chief financial officer, told reporters, 'It's too early to get projections and numbers, but Muhammad Ali is arguably the most recognisable sports person in the world.'

* * *

Arthur Morrison was arrested in Newark, New Jersey on 29 July and charged with making threatening phone calls to former girlfriends, their employers and associates. Still styling himself the president of Champion World Brands, the litany of allegations included harassment, extortion and breaking into an ex's apartment.

* * *

Muhammad Ali and leaders of various Muslim organisations across America came together for a press conference at the United Nations on 18 August to highlight the plight of Muslims in Bosnia-Herzegovina in the ongoing Balkan conflict. The group met with Muhamed Sacirbey, the nascent country's ambassador. 'When Ali came to see me at the UN, more accurately to symbolise his solidarity with Bosnia & Herzegovina, his legendary art of the word was largely subdued by Parkinson's, but his intellect and humour were more than intact,' wrote Sacirbey. 'He sought me out as an individual in our brief interaction, seeing beyond my heavy responsibilities as the very young representative of BiH and its suffering people. He did this amazing physical illusion which made him appear to be floating.'

The group called for an end to the Serbian concentration camps and for a lifting of the arms embargo so the Bosnians could better defend themselves. Ali was present for all of this but never spoke a single time, allowing Jamil Al-Amin, the 1960s radical formerly known as H. Rap Brown, to do all the talking in front of journalists. As they were leaving, one reporter asked Ali how he was feeling. 'Tired,' he responded.

* * *

At one point during 'Breakfast with Muhammad Ali' at the Women's Improvement Centre in Sacramento, Ali whispered an instruction to one of his entourage. Minutes later, the kitchens emptied and every dishwasher, server and chef emerged into the dining area. Still wearing aprons, they formed an orderly line to shake his hand. Each then departed with a signed brochure outlining the teaching of the prophet. 'He doesn't talk but he doesn't have to,' said Steve Lawrence, a member of the catering crew. 'He knows how much it means for people just to shake his hand and get their picture taken with him. No matter what, he still loves people.'

It was Friday, 21 August and tickets for breakfast with Ali cost $20 each, all proceeds going to the local Muslim community's effort to fund a new mosque. It marked the start of 'Muhammad Ali Weekend' in the California city, with events ranging from inaugurating the East-West Shopping Plaza to 'An Intimate Evening with Ali' at a private home in Carmichael. Entry to that was $250 per person.

Ali was invited by Imam Enrique Rasheed, who he'd first met at a mosque in Oakland nine years earlier. The version of Ali who turned up for breakfast in Sacramento was tired and weary and didn't speak from the podium. While several community leaders held forth eloquently about his legacy and particular significance to American Muslims, Ali remained silent.

On a visit to the state capitol hours after the breakfast, Ali met Summer Sanders, the local girl just returned from winning two swimming golds, a silver and a bronze at the Barcelona Olympics. On Saturday, his presence caused a stir at William Land Park, which was hosting the Hoop-it-Up three-on-three street basketball tournament. The funniest moment of the weekend came at a party where Fahizah Alim, a reporter with the *Sacramento Bee*, had brought along his five-year-old son Rashad. When the child got tired, Ali invited him up into his arms and the little boy promptly fell asleep there.

* * *

The inaugural class at the Madison Square Garden Walk of Fame gathered for induction on 14 September. The 25 honourees included Wilt Chamberlain, George Mikan, Oscar Robertson, Bob Cousy, Red Holzman, Maurice Richard and Gordie Howe, some of the biggest names in the history of American sport. Then Marv Albert, MC for the occasion, introduced Muhammad Ali: 'There are only two words to describe this next man – The Greatest!' The applause was louder and more sustained. Even the media clapped and all the other iconic athletes rose from their seats in acknowledgment of Ali. 'I am from Argentina,' said a young man in the crowd as Ali walked past. 'I love you!'

Ali didn't respond, stopping only to hand the admirer a signed pamphlet about Islam. He moved slowly throughout the event and didn't talk, even as he posed for photographs in front of the plaque bearing his name. 'Boxing has made me famous,' said Ali at a reception upstairs afterwards. 'But this is the real goal. My goal is to be the world's greatest ambassador, to spread the word of Islam. I want to get to at least two million people. That's my main goal. My life has just started.'

Estimating that he'd taken 182 flights over the previous year, he outlined a forthcoming itinerary that included an autograph session in Miami and proposed goodwill trips to Bosnia, Russia and Somalia. All answers were delivered falteringly, many of them punctuated by long silences. 'His hands tremble constantly,' wrote

Bert Rosenthal for the Associated Press. 'His speech is slurred and repetitious. His memory is faded. He walks with a shuffle. His face is puffy. Generally, his expression only becomes animated when he discusses religion. Otherwise, he is subdued and low-key when he speaks. There are times, however, when he won't even talk at all.'

That night, Ali was back at the Garden for the 20th annual National Multiple Sclerosis Society Dinner of Champions. 'I was seated at table 90, the most popular table on the floor because the champ, Muhammad Ali, was there,' wrote Bill Gallo in the *New York Daily News*. 'I thought, "Where have you gone, Muhammad Ali?" There was Ali looking youthful and healthy, greeting all the people who lined up to get his autograph. Women – young, middle-aged and old – hugged him and kissed his cheek. They were the kisses of mothers to their sons, brothers or nephews. Ali is like one giant cuddly bear. I even saw tough, old guys hug him and plant kisses on him.'

* * *

The residents of Joe DiMaggio Children's Hospital in Hollywood, Florida were treated to a magic show by Muhammad Ali on the first day of October. In town to attend a reception for the Memorial Classic, the facility's annual fundraiser, Ali spent time with the children on the fourth floor and performed some of his favorite sleights of hand. 'I've been doing magic for 25 years and it's just for the children,' said Ali, who also threatened to go a few rounds with hospital administrator Zeff Ross. 'And they love it.'

He was especially taken with five-year-old Jeremy Pittman, examining the boy's arms so he could check out his muscles. 'I don't think I'm stronger than he is,' said Pittman. 'But my dad is stronger than me and I think he's stronger than him too.'

* * *

Geoffrey C. Ewing had been playing the title character in an off-Broadway production of *Ali* for over two months when the boxer upon whom the one-man play was based turned up in the audience at the Sheridan Square Playhouse on Tuesday night, 27 October. Afterwards, Ali went backstage to congratulate the actor, who had also co-written the script. 'You're good,' he told Ewing. 'You're just like me but you're not as pretty as me.'

Ewing's girlfriend was also present. 'Are you with him?' asked Ali. 'Yes,' she replied. 'Well, you come with me,' he joked. 'I'm the real thing.'

* * *

The patients at the Children's Hospital of Oklahoma were visited by Muhammad Ali on 11 December. Ahead of his visit, they hung the room with banners. One read, 'Float like a butterfly, sting like a bee. You're the greatest!' Another said, 'Merry Christmas Muhammad Ali!' Children who were not even born when he last held the heavyweight title referred to him as 'Champ'. 'It is really nice of him, since he has his own problems, to give of his time,' said Gail Breckle, whose 11-year-old daughter was one of those Ali made giggle with his antics.

Ali was visiting town to promote Fight Night I, a black-tie affair where all proceeds were going to the Junior Achievement of Oklahoma City. At a luncheon held in his honour at the Lincoln Plaza Hotel, reporters joked with him about his new-found reticence, to which he responded with a smile, 'I'm all washed up!'

ROUND TWELVE

1993

*Muhammad Ali's visit to London this week will
reinforce the view that he represents the sad end
product of the most unforgiving business on earth. It is
Ali's burden to be both the fight game's most eloquent
defender (from his days of beautiful, loud menace) and,
in his tired state now, its walking tombstone. The soft
voice heard will be more like a whisper of death than
a proclamation of boisterous ego and eccentric skill
from long ago*

Kevin Mitchell, *The Observer*, 13 June

ON NEW Year's Day, Larry Smith and his fiancée Rita attended
the Orange Bowl (OB), one of the annual college gridiron
showpieces in Miami. A neophyte sportscaster with WPTVI in
Palm Beach, Smith couldn't believe his luck when he discovered
his seats were next to his hero. Muhammad Ali had earlier served
as grand marshal for the various ancillary festivities and parade
that make up the OB Jamboree, hyping up the build-up to the big
game. During breaks in play as Florida State University defeated
the University of Nebraska, Ali chatted to the excited young
couple and performed magic tricks for them.

* * *

A total of 1,700 exhibitors and an estimated 80,000 retailers turned up for the Winter Consumer Electronics Show at the Las Vegas Convention Centre over the second weekend in January. On Saturday, the star attraction was not a new piece of technology or a ground-breaking television screen but a retired boxer, signing autographs and promoting the release of *Muhammad Ali Heavyweight Boxing*. Designed for the Sega Genesis System, it allowed players the opportunity to fight as Ali against nine different opponents, their names derived from some of the best in the division at that time.

The cover blurb showed Ali delivering a straight right and promised players the chance to 'float like a butterfly and sting like a bee', providing 'you and a friend the chance to take turns trying to fill Ali's gloves'. Ali did not participate in a demonstration of the product but did pretend to spar with more than one gamer.

* * *

On one of his regular visits to Muhammad Ali's farm in Berrien Springs, Davis Miller brought along his six-year-old son Isaac. They watched Ali play with his adopted 22-month-old Asaad, got a glimpse of the fan mail piled up in his office and sat together watching a tape of his 1975 fight with Chuck Wepner. Miller was so much regarded as one of the inner circle now that, as Lonnie mocked her husband's addiction to chewing gum, she told him to check out under his desk. There, he found the mahogany pockmarked with dozens of scraps of chewed gum stuck there by Ali. Before he departed, Miller got out his video camera. 'This is Muhammad Ali in Berrien Springs, Michigan,' said Ali, staring down the lens. 'Today is the 8th of February, 1993. Ain't nobody else like me. Joe Louis, Sugar Ray Robinson, they just boxers. I'm the biggest thing that ever happened in sports. I ain't boastin', it's just the way it is. From Adam until now, I am the greatest in the recorded history of mankind.'

* * *

Delta Flight 655 from Atlanta touched down in St Petersburg, Florida in the early afternoon of 19 February. When he walked slowly up the ramp from the plane, Muhammad Ali was carrying a bulging briefcase in his left hand while his right hand shook with tremors. He was a shadow of the man he used to be. Then he spotted a young toddler coming towards him, scooped him up into his arms and kissed his face. Suddenly, he was his old animated self, the mere presence of a child invigorating him. Again. Always.

Ali had arrived in Tampa Bay for a three-day visit. Aside from receiving the key to the city from Mayor David Fischer and two autograph-signing appearances at the Bay Area Outlet Mall, where patrons paid $50 per signature, he was the star guest at a gala raising funds for Operation PAR (Parental Awareness and Responsibility), a drug-treatment and prevention programme. Patrons might have been dressed formally for that grand occasion, but once jazz singer Belinda Womack finished her rendition of 'Amazing Grace', the crowd chanted 'Ali! Ali! Ali!' as they waited for him to enter the room.

Similar adulation and fervour greeted his appearances at Bruce Allen's Sports on Saturday and Sunday. Scheduled to visit the store for two hours each time, Ali stayed for six on both days. As long as people kept coming forward, he kept signing. He didn't talk much but posed for every shot, still smiling. Special overflow parking had to be introduced. 'Many people are in this for the money,' said Andre Darby, clutching a *LIFE* magazine cover newly blessed with the Ali signature. 'I don't see it that way. Ali is the only athlete in the world who is worth going out of your way to meet. You can still see that love. He hasn't lost his love for people.'

* * *

America's Leeonzer Barber retained his World Boxing Organisation light-heavyweight title with a unanimous points decision over his compatriot Mike Sedillo in a fight known as 'The Brawl at the Wall'. Fifteen thousand Chinese, some of them paying the equivalent of $90 for ringside seats, filled the Capital City Gymnasium in Beijing on 27 February for the country's first professional boxing card since 1949. The government had lifted a ban on the sport back in 1985, a move prompted by Deng Xiaoping meeting Muhammad Ali. Fitting then that the largest cheer of the night greeted Ali's arrival into the venue as guest of honour.

He had caused a similar stir around the city over the previous days. The sport might have been prohibited during his pomp but the locals knew enough about Ali to swarm around him, offering various paraphernalia for him to sign. The items pressed into his hands at the hotel included T-shirts and 10-yuan notes (then worth about $1.70). 'I stayed after work to see Muhammad Ali,' said Yang Jie, a bathroom attendant at Ali's hotel. 'The best fighters of all time are Ali and Bruce Lee.'

Ali played the crowd the same way he played every crowd, no matter the language barrier. 'I don't like China,' he said, then pausing long enough for anticipation to build before declaring, 'I love China!'

There was a visit to a school too, police escorting Ali down a tiny street where 2,000 pupils were gathered, waiting. They waved white silk handkerchiefs in the air and chanted the words, 'Ali! Ali! Ali!' One photograph captured him, an enormous figure, an island in a sea of adoring children. 'I've been around Ali for a lot of years and I know what moves him,' said Harold Smith, a member of his entourage during that trip. 'That day, that morning, he was moved. He was deeply touched. I remember looking over at José Torres and seeing tears running down his cheeks. It was a moment I'll never forget.'

There were other cameos of wonder too, like the elderly woman who climbed out of a rice paddy in rural China and showed she knew exactly who Ali was. 'She starts moving her hands back and forth like she is boxing,' said Howard Bingham. 'Most amazing thing I've ever seen. He's been on more film than the Beatles, the pope, the president, all put together.'

* * *

North Carolina declared 12 March to be Muhammad Ali Day. Arriving at Raleigh-Durham Airport the night before, he was greeted by a crowd of grandee politicians and local fistic hero James 'Bonecrusher' Smith. As he made his way through the terminal, Ali distributed signed pamphlets about Islam. He also performed his disappearing handkerchief trick. 'I am the greatest of all time,' he declared when he made the swatch of red cloth reappear from between his fingers. 'Wherever he goes, he draws a crowd and keeps its attention,' wrote Foon Rhee in the *Charlotte Observer*. 'He tells jokes and kids around, vowing a comeback in the ring. He mugs for the cameras. He does sleight of hand tricks. He gets a pretty waitress to buss him on the cheek, then stumbles backward in mock surprise.'

As was now normally the case, some were aghast at his stilted gait, his speech soft and slow. It was evident too, however, that his pace quickened up around people and fulfilling a typically punishing schedule was not a problem. He visited Fike, Hunt and Beddingfield High Schools in Wilson, a city of 37,000, 45 miles from Raleigh. While there, he also dropped in at the Eastern North Carolina School for the Deaf and spent time at the Opportunities Industrialisation Centre, a job centre established by Howard Jones, organiser of the event. Everywhere he went that day, Ali spoke little but repeated the same, simple mantra to children who crossed his path. 'Stay in school,' he said. 'Be no fool!'

* * *

Muhammad Ali travelled 15 miles north from Berrien Springs to the McDonald's in St Joseph on Saturday, 27 March. There, he sat for several hours, signing autographs and posing for pictures. If customers arrived without something to sign, they could purchase small cards with Ali's photograph for $3 or a larger drawing of him that cost $5. Every dollar raised was to benefit Ronald McDonald House, a charity that helped defray costs incurred by the families of sick children during hospital stays. 'We would like him to take back with him at least $5,000,' said Tom Potts, owner of the McDonald's.

A queue had formed outside the building by 8.30am. Some were old enough to recount every detail of his career, others were youngsters press-ganged into attending by parents who knew one day they'd be grateful to have been there. Jim Colerman of Stevensville came bearing *LIFE* and *Sports Illustrated* magazines from 1964 with the fighter then known as Cassius Clay on the covers. 'I've just been a fan for years,' said Colerman. 'I've met him a couple of times.'

Not everybody wanted memorabilia signed. A few came for the thrill of meeting the biggest celebrity who lived in the area. No matter their motive, Ali smiled and interacted with all. At one point, he did shout out, 'I'm only doing this for charity!'

* * *

On 10 April, Chris Hani, general-secretary of the South Africa Communist Party, was assassinated as he got out of his car at his home in Dawn Park with his 15-year-old daughter Nomakhwezi. Shot four times by Janusz Walus, a Polish immigrant and far-right extremist, he died at the scene. His killing sparked intense rioting all over the country, prompted a one-day national strike by six million black workers and near enough plunged South Africa into civil war. That was the same date Muhammad Ali happened to touch down for a long-planned visit. 'The following two weeks, the time Ali spent in South Africa, proved to be the most tumultuous, taut and politically nerve-racking in the three years since President F. W. de Klerk decided to open the floodgates and initiate talks with the ANC (African National Congress),' wrote John Carlin. 'Somehow, all went well. If anything, Ali's trip was the richer. He saw the anger and the tragedy of black South Africa, as well as the exuberance.'

At the Elgangeni Hotel in Durban one evening, Ali asked the personal assistant to the manager to type up a letter he wanted sent to Nelson Mandela, reflecting the traumatic events of the previous few days.

'Dear Mr Mandela,

Allow me to extend to you and the ANC my deepest regrets upon hearing of the death of Chris Hani. My prayers go out to Mr Hani's family and the people of South Africa during these difficult days.

I am providing you the following information regarding my itinerary should you desire to contact me (prior to our scheduled meeting on 19 April, 1993): -

CAPE SUN-13 TO 16 APRIL – TEL 021 238844 FAX: 021 238875

JOHANNESBURG GARDEN COURT – 16 TO 22 APRIL – TEL: 011 297011 FAX: 011 291515

Inshallah, I pray that God keeps you safe.'

Yours Sincerely,

Muhammad Ali.'

The man typing the letter was so nervous about the task that he initially misspelt Muhammad with an 'e'. It was only after it had been signed by Ali that somebody noticed the mistake and requested a new, amended version be produced.

Fareed Hoosen, a 20-year-old working for a VIP security firm, suddenly found himself part of a detail travelling with Ali throughout the country. On the first day they met, Hoosen confessed to the man he was supposed to protect, 'When I was a kid, I watched all your videos.'

Ali smiled, tapped him on the back and said, 'I'm just a regular guy.'

And, in this case, very much a wide-eyed tourist too. 'He loved going to the Bo-Kaap, the mosques, to Gugulethu,' Hoosen said. 'We drove him on Chapman's Peak Drive. He said it was the most beautiful ever. He wanted to see Sea Point, the lights of Sea Point. So, we took him [at] around 7pm or 8pm. Once, standing at the Waterfront, he looked at the top of Table Mountain and said, "It's very interesting that it's a flat mountain. But how did they build the cable car house at the top? Did they first build the cable car, then take up the bricks?" We laughed, but then we thought about it.'

As the country came to terms with the violent aftermath of the killing, Ali, a veteran of the civil rights struggle of 1960s America, turned up for a protest march in Cape Town on 14 April, alongside the likes of Bishop Desmond Tutu. While most of those involved remained peaceful throughout, there were reports of looting. One black youth was killed, a policeman was shot and a peace monitor was stabbed. After the march had ended, a group of young men on the rampage surrounded the bus carrying Ali and appeared bent on doing damage. At least until they realised who it was carrying. Then, they raised their clenched fists and chanted, 'Ali! Ali! Ali!'

No matter which city he was in, Hoosen and the security detail were instructed again and again to stop the convoy in poor neighbourhoods so Ali could get out and meet ordinary people. In the Soweto township in Johannesburg, he visited a mosque, an orphanage and the famous Dube boxing club. There, he excused himself from sitting with dignitaries to go outside, where a group of youngsters were sparring on the grass. Mandal Mahlalela was the smallest of the boys and he was the one Ali chose to engage, squaring up to the diminutive pugilist and warning, 'I'm gonna get you, Joe Frazier!'

Mbongeni Ngema and Laura Jones had co-written a musical called *Magic at 4am*, the story of a South African goldminer and enthusiastic amateur boxer who based his entire life and personality on Ali. The man himself turned up for the premiere, sitting in the mayor of Johannesburg's box, and at the end he went onstage to dance and spar with the lead actor. They brought the house down.

There was serious business to be attended to as well. Ali visited Hani's widow Limpho, met the former minister Tokyo Sexwale and, despite concerns that it might degenerate into violence, he insisted on attending the funeral at a football stadium in Soweto. There, he spent time consoling Hani's children and also issued a statement, calling for those hurt by the assassination to keep pursuing their goals through politics rather than violence. 'The call of democracy is too important,' he said, 'and your future too precious to allow the act of a single man to interfere with your destiny.'

Amid all this chaos and tumult, there was a summit with Mandela himself. The men had met for the first time in Los Angeles, shortly after his release from prison in 1990. The leader of the ANC had made it known in interviews that Ali was one of his heroes (on Robben Island, he used to copy the boxer's poses when he saw them in magazines) and an inspiration to millions of black South Africans during the decades of the struggle against apartheid. Now that he was finally in his country, Mandela poured him tea and the two men enjoyed a respite from the conflict going on all around them. 'When I met Ali for the first time, I was extremely apprehensive,' said Mandela. 'I wanted to say so many things to him. He was an inspiration to me even in prison because I thought of his courage and commitment to his sport. He used mind and body in unison and achieved success. I was overwhelmed by his gentleness and his expressive eyes. He seemed to understand what I could not say and, actually, we conversed very little. When he came to South Africa, I was proud of how the hero of millions of young people was received here. Ali is my hero and will remain the master of boxing to me.'

Mandela kept a photograph of the boxer in his office for the rest of his life.

* * *

On 29 April, Muhammad Ali and Joe Frazier sat across from each other at Nelson's Buffeteria in downtown Tulsa. Before tucking into baked chicken (Frazier) and chicken fried steak (Ali), Smokin' Joe bowed his head and said grace. The old adversaries were in Oklahoma to lend their celebrity wattage to Fight Night II, a fundraiser for the local boys' home that night. Earlier in the day, they'd visited the charity home and, under the watchful eye of Bill Connors, a journalist, hammed up their rivalry once more. 'You are still ugly,' said Ali. 'You're still stupid,' replied Frazier.

Then they hugged.

* * *

When Muhammad Ali touched down in Tehran on 6 May, he was welcomed at the airport by Ahmad Nateq-Nouri, head of the Iranian Boxing Federation. The purpose of his visit was not solely to do with a sport that had only been made legal again in the country in 1989. He had come to try to organise an exchange of prisoners between the Iranian and Iraqi regimes, men caught by the other side during their nearly decade-long conflict that ended in 1988. Not everybody was thrilled by his arrival, however. 'For many years, Muhammad Ali's fame has been used as a tool to promote the political wishes of the United States government,' declared *Salam*, regarded as the most hardline opposition newspaper, in an editorial criticising the visit.

During a two-week stay, he attended the sixth Tehran International Book Fair held at the city's Permanent International Fairground. There, he presented Manouchehr Basir, who translated *The Greatest – My Own Story*, his first autobiography (ghost-written by Richard Durham), from English into Persian, with an original signed copy of the work. IRNA, Tehran's official news agency, also reported he laid a wreath at the tomb of Ayatollah Ruhollah Khomeini, and prayed for the soul of the late leader of the 1979 Revolution. It quoted him as saying, 'I have been to many countries, and Iran is the greatest!'

* * *

A white Rolls-Royce carrying Muhammad Ali pulled up to the front of the Mermaid Theatre in Blackfriars, London on 16 June for a special gala performance of Geoffrey Ewing's play, *Ali*. 'It's good,' he told reporters, while distributing signed leaflets about Islam. 'It's good.'

As part of the evening, Ali posed in a ring on stage with his former opponent turned good friend Henry Cooper. 'He was a great champion,' said Cooper. 'No man that size was ever that quick in a ring. It was like fighting a middleweight.'

* * *

On 7 July, Muhammad Ali arrived in Baghdad following another visit to Tehran in his ongoing efforts to negotiate an exchange of prisoners of war between Iraq and Iran. During 14 days at the Rashid Hotel, Ali met Izzat Ibrahim, a deputy to President Saddam Hussein, and received assurances from him that the Iraqi government was willing to free all Iranian prisoners if such a deal could be arranged. Although Ali's party went public with that information, there was no official government statement. 'Ali's long-time dream: Islamic nations must stop quarrelling among themselves,' said Shahi Ahmed Raza, somebody described as a spokesman for Ali. 'His immediate goal: repatriation of Iran-Iraq prisoners of war.'

At one point during his stay, photographers captured Ali leaving his hotel and walking across a mosaic on the street that was a portrait of President George H.W. Bush containing the words 'Bush is criminal!' He departed for the 600-mile journey to Tehran by car with reports that the border between the two countries was going to be opened specially to allow him through. 'A man who is not courageous enough to take risks will never accomplish anything in his life,' said Ali through a spokesman.

While in Tehran, Ali climbed into a boxing ring for an exhibition bout with Al Kezami, watched by several hundred fans. Moments before the start of the fight, Kezami, still wearing his Olympic singlet from the Barcelona games the previous year, bowed and touched Ali's feet with his glove, a way of showing respect for his opponent. Then he kissed him on both cheeks and patted his head.

Once the bell went, Ali, wearing a tight yellow long-sleeved T-shirt and red shorts, moved much better than he had when entering the ring, extending a left jab that never reached and threatening several wind-up uppercuts with his right. At one point the referee admonished him, so he turned and made as if to fight him instead of Kezami. For his part, the local hero played the straight foil to the pantomiming Ali perfectly, never throwing an actual punch in riposte, even when Ali followed him into the corner at a break in the action.

At the finish, the third man (who had incurred more than once punch from Ali) raised Ali's hands in victory and the gym echoed to the sound of 'Ali! Ali! Ali!'

* * *

Brent Gresham was a fourth-grader at Orange City Elementary School in Florida. On Friday, 17 September, his teacher had scheduled a math test. Unbeknownst to her, Brent's father Rudi had also organised an impromptu class visit by Muhammad Ali. 'I picked him up at Orlando Airport and to get out of there and to your car would take, what, about ten minutes? With him, it was an hour,' said Gresham, a former senior adviser to the secretary of Veterans Affairs, who became friends with Ali at the 1988 Republican Convention. 'He'd take time out for everybody. Everybody walked up to him. He turned nobody down. He was respectful to all the people, no matter who it was. He'd be sweet. He treated everyone well.'

The two men were sitting down at the Gresham household when Ali came up with an idea. 'Rudi, you're always talking about your children, let's go visit them.'

So, they headed for the elementary school. Ali barely spoke and didn't need to. His very presence in the corridors had teachers all in a tizzy and nobody minded the poor quality of the autographs on the cards he handed out to every child either. After performing the disappearing handkerchief magic trick, Ali was on his way back to the car and down the road to Deland Middle School to drop in on Lily and Jeffrey Gresham, Rudi's older children.

* * *

In Richmond, Virginia, the Committee to Save the Children of Iraq held a $50-a-plate charity dinner on 2 October to raise funds to help children injured in the Gulf War. 'I spent two months in Iran and Iraq this past spring and summer, trying to bring about a peaceful solution to the hostage situation,' said Muhammad Ali, chairman of the committee, before inviting guests to make further donations to the charity. 'Therefore, I know the tragedies and hardships Iraqi children face daily and have seen the suffering first hand.'

While in the area, he was on his way to visit Sisters Constantine and Helen at the Greek Orthodox Cathedral when he met Carroll Sample. A former Virginia amateur welterweight champion, Sample heard his hero was coming to town while working a shift washing dishes at the Crazy Greek restaurant and pestered the church for details so he could bring his children to meet Ali. Once Ali hovered into view, Sample introduced himself and offered a flavour of the mean impression of him he'd perfected over the years.

> *'Joe's going to come out smokin'*
> *And I ain't gonna be jokin'*
> *I'll be peckin and a-pokin'*
> *Pouring water on his smokin'*
> *This may shock and amaze you*
> *But I will destroy Joe Frazier.'*

Ali responded to the performance by throwing a right jab, smirking.

* * *

A line began to form outside Walden Books in Lower Manhattan at 10am, a full hour before Muhammad Ali's flight was due to

land at La Guardia Airport and two and a half hours before
he was due at the store to promote Howard Bingham's new
book *Muhammad Ali – A Thirty Year Journey*. Containing 182
of Bingham's photographs, the publication was a portrait of
the enduring friendship between the two men. Michael Katz,
boxing correspondent of the *New York Daily News* captured
the relationship perfectly in a brief exchange that morning of 4
October.

'Your name is over my name,' said Ali.

'I'm the star,' said Bingham.

'Alright, I won't show you up.' 'No, no,' smiled his friend,
'you're the star.'

Six hundred people waited to have Ali sign the book, the
one-hour scheduled appearance taking three times that long. He
signed each one placed in front of him, his voice never rising above
a whisper and his debilitated condition impacting on fans. 'It's
sad,' said Doug Henderson, a businessman who waited an hour
and 45 minutes to have Ali autograph two books. 'One is for my
wife. She's idolised him for 20 years. I'm not a boxing fan but I
admire the man. It was worth the wait.'

The way Ali carried himself also impressed the staff, who had
plenty of experience of celebrities of lesser wattage behaving with
far less grace. 'Muhammad Ali is the biggest draw we've had,' said
Sandra Peterson, the assistant store manager. 'He's a dream to
work with. We've had other celebrities who were rude and mean.
But Muhammad Ali truly lives up to being a living legend.'

Bingham sat beside his pal while Bernie Yuman, another old
friend, performed the task of opening every book for Ali to sign.
By accident or design, Yuman opened each one on a photograph
from 1968 showing Ali in a suit and tie, at his most dignified and
defiant during his enforced exile from the ring. A reporter asked
Bingham what he saw now in that shot. 'I see him during his

prime and wishing he could stay that way forever,' said Bingham. 'But Ali has no end. The crowd today tells you that. This is how it's been all day, every day for 30 years.'

* * *

A young reporter with the *Greenwich Time* in Connecticut, John Breunig received a tip from Paul Ardaji, a local restauranteur, that Muhammad Ali was going to be visiting with a group of special Olympians at the local police department on 12 October. At the front desk of the station, the officers had no interest in letting a journalist inside but Breunig ran outside when he saw the car carrying Ali pull up. He stuck his foot in the metal door as it was closing, and the moment some officers complained about his presence, Ali waved him in. 'He entertains the special Olympians with a few jokes and magic tricks, always remaining true to his Muslim faith by revealing his secrets,' wrote Breunig. 'When we leave, he turns his back on a waiting limousine when he hears a small group of men outside the cigar shop across the street start bellowing "Champ." Ali follows the sound of the cheers, rewarding fans with autographs and memories. This is the street where movie stars and billionaires shop and gawking is considered gauche. Yet cars pull over and strangers stop to stare at Muhammad Ali.'

As he accompanied Ali that day, Breunig happened upon a world exclusive. Ardaji, chief executive officer of MEAM CO, a New York advertising agency, was producing an epic movie of the boxer's life. In a film with a proposed $40m budget, the Ali story was finally going to be told properly on the big screen. Ali said the problem with the previous attempt to do that (*The Greatest* in 1977) was that the script had been too concerned with just boxing and his girlfriends. 'It just wasn't done right,' he said.

At one point in the conversation, Breunig told Ali, 'I've interviewed a lot of famous people, but you're the only one I ever really wanted to meet.'

Ali's eyes widened, he smiled and replied, 'I know.'

* * *

Ally McCoist was 31 years old and still near enough at the top of his game for Rangers FC in the Scottish Premier Division. When he heard Muhammad Ali was visiting Waterstones bookshop in Glasgow on 19 November to promote Howard Bingham's book, McCoist, the great goalscorer, went in search of a great score. He wanted a photograph with the boxer he had worshipped since listening to *The Rumble in the Jungle* on the radio two decades earlier. On his first visit to the city since 1965, Ali, as was his form, stayed for hours to satisfy every autograph and to pose for every picture, including one with the only man in the building to rival him for celebrity, at least in Scotland. 'I was like a wee boy in his first Christmas,' said McCoist, who wore a shirt and tie and his trademark cheeky grin for the encounter. 'There's a couple of pictures I've got where I'm just staring at him thinking, "This is unbelievable." I will never forget that sparkle in his eye. In one of the pictures I got with him, I could swear he wants to put one on my chin. He's looking at me and we've got our fists clenched. He's looking at me as if he wants to land one on me – it's brilliant.'

* * *

Mayor Rick Cole of Pasadena declared 18 December to be Muhammad Ali Day in the Californian city. Outside the Black and Latino Multicultural Centre on Mentor Street, which had been closed for traffic, Ali was presented with a proclamation to that effect. 'I came all the way from Germany through the snow and blizzard,' said Ali, upon receiving the certificate, 'and this is all I get!'

A jazz band entertained fans who lined up to purchase and sign copies of Howard Bingham's book. 'He's done politics, human affairs, sports,' said 32-year-old Lori Jones, as she waited for her audience with Ali. 'He's crossed every boundary. If our youth had him as a role model instead of Snoop Doggy Dogg, then maybe we wouldn't have so many problems.'

* * *

On the day before Christmas, Muhammad Ali filed a lawsuit with the Cook County Circuit Court in Illinois, seeking to nullify a 1991 agreement between himself and Herbert Muhammad, his erstwhile spiritual and business adviser, and head of the Chicago-based Muhammad Ali Foundation. Ali alleged his signature on the document had been obtained 'under undue influence or duress' during a trip to the Middle East when he was unwell due to fasting with the Grand Mufti in Damascus and going without his prescribed medication.

Documents filed with the court stated, 'He has no recollection of the contents of the purported agreement.' Further alleging his signature had been forged on fundraising letters, Ali sought a court order preventing Herbert Muhammad and the foundation from using his name and likeness, and also requested payment for damages incurred by his reputation.

ROUND THIRTEEN
1994

For too long, the sport of boxing has had a shadow cast over it because of the lack of regulation from a respected central governing body, which gave opportunity for many young boxers to be abused and taken advantage of by seasoned professionals in the business ... I firmly believe with the passage of bill S. 1991, the Professional Boxing Safety Act, the sport can be made a clean sport, leaving behind the stigma that has followed it for far too long.

Muhammad Ali, Letter to Senator John McCain, 3 August

TWO NIGHTS before the Dallas Cowboys trounced the Buffalo Bills in Super Bowl XXVIII at the Georgia Dome, the NFL held a party and laid on buses to ferry guests from their hotels. Muhammad Ali walked up to one such vehicle, hauling a large black suitcase behind him up the steps. Then he stopped to shake hands with the driver, calling him, 'My man!' None of the other passengers had even acknowledged the man's existence when they boarded.

Ali was sitting halfway down the bus when three couples in their 20s got on. The men recognised him and immediately started yelling, 'You're the greatest of alllll tiiiiiimme!' He smiled at their antics and told them, 'You crazy!'

Suddenly, everybody on board wanted an interaction. Another gentleman told Ali he'd been a fan since his first fistic memory, the defeat of Zora Folley in 1967, the last fight before his enforced exile from the ring. 'That's how far back I been a fan of yours,' he said. 'You knocked him out quick.' 'I bet you made some money on that,' replied Ali, the voice soft but with an impish grin on his face.

A journalist was next to try his luck. 'Champ,' said the hack, 'I want your autograph.' 'How badly you want it?' asked Ali.

'Real bad!' 'Then I'll give you two.' Ali handed over two pamphlets about Islam that contained his signature and the year.

At the party, Don Shula, coach of the Miami Dolphins, spotted Ali in the crowd and shot across. He shook Ali's hand, beseeched him to come and meet Shula's new wife Mary Anne, then asked him to pose for a photograph. 'Ali smiled,' wrote Ron Borges in the *Boston Globe*. 'Shula's wife smiled. And, believe it or not, Don Shula smiled more broadly than both of them. Muhammad Ali's presence can have that effect.'

* * *

The Ted Williams Museum and Hitters Hall of Fame at Citrus Hills, Florida opened on 9 February. The night before, there was a gala dinner attended by 30 baseball icons, including Stan Musial, Joe DiMaggio, Enos Slaughter and Brooks Robinson. When introduced to the crowd, each drew loud cheers. Yet the loudest reception of the evening came when Muhammad Ali rose from his seat. Energised by the adulation, he unfurled the Ali shuffle and that only drove the volume up.

At the official dedication ceremony the next morning, Peter Kerasotis, a journalist with *Florida Today*, observed Ali. 'His hands vibrate continually,' wrote Kerasotis. 'His face wears the plastic expression of a mask. His head doesn't seem to belong to him but to one of those toy dolls with the bobbin' noggin.'

* * *

On 6 March, 19,100 runners gathered outside the city's fabled Coliseum for the start of the ninth annual Los Angeles Marathon. Mayor Richard Riordan was charged with firing the starter's gun, assisted by Muhammad Ali. As the participants waited nervously for the off, an impromptu 'Ali! Ali! Ali!' broke out. He smiled and pointed at the runners as they strode past, staring up at him. Of all the hopefuls, Noelle Brown had more reason to smile than most.

When she and a friend turned up at the Los Angeles Convention Centre to collect her number earlier in the weekend, they walked through the Runners' Expo and discovered a large crowd milling around one table. Brown stuck her head into the throng and discovered the people were queuing to get Ali to sign copies of Howard Bingham's book *Muhammad Ali – A Thirty Year Journey*. So many were in line that a limit had already been placed on how many copies he could write his name on.

Brown inveigled her 5ft 2in frame into the melee until she reached the table where Ali was sitting. At that point, her stealthy progress was interrupted by two security men who reached in and started to remove her from the scene. Ali noticed what was going on and a word in the ear of one of his entourage bought Brown a reprieve. Then he gave her the signal to come forward. 'In a sputter of excitement, I remember saying to Ali that I was a fan,' wrote Brown. 'By that point, my friend stepped up behind me and handed me the marathon poster, which I rolled out in front of him. Always gracious, he asked me to spell my name, which I did. As he signed his name, he drew a small heart by his signature. Then he did something incredible. He pointed to his cheek, signalling for a kiss. I leaned over the table and gently kissed him on the cheek. He clutched his fist to his heart like I had knocked him out! And then, he smiled at me with a smile that lit up the room.'

* * *

On 10 March, *The State* newspaper in South Carolina reported the FBI had demanded medical records kept by Dr Rajko Medenica at Hilton Head Hospital. A group of fellow doctors had openly questioned the Yugoslav's outrageous claims about the success of his unorthodox treatments. They had discovered his résumé was riven with falsehoods and there was a disturbing lack of peer-reviewed findings to back up his boasts about curing various ailments, including cancer, with revolutionary methods.

Just three weeks earlier, Dr Medenica gave yet another interview asserting Muhammad Ali's medical problems were caused by pesticides. Claiming the 'pesticides have an affinity for neurological cells' and the toxins had specifically invaded Ali's body, he also reiterated that there had been a huge improvement because Ali was, by then, still shuttling between his South Carolina and Denver offices every three weeks to see him.

* * *

Since 1932, the Aquinas Institute for Education in Rochester, New York hosted the Mission Bouts, an annual boxing tournament to raise money for the missionary work of the Basilian Fathers in Mexico and Colombia. When the school's sports boosters gathered at Bathtub Billy's sports bar to plan for the 1994 edition of the event, they were determined to come up with something special as it was the first to be held at the school's freshly built Wegman-Napier Centre. 'Get Ali!' suggested Joe Giordano, co-owner of the pub. 'Get Ali and while you're at it dig up Rocky Marciano,' said boxing coach Dom Arioli, thinking the whole thing ridiculously far-fetched. They asked. He came.

On 10 March, Muhammad Ali was ringside in a crowd of 1,500 to witness 13 bouts and to cause the usual mayhem. He had given the Aquinas Institute permission to sell T-shirts with his image on them, agreed to sit for a VIP picture and autograph session at Bathtub Billy's, and helped to raise a record $7,000. 'You the coach?' he asked Arioli when they were introduced. 'Yes,' said Arioli. 'Don't screw it up,' Ali warned, with a wink and then a smile.

The loudest cheers of the evening came when Ali stepped towards sophomore Chris Schwab and invited him to fight. Suddenly, he was dancing around the ring letting jabs fly and the boosters worried the noise might take the roof off the new venue. He did not speak much during his first day in Rochester but, at the student assembly in the institute next morning, he delivered brief remarks. 'My purpose was to be a great boxer,' he said, 'so I could use it for other things.'

* * *

Charles Jenkins Bilal was elected mayor of the south-eastern Texas town of Kountze (pop. 2,000) in 1991. The first Muslim to hold the office in any municipality in America, Bilal's status was enough to bring him to the attention of Muhammad Ali, who flew in for a three-day visit on 19 March. So few locals believed Bilal about the imminent celebrity visitor that he needed a letter of confirmation from Ali before he was allowed to reserve the top floor of the Hilton Hotel off Interstate 10.

Ali came to Hardin County, a place with a racially charged history, because he'd been told Bilal needed to raise money to build a new water-well, his efforts to do so having been stymied by the predominantly white local council. Eventually, it was decided that with the most famous athlete on earth visiting, enough money might be raised to go even further and to underwrite the construction of a new youth centre. Ben Rogers, a local businessman, philanthropist and huge boxing fan, loaned a convertible limousine as a fitting mode of transport and Ali was paraded through town with the grinning mayor sitting beside him in the back.

The entourage stopped at a house where seven-year-old Jemiah Richards was with his great-grandmother. The child was besotted, watching Ali 'levitate'. At one point, he leaned over and told the boy, 'Greatness is inside'. Two decades later, Richards was a nationally ranked amateur lightweight. There were plenty other stops on his whistle-stop tour too, his drop-in bringing predictable havoc to the Parkdale Mall, where hastily purchased polaroid cameras were used to snap pictures of Ali. 'He would put a ball in his hand and have someone try to guess which hand it was in,' said Derek Woods, working at the Camelot music store when Ali popped in. 'He was very nice and you could tell he liked to be around people.'

A banquet at the local high school featuring Ali as the star attraction raised $7,000, yet after the state paid for the water-well the council could not agree on how to spend the cash. The youth centre was never built and the money sat in a bank account gathering interest for years. It was eventually used to construct a plaque to Ali at the site of the former George Washington Carver School, where black children were educated before the district integrated.

* * *

Perry Holloway was a 39-year-old forklift driver for the Dixie Warehouse and Cartage Co. and traced his Muhammad Ali obsession back to the night three decades earlier when he'd eavesdropped a crackling radio signal of Cassius Clay defeating Sonny Liston. Holloway regularly cruised Buechel Bank Road in Louisville, hoping he'd catch a glimpse of Ali visiting his mother Odessa Clay at her house there. On 24 April, another fruitless drive-by elicited no sighting but this time he stopped to ask a neighbour if he was even stalking the right place. 'Do you know where Odessa Clay lives?' shouted Holloway at a large man standing on a faded redwood deck behind a red brick house.

The man turned and glared back at him. The man was Ali.

Back in his hometown because his mother had suffered a stroke that put her in Audubon Regional Medical Centre, he put on his famous stare until the face creased into a grin and then he threw a playful punch in Holloway's direction. After all this time hunting his quarry, Holloway struggled to speak, finally getting the words out to ask if Ali would sign his copy of *The Greatest*, which he always kept in the car just in case. He would and he did. For 15 minutes, the pair of them stood there chatting until a phone call brought Ali back inside. 'It was magic,' said Holloway. 'The best moment of my life!'

* * *

As the flight descended into Hanoi Airport on 11 May, Muhammad Ali turned to Albro L. Lundy III, a 34-year-old sitting in the seat next to him, and said, 'I can't believe I am here. I spent so much of my life fighting not to come. But now I am here to bring your dad home.' 'Thank you,' said Lundy, who was ten when the Skyraider plane being flown by his father, USAF Major Albro L. Lundy Jr, was shot down in Laos during the Vietnam War on Christmas Eve 1970.

Having received various messages over the years telling him his father was still alive and a prisoner of war, he had finally decided to go and see for himself, joining an expedition led by a non-profit called 'Let Freedom Ring'. Carol Hrdlicka, 56, of Conway Springs, Kansas, had come to search for her husband, Capt. David Hrdlicka, last seen being led away after he was shot down on 18 May 1965, also over Laos.

An ambitious attempt to bring closure to some long-suffering families of the 1,643 Americans termed MIA (Missing in Action), the project had been lent considerable weight by Ali agreeing to travel to the country with whom his legend and career were so intertwined.

'We welcome you because the Vietnamese people understand you as a champion boxer,' said Vu Chi Cong, director of the Vietnamese Office For Seeking Missing Persons, 'and also as a fighter for peace.'

Ali and the rest of entourage met with Vietnamese officials to discuss the cases and to elicit some more information about the possible whereabouts of the missing pilots. 'I will always remember Ali describing to the Premier how the world was his home and each country was a room within it,' said Albro Lundy. 'And we, as family living in that home, should work together for peace. Then he brought up my father and asked if he was held by the Vietnamese [who ruled Laos], [and] would they release him? And I can remember so clearly the Premier saying, "Champ, if this was between our peoples, we would have resolution. But this is between our governments. And out of my and your hands."'

Afterwards, the American visitors were brought to a house to meet Luu Van Chanh and his wife Dang Thi Cuc, an elderly couple who had a pair of sons still listed among the 300,000 missing from the Vietnamese side. As the group wended their way through the streets of Hanoi, Ali handed out money to the children swarming around him, which only caused more and more to appear. 'Muhammad is a man of peace and goodwill,' explained Arnold Beizer, a Connecticut lawyer who helped organise the trip, to the grieving parents. 'He came here to build a bridge of friendship between our peoples. He's got medical problems himself and he gets tired very easily. His mother at home is very sick and he came all the way here to meet with you people to tell you how important establishing better relations between us as a people is.'

The conversation between the Americans and the Vietnamese couple took place in a tiny, cramped room that was unbearably hot and dark due to a power outage. While Ali didn't speak at all and one reporter present described his condition as 'wrenching', there was a back and forth between the locals and their visitors, with an interpreter helping to surmount the language difficulty so the stories could be shared. 'We have hatred for the war,' said Dang Thi Cuc. 'We understand your losses because we also have losses. As for the mothers, of course, we miss our children very much.'

Predictably, the mission to bring home the missing men to their families failed, yet Ali still felt something had been gained from the trip. 'People who were bitter enemies towards each other sat down and came to terms and made peace,' he said.

* * *

When Muhammad Ali fought Sonny Liston at the Central Maine Youth Centre in Lewiston in May 1965, Bryan Carlson, a freshman at nearby Bates College, snuck into the venue by carrying a typewriter and passing himself off as a journalist. He even ended up in seats next to Ali's parents and his then wife Sonji. 'Write this down,' said Cassius Clay Sr to the undergraduate. 'If Cassius says a mosquito can pull a plough, just hook him up and don't ask how.'

Carlson transcribed the quote and was an Ali fan thereafter. Twenty-nine years later, he was president of Mount Ida College, a leafy private school just outside Boston that awarded Ali an honorary doctorate for 'his courage, generosity, leadership and spiritual and personal integrity in his life'.

The night before the ceremony, George Kimball of the *Boston Herald* spent time with Ali, Lonnie and Howard Bingham in their hotel suite. When the reporter rose to leave, Ali struggled to climb from the armchair and drool dripped from his mouth. Noticing the shocked look on Kimball's face, Lonnie explained that he hadn't taken his medicine that day. Still, the veteran boxing scribe was worried.

'Howard,' he said to Bingham in the corridor. 'I've known for some time that he has good days and bad days but until this moment I never knew just how bad the bad days could be. Are you sure he'll be alright tomorrow?'

'He'll be fine,' said Bingham.

And he was. The ceremony took place in a banquet tent on the college grounds on Saturday, 28 May. Aside from Lonnie, their son Asaad and Bingham, Ali was accompanied by Wilbert 'Skeeter' McClure, the Massachusetts state boxing commissioner and a former team-mate from the 1960 Olympics.

'He tried to disrupt the old order,' said Carlson in his speech. 'He has spoken with his fists, spoken with his words, he has spoken with his deeds.'

Wearing a cap and gown, Ali stood alongside other recipients of honorary degrees, including Tansu Ciller, the first female prime minister of Turkey. After Mount Ida announced the establishment of 'The Muhammad Ali Award' to be given each year to the student who contributed most to promoting a multi-racial community on campus, Ali made his way to the rostrum. 'I've been called the king,' he said. 'I've been called the greatest. I've been called champ. And now I can be called the doc.'

* * *

With an estimated one million Americans battling it, seven days each year had been designated 'Parkinson's Disease Awareness Week' in order to raise its profile so politicians would fund research into a cure. For the first time ever, Muhammad Ali agreed to participate in the event in Washington, DC and on 13 June he strolled down a hallway in the US Senate, flicking the ear of one of his entourage then pretending he hadn't done any such thing. 'Champ, great to see you,' said Senator Orrin Hatch of Utah, his old friend. 'How are you? You doin' good?'

'No,' Ali whispered.

Ali's presence in Washington was down to Dr Abraham Lieberman, the Phoenix-based national medical director of the American Parkinson's Disease Association. Earlier in the year, Lieberman, who had known Ali for about a decade, travelled to Berrien Springs to ask Ali to lend his name to the cause. Although Lonnie liked the idea, Ali was reluctant and didn't want to become the public face of the illness. Others had tried and failed to coax him on board before but eventually he asked Lieberman to write him a letter, outlining the case.

Instead of a letter, the neurologist composed a poem in which he praised Ali, writing, 'The image, the legend, the symbol of Muhammad Ali is ageless. A part of the world, like the pyramids and the Grand Canyon. This can never change.'

After the paean he gave the hard sell, outlining what Ali's celebrity was worth to the campaign.

'You have the ability to help people with Parkinson
And you must meet this challenge
When you go to your grave, as we all must
It will not be enough that you were the greatest champion in
history
If Parkinson's disease lives on'

Ali agreed to get involved. The night before his visit to the Senate, he was guest of honour at a small dinner party at the Watergate Hotel. His mood was characterised by one attendee as 'outgoing, droll and generous', growing particularly excited when one guest brought out a poster advertising his 1976 bout against Jean-Pierre Coopman in San Juan. If there was plenty of the old Ali present that evening, he cut a less robust figure at a press conference alongside senators Hatch, Mark Hatfield and John McCain (who was sponsoring a bill to clean up professional boxing and protect fighters' welfare) next morning. 'As McCain spoke,' wrote James Warren in the *Chicago Tribune*. 'Ali slumped in a chair, gingerly fingered a pair of sunglasses and put them on. When he was introduced, he tried to get up but his balance was off. He rose a few inches, then slipped back down. And yet, when the ceremony concluded, a likely tendency to see him as a mournful, even tragic figure, was dissipated by Ali himself. He spotted a young boy, beckoned him over and then opened the palms of his hands, towards the youngster. Then he closed the left hand into a fist, and with the right, plucked out a red handkerchief. Abracadabra! The boy was enchanted. The champ smiled broadly.'

The tableau played out in front of a gallery of young Senate staffers, rapt by the transformation of somebody who had seemed to be struggling to get through the press conference. 'Pretty amazing,' quipped one onlooker. 'He really still looks like Muhammad Ali!'

* * *

Over the course of Father's Day weekend, Sawgrass Mills Mall in Fort Lauderdale, Florida hosted SuperExpo XII. Billing itself the state's largest sportscard, comic and memorabilia show, Muhammad Ali was the star attraction, signing photographs for $50 each. Among the 500 people who bought tickets on Saturday, 18 June were Greg and Shana Beckno from Coral Springs. They stood in line with their four-month-old daughter Kayla, and as they approached the table where he was signing, Shana, a native of Malawi, said, 'as-salamu alaykum'. The Arabic greeting, 'peace be upon you', got Ali out of his seat. Either that or the sight of a new-born baby moved him, as always. He asked for permission to take Kayla in his arms. 'There are only two idols I have had,' said Greg Beckno, 'Nelson Mandela and Muhammad Ali. I missed Nelson Mandela when he was in Miami Beach. I decided I was not going to miss Ali.'

* * *

Before a night of boxing at the Pennsylvania Convention Centre on 1 July, Mayor Ed Rendell of Philadelphia introduced Muhammad Ali to an audience attending a dinner in his honour. Rendell pointed out that Ali would make a wonderful politician because of his special relationship with the public and the fact he always symbolised what is good. Then he described him as 'one of the greatest fighters of all time'. Big mistake. 'Not one of the greatest,' said Ali. 'The greatest!'

Joe Frazier, a native of the city and a man liable to argue that point, had turned up late for the affair. As he walked in, Ali rose from his seat and assumed a fighting stance. The pair bobbed and weaved, and the crowd roared. Frazier reminded the audience his great rival had lived on Philadelphia's Main Line for a time in the 1960s. When Rendell went to present Ali with a commemorative bowl, he grabbed the microphone from ring announcer Michael Buffer and said, 'I came all the way from London, and all you give me is a bowl!'

* * *

In Beaufort, South Carolina on 21 July, United States District Judge Cameron Currie dismissed a lawsuit accusing three Hilton Head physicians of trying to put Dr Rajko Medenica out of business. Among the plaintiffs attached to the case on Medenica's behalf was Muhammad Ali, who the Yugoslav still claimed did not suffer from Parkinson's syndrome but was merely battling toxins that had invaded his body.

* * *

On 24 August, Odessa Lee Grady Clay was laid to rest at Green Meadows Memorial Cemetery in Louisville, Kentucky. Muhammad Ali's mother had died four days earlier at the Hurstbourne Health Centre, a nursing home where she had lived since being disabled by a stroke in February. 'Without the mother, the tree could not have stood so tall,' said Reverend Kevin Cosby, pastor of St Stephen Baptist Church on 15th Street. 'It's only right we say thank you to the roots of greatness. If the tree stood tall, it was only because of the roots.'

Hundreds of people had swarmed A.D. Porter and Sons funeral home the previous night to pay their respects to the 77-year-old known as 'Mama Bird'. In the early days of her son's boxing career, she walked into gyms where few women had ever been in order to check on his welfare. When he turned pro and became world heavyweight champion, she travelled the world to watch him fight. For the duration of her illness, he'd been back and forth to Louisville to visit her. 'Everybody thinks their mother is the greatest,' said Ali.

* * *

Muhammad Ali arrived at Hong Kong international Airport on 30 August en route to Macao, the tiny Portuguese territory across the Pearl River Delta. Aside from being named 'Fighter of the Century' by the Macao Sports Institute, Ali visited the Portuguese Consul-General, and the office of Jorge Rangel, secretary for public administration, education and youth.

He spoke very little during his public appearances but pleased the large crowds that followed him around Macao by repeatedly performing the magic trick of the disappearing handkerchief. After many formal events, Ali asked to be driven to an orphanage, where he found a Catholic nun and her helpers caring for 30 children between the ages of three months and ten years. He told everybody in his entourage that day to empty their pockets and donate what money they had to the nun. An estimated $1,400 was collected, a sum she assured the donors was enough to cover the charity's expenses for a year.

* * *

The limited-edition Muhammad Ali Fossil watch, a water-resistant timepiece with quartz movement and a leather strap, presented in a collectible tin placed inside a mahogany wood box, retailed for $200.

Just 7,500 were produced and every purchase came with an opportunity to be photographed with Ali. Among the 300 people who lined up outside Macy's at Roosevelt Field Mall in Garden City, Long Island on 10 September was Chuck Everson, a 7ft 1in centre on the University of Villanova basketball team that won the 1985 national championship. 'He's one of the greatest athletes I've ever seen and I just wanted the opportunity to shake his hand,' said Everson. 'I wanted his picture taken with my son. He was great with the baby.'

Ali was in fine form, shadow-boxing customers and throwing his hands in the air pretending to be arrested when a uniformed Nassau County police officer reached the top of the queue. After the last watch had been sold, autographed boxing gloves were auctioned off for the Parkinson's Disease Foundation. As fans chanted 'Ali! Ali! Ali!' Jamie Nelson, a sports performance trainer from Levittown, stumped up $2,700 for the pair. 'As soon as I went up there,' said Nelson, 'I started shaking. I got chills. He had me on my heels, as they say in boxing.'

* * *

As part of its 40th anniversary edition on 19 September, *Sports Illustrated* asked its journalists to vote for the top 40 most influential sports people of all time. Out of 300 nominations, Muhammad Ali finished first, just ahead of Michael Jordan in the voting. 'We looked for people who not only performed but also impacted the sport, both on and off the field,' said Mark Mulvoy, editor of the magazine. 'One athlete has bridged the 40 years with us – Cassius Clay-Muhammad Ali!'

* * *

The Centre for the Study of Sport in Society celebrated its tenth year as part of Northeastern University with a banquet for 700 in Boston on 2 November. Muhammad Ali attended the event, accepting a doctorate recognising his public service and becoming the first inductee into the centre's Hall of Fame. 'But for most of the evening, the 52-year-old former champion sat at his table, his rigid moon face drooping on his chest, dozing,' wrote Robert Lipsyte in the *New York Times*. 'He autographed with a shaky hand. The unerringly light-touched master of ceremonies, Dick Schaap, had to explain Ali's Parkinson's syndrome. Ali was originally scheduled to come to the podium to receive his award as the centre's first Hall of Fame inductee. At the last moment, the presenters went to his table instead, where he received the plaque almost stuporous in the glare of TV lights. The audience sighed sympathetically.'

Then John A. Curry, president of Northeastern University, and George J. Matthews, chairman of its board of trustees, began the ceremony in which they were to confer his honorary degree.

As soon as they began speaking, Ali jumped to his feet and ran down the aisle. To the disbelief and delight of the audience, he climbed up on to the podium, grabbed the microphone and said, 'Now! You got to call me doctor!'

* * *

At lunchtime on Friday, 5 November, Muhammad Ali and Joe Frazier strode past the crowd at the City Place Mall in Silver Spring, Maryland and through the doors of the newly opened rotisserie chicken restaurant bearing Ali's name. The brainchild of Talib Rashada, an old friend of Ali's who'd come up with the idea after tasting the greatest roast chicken of his life during a trip to Saudi Arabia the previous year. Rashada bought the recipe and then, in return for equity in the company, invited Ali to lend his name to an enterprise he envisaged becoming a global chain.

Conrad Cheek Jr, one of those who came to sample the chicken and meet his hero, was accompanied by his wife. As they lined up to order food he pointed out Ali over in the corner, where a gaggle of people were waiting. At that point, Mrs Cheek lost it. 'Muhammad! Muhammad!' she screamed, marching towards him, bellowing about an uncle of hers who had fought pro in Kansas City back in the day. 'Let her through,' mumbled Ali, who extended his hand. 'Ali was holding her hand as she – being tall, shapely, beautiful and intelligent – introduced me as her husband,' wrote Cheek. 'He gave me a look and made a growling sound like a pitbull, as though I was the next contender that he was going to meet in the ring! I puffed my chest, balled up my fists, looked him in the eye and yelled at him assertively, 'That's *myyyyyyyyy* wife!' He let go of her hand, smiled and welcomed us to his restaurant.'

The 3,000-square-foot space had several large television monitors suspended from the ceiling, and seating in the shape of a boxing ring. Aside from rotisserie chicken, the menu included family-style macaroni and cheese, candied yams, collards and cornbread. With a logo featuring a butterfly and a bee, every purchase of a Three Whole Rotisserie Chicken Ali Value Meal came with an autographed black-and-white photograph of the part-owner.

* * *

Frank Liles retained his WBA super-middleweight crown with a unanimous decision over Michael Nunn while Segundo Mercado and Bernard Hopkins fought a 12-round draw in their IBF middleweight championship clash at the Coliseo General Rumiñahui, in Quito, Ecuador on 17 December. To add glamour to the country's first-ever hosting of world title fights, Don King had brought Muhammad Ali for his first visit to the South American country. In a photograph reproduced in newspapers across America, Ali and King were pictured sitting together ringside licking lollipops while watching the action.

ROUND FOURTEEN

1995

*The man whose movements were so fast they seemed acts
of sorcery now has trouble with a slow shuffle. The voice
whose words once flowed like a mighty river has been
reduced to a hesitant whisper. A magician named Ali
once upon a time created the illusion that this was sport.
But it was an illusion. Boxing is no sport and it has no
place in civilised society. Ban it. Ban it now!*

John Head, *Atlanta Journal-Constitution*, 12 June

A POLICE escort took Muhammad Ali's limousine to the front
door of the Dunbar Community Centre in Lexington, Kentucky
on Saturday morning, 18 February. There, he spent three hours
meeting with a crowd of over 300. Some came to beseech him
to autograph memorabilia (one lugging along a Muhammad
Ali pinball machine), more wanted handshakes, hugs or kisses.
All were eager just to be in his presence. The front page of the
next morning's *Lexington Herald* showed Ali, in black shirt and
slacks, receiving a baby being passed to him by a delighted mother.
'Muhammad Ali coming to town and being here and the diversity
and the enthusiasm of this crowd is really something special,' said
Urban County councilman George Brown. 'He's still a profound

and magnetising figure. There's just an aura about him. I was so excited this morning that my palms were sweating.'

Upon arrival, Ali had been greeted with a red carpet strewn with rose petals and a chair prepared for him was draped in African Kente cloth. He moved slowly and barely spoke, even during a presentation ceremony in which representative Jesse Crenshaw awarded him the Governor's Outstanding Kentuckian Award and councilman Brown gave him the key to the city. To the amusement of the crowd, he squinted at the smallness of the key as if it couldn't be real. 'I just told him that I thought he was the greatest and God bless him,' said 45-year-old Tim Soulis of Lexington, after queuing for an hour. 'His hands were so soft. His fists have done such damage in the ring, and yet his hands are so soft.'

Ali's departure from the centre was a truncated affair, his progress to the limo checked by constant interruptions and requests he couldn't possibly refuse. After climbing into the backseat ready to depart, he still couldn't resist getting back out to shadow-box some youngsters gathered on the sidewalk.

Later that day, the University of Kentucky basketball team entertained the Florida Gators at the Rupp Arena. Ali turned up just before tip-off, sat on the home team's bench and never left. 'It was the thrill of a lifetime,' said coach Rick Pitino after his team had won by ten points.

At one juncture, Kentucky guard Jeff Sheppard got a cut on his nose and had to be brought to the bench for treatment. As Ali stared at the blood dripping from the boy's face, Sheppard quipped, 'I got punched in the nose.' Ali laughed.

Later, a reporter asked Pitino's assistant Jim O'Brien how come Ali got to sit in the middle of the bench during an actual game. 'Who's going to tell Muhammad Ali where he can sit?' answered O'Brien.

After the game, Ali had dinner with former Kentucky Governor John Y. Brown Jr at Bravos, the restaurant Pitino owned. During the meal, Cawood Ledford, the legendary voice of Kentucky basketball, dropped by the table, unsure if the boxer he covered during his early days as Cassius Clay would even remember him.

'Cawood,' whispered Ali, placing his arm around him, 'we're getting to be old-timers.'

* * *

At 6.16am on Saturday, 25 March, Mike Tyson walked out of the Indiana Youth Centre where he had served three years for raping beauty pageant contestant Desiree Washington in an Indianapolis hotel room in 1991. Flanked by Don King and co-managers Rory Holloway and John Horne, and wearing a white Muslim prayer cap, Tyson walked through a crowd of well-wishers and climbed into a black limousine. The car sped two miles to the Islamic Society of North America Mosque on County Road where Muhammad Siddeeq, his new spiritual adviser, the rapper MC Hammer and Muhammad Ali were waiting to greet him.

A large banner draped from the ceiling read, 'May Allah Bless Mike Tyson'. The original intent was for the morning prayer ceremony to take place in private but that idea had to be abandoned as hundreds of fans swarmed the property. Eventually, all who wished to enter were allowed in to participate. Ali and Tyson sat in the front row of the service led by Siddeeq. King, who didn't want the mosque included on the itinerary, bristled in the second row.

Afterwards, there was a private breakfast where Ali had some issues. 'Muhammad Ali was just having a little difficulty with his plate,' said Siddeeq. 'As Ali was trying to sit down, Mike interrupted what he was doing to take the plate from Muhammad

– very gentle and placed the plate down. And then he went over to pull the chair out for Muhammad Ali and let him sit in the chair, and then they sat there together.'

As the two former champions ate together, Ali turned to Tyson and said, 'Brother, Islam is a firm handle, it will not let you go, if you don't let it go.'

Tyson replied, 'I won't let it go. It's going to be my way of life.'

* * *

Howard Cosell, Ali's verbal sparring partner in so many encounters that gripped American sports fans, died at the age of 77 in New York's Hospital for Joint Diseases on 23 April. 'Howard Cosell was a good man and he lived a good life,' said Ali in a statement. 'I have been interviewed by many people but I enjoyed interviews with Howard the best. We always put on a good show. I hope to meet him one day in the hereafter. I can hear Howard now saying, "Muhammad, you're not the man you used to be." I pray that he is in God's hands. I will miss him.'

At Cosell's memorial service, Ali sat next to the comedian Billy Crystal. 'Little brother, do you think he's wearing his hairpiece?' he asked at one point.

'I don't think so,' replied Crystal.

'Well, how will God recognise him?'

'Champ,' said Crystal, 'once he opens his mouth, God will know.'

The two of them cracked up and then Ali leaned over and said, 'Howard was a good man.'

Later in the service, after Jill Cosell delivered a touching eulogy for her father, she sat on the other side of Ali. 'Muhammad patted me,' she said. 'He had tears streaming down his face. I told him, "It's okay, Muhammad".'

* * *

On Friday, 28 April, 150,000 North Koreans shoehorned into the May Day Stadium to witness the opening of the Pyongyang International Sports and Culture Festival for Peace. They had come to watch wrestling matches involving famous Japanese and American grapplers. That the natives weren't huge fans of either country didn't diminish their enjoyment at the spectacle headlined by the likes of Ric Flair, Chris Benoit and Antonio Inoki.

The event was the brainchild of Inoki. Famous in the West for having fought Muhammad Ali in a cross-sport debacle in 1976, he had embarked on a political career in Japan and was always trying to break down barriers with the communist neighbours.

Just one year into his reign as Supreme Leader of the troubled nation, and with a famine that would kill millions taking place on his watch, Kim Jong-il bought into the idea of an eye-catching promotion to showcase North Korea to the world. This explained the presence of Muhammad Ali in the stadium that day.

Inoki had wanted Ali to be involved from the outset, reaching out to Eric Bischoff, then president of World Championship Wrestling (WCW) in the US, to see if it was possible to bring some big names from his talent roster and the most famous athlete on the planet as an added bonus. The first part was easy enough and once Bischoff raised the possibility of visiting a country that rarely opened its doors to visitors with Ali and his handlers, his enduring thirst for adventure meant there was only going to be one answer.

The journey to Pyongyang was complicated by the US State Department banning direct flights to North Korea. As a result, the travelling party convened in Nagoya, Japan before making the last leg of the trip to the most cloistered society on earth. There, Scott Norton, a 6ft 3in, 360lbs behemoth, caught his first up-close glimpse of Ali. 'We're sitting there waiting for the plane and you hear this huge commotion and it's Ali with his entourage,' said Norton. 'He's pointing at us. He kept saying, "I want you! I want you!" I'm kind of looking around and, all of a sudden, I'm realising he's talking to me. This is the most unbelievable thing. The cameras are clicking and people are going nuts. He's got his dukes up. This is Muhammad Ali, man. I'm just some greenhorn in the business. I had so much respect – I mean, I watched every single round this guy had ever fought. It was unbelievable. He had time for everybody. He was so cool. He shook everybody's hand.'

On the flight across the Sea of Japan to Pyongyang, on a rickety old prop plane that often seemed like it might not be quite up to the job, Ali talked about his love of wrestling with Bischoff and did magic tricks for anybody else who wandered into his airspace. It was a welcome distraction during a fraught couple of hours.

In North Korea, the itinerary included a visit to the Mansu Hill Grand Monument. Originally built in 1972 to commemorate the nation's struggles, the centrepiece was a statue of Kim Il-Sung, the nation's founder. While the American wrestlers had all noticed the seriousness of Ali's battle with Parkinson's syndrome and his obvious physical decline, once he approached the steps leading up to that plaza, they witnessed him turning back the clock. 'We were walking up these – it seemed like a thousand steps, maybe more – to worship their first dictator, who started all the crazy shit over there,' said Norton. 'Muhammad Ali, he's kind of having a hard time. The next thing you know, he starts kind of bouncing around. You always kept an eye on that guy when he was around you because it was so prestigious. He snaps out of the Parkinson's and took his jacket off – I watched this, I was amazed. He took his jacket off and untied his tie, and he started jogging up these stairs.'

Another excursion involved a pilgrimage to the birthplace of Rikidozan, the Korean-born father of Japanese wrestling and one-time mentor to Inoki. 'We went to visit Rikidozan's home,' said Sonny Onoo, WCW's Japanese-American consultant who also worked the trip. 'As I was walking back to our vehicle, I feel something on the back of my head. Somebody's tapping me. I turn around and it's Muhammad Ali, punching me on the back of my head. So, I got a picture of me and him squaring off. I will always cherish that.'

Huge stars in their own firmament, being in Ali's orbit turned the wrestlers back into childish fans. 'Even with his hands shaking, when he signed his name, his name was perfectly signed,' said Too Cold Scorpio. 'It was perfect handwriting – better than mine. I was just blown away to get his signature. To actually take a picture with Muhammad Ali meant more to me because my dad, when he was younger, he used to spar with Cassius Clay as a semi-pro boxer.'

At the May Day Stadium, there were two days of performances, each show preceded by choreography involving every person in the venue holding up different coloured cards. On cue. In perfect sync. When that finished, Ali was introduced to the crowd. The reaction was polite cheering. None of the Americans knew if the men and women on their feet had even heard of the man or his career or were just applauding because they were under strict orders to do so.

The visit was not without its flashpoints. During one state dinner, a North Korean government official gave a speech boasting about the military capability of the country, reckoning it now had the firepower to take out Japan or the United States at any given moment. Around the tables of the American wrestlers, that assertion was greeted by much eye-rolling, and Ali reacted by turning to Ric Flair sitting next to him and whispering, 'No wonder we hate these motherfuckers!'

* * *

The Muhammad Ali Museum and Education Centre opened at the Louisville Galleria on 29 April. A single room filled with memorabilia from his career, much of it donated on loan by Ron Palloger, a California-based collector, and other artefacts contributed by John Ramsey, a radio announcer with WRKA in the city. Admission was $4 for adults and $2 for children between the ages of 6 and 11. Fourteen stations throughout the exhibit told the story of the different phases of his life, from his childhood right through the glory years of his stints as heavyweight champion.

Five days after the first visitors shuffled through the door, Ali – freshly returned from North Korea – formally opened the museum in what was once a clothing boutique. 'We watch Ali,' wrote Joe Posnanski for Scripps Howard News Service. 'We take his picture. We beg for his autograph. We follow him around the room. We look for his eyes. We tell him our dreams. Everybody has a story. The young man in the suit wanders up to tell Ali about being ringside at the Ken Norton fights. Mike Ward, the Louisville Congressman, tells about walking into a store in the heart of Africa and seeing Ali's picture. Everybody tries to explain how much he changed their lives, but the words plink off key. How do you thank somebody for filling your childhood, for giving you something to talk about with your father, for being splendid?'

People pressed forward asking Ali to sign his name across various items. One young man emerged from the crowd, bearing nothing except the desire to envelop him in a hug. 'Thank you for being my hero,' he said. 'Do good,' whispered Ali in his ear.

While happy that the museum had opened at all and acknowledging plans to raise funds for a permanent home in a dedicated building, there was a view abroad in the town that Ali and his legacy deserved much better than an interim space in a shopping mall. 'Louisville owes Muhammad Ali a lot more than Muhammad Ali owes Louisville,' wrote Bette Winston Baye in the *Louisville Courier-Journal*. 'At the very least, Louisville owes its native son a permanent and fully endowed Muhammad Ali Museum and Education Centre. And it needs to become a reality while Ali is still with us and can walk through it and smell the sweet fragrance of all the roses he so richly deserves.'

* * *

John Petek, a world-renowned sculptor of athletes, had been commissioned to produce three new bronze figures of Muhammad Ali. For the unveiling, Ali travelled to Billings, Montana for the first time, arriving in town on 11 May for a Growth Thru Art Benefit at the Holiday Inn Trade Centre. There, his slow, deliberate entry into the room was sound-tracked by the crowd chanting his name. One woman burst into tears at the sight of him and a local newspaper reported that 'every socio-economic group' in the region appeared to be represented.

Ali never spoke a word in public during his appearance but when Petek whipped the cover off the first sculpture, Ali jumped back, feigning surprise at the representation of his young self. Then, two lines formed of people wanting to get autographs and photographs. Eventually, those around Ali announced he was taking a break, assuring those who had yet to have an audience that he would return for a second act. And, of course, he did.

Most in the room surmised he'd grown tired and needed to recuperate but, in actual fact, the interval was pre-planned so he could sit for Petek to paint a watercolour of him, the work to be auctioned off later in the evening. 'The good I feel bringing happiness to people,' said Ali to Petek in their private conversation. 'Boxing was my life. Now my life is my religion and children.'

Petek recounted the conversation in an angry letter to the *Billings Gazette* in the week following the event. He and others who had worked with Ali on the night were annoyed by a column that appeared 48 hours after the event, in which Joe Kusek, a local sportswriter, expressed sadness about Ali's diminished physical condition. 'He acknowledged the crowd but did not seem to know why, always glancing towards his aide for help,' wrote Kusek. 'The man who once had the attention of the world was now a silent observer. Does he need to do this? To be flown from town to town for a few dollars, being shown like someone's prize animal at a fair. The man's dignity is worth more than that. As he disappeared behind the curtain Thursday night, I could only think, "Take care Muhammad. You deserve better." And our memories deserve better.'

Kusek mostly reported what he saw, which was a hero in serious decline. But the image he used of a helpless man being led around by others bent on wringing money from his celebrity was wide of the mark. It provoked several letters to the editor, all taking him to task for failing to appreciate that part of Ali's enduring greatness was his willingness to still engage with the public even when his hands shook and the mouth that roared had been reduced to a whisper. 'Mr Kusek saw a much different Muhammad Ali than we did,' wrote Phil and Ty Keeter of their experience of the evening. 'We all saw a man play the room, performing a few simple magic tricks for those lucky enough to gather around him after the autograph session. Ali winked and smiled as we laughed and applauded his skill and showmanship. There were many words said by others that night. Ali did not talk but no one "spoke" to us like Muhammad Ali!'

* * *

When Madonna took to the stage at the Marriott Marquis in New York City on 1 June, most of the people sitting at tables that cost $25,000 each turned their backs on her. They had eyes only for Muhammad Ali as he rose from his seat. Wearing a demure powder blue outfit, the singer had been tasked with presenting Ali with a silver plaque to acknowledge his charity work by the Parkinson's Disease Foundation. Once she finally had the audience's attention, Madonna explained why they'd chosen her for the job. 'I have more pictures of Muhammad Ali in my home than anyone else, including my family,' she said. 'And my favourite is the one that he autographed to me. It's a picture of Ali standing in the ring in Lewiston, Maine after he knocked out Sonny Liston and it says, "To Madonna, we are the greatest!" And I have to agree. Because we are both arrogant. And we do have a lot in common after all, except for one thing. Ali is something I will never be. He is the greatest living boxer in the world. And that is why it is my pleasure to present this award to a great role model and a great man – Muhammad Ali!'

When Ali reached the dais, Madonna smiled and perhaps for the first time in her professional life asked, 'Do you remember me?'

Ali grinned.

As they left the stage, she linked his left arm and they posed for more photographs, a shoot during which Ali's four-year-old son Asaad stole the show. As journalists shouted for Madonna to look this way and that in their direction, Ali, as he had the entire night, remained stoic and never said a single word.

* * *

At the 16th Annual National Card-Collectors Convention in St Louis, the roster of stars lined up for Tuesday, 25 July included Dick Butkus, Ed O'Bannon, Bryant Reeves, Shawn Respert, Manon Rhéaume and Muhammad Ali. Those who lined up for Ali's autograph came away with something a little more than a signature. On that particular day at the Cervantes Convention Centre, he used a new Sports DNA pen containing some of his own genetic material.

Harlan Werner, representing an outfit called Sports Placement Service, told reporters a hair from Ali had been taken to a laboratory where his DNA was isolated and later infused into the ink mixed for the pen. In an era when counterfeit autographs were growing more and more commonplace, this was one of several new anti-fraud measures the company was introducing to protect what was now a multi-million-dollar industry.

* * *

When the Professional Bowlers Association (PBA) swung through Louisville on 8 August, Randy Pedersen defeated Mark Williams to take the Executive Bowl title with a 244-203 win. The morning after the final, Bobby Dinkins, PBA Director of Operations, was chatting to Al Hayden, one of the local staffers brought in to run the event. Hayden mentioned that Muhammad Ali was his brother-in-law and Dinkins confessed that he might just be the only person in the world he would one day love to meet. As it happened, Ali was in town that week too. Within minutes, Hayden had him on the line and was pressing the phone into Dinkins' hand.

Suddenly, he was asking if he could drop by to visit. 'Yeah!' whispered Ali. 'You and me, we'll go a few rounds.'

Pushing his luck, Dinkins asked if it would be alright to bring some memorabilia for him to sign too. 'Yeah,' said Ali. 'No problem.'

Dinkins put the receiver down, turned to Hayden and exclaimed, 'Holy shit! I just talked to Muhammad Ali!'

At the Louisville Marriott next morning, Ali answered the door in a T-shirt and boxer shorts. Hayden, making mischief, pushed Dinkins into the room first and Ali balled up his fists to throw punches at the visitor. Then, he started to entertain the entire entourage with his magic tricks. When that was over, he changed into his clothes for photographs and requested that Dinkins read a passage from the Koran and a passage from the Bible in order to compare the two.

Dinkins did as he was asked, then showed Ali the Everlast gloves and a copy of Jack McGonagle's unauthorised biography *To Touch the Sun – A Portrait of Muhammad Ali*. He'd purchased those items in a hurried visit to a mall the previous night, so he'd have stuff for Ali to sign. The pen came out and Ali started to flick through the book, smiling at photographs of his younger, more ebullient self. 'I vividly remembered Ali drooling due to his advancing Parkinson's and speaking difficulty,' said Kevin Shippy, Dinkins' assistant with the PBA.

Others in the party were taken aback by his appearance too. 'I remember thinking that he would be bigger,' said Dave Schroeder, the PBA publicity director. 'He didn't seem as "big" as what you saw on TV. And I also remember being struck how the Parkinson's made him shaky, and how it seemed to make him reluctant to speak. He didn't speak much and spoke in kind of a whisper.'

They had no difficulty understanding him, however, when somebody asked if he could beat Mike Tyson. 'I'd kick his ass,' whispered Ali.

* * *

As part of the festivities to mark Lewiston's bicentennial, Muhammad Ali was invited back to the building now called the Maine Central Civic Centre, the very place where he had downed Liston with the so-called phantom punch in 1965. On Friday, 22 September, he was guest of honour at a banquet where 500 people paid $200 a ticket.

Claudette Chamberland, one of the organisers of the event, boasted a special link with the bout three decades earlier. As a then 13-year-old, she got to touch Ali's robe and boxing trunks when they were in a local laundromat where her friend's father had the job of washing them before the fight. 'God, they were gorgeous,' said Chamberland.

All these years later, Ali remained magnetic and charismatic enough to draw a crowd, many of whom broke into 'Ali! Ali! Ali!' during the evening. Of course, he was not quite his old self. One reporter compared him to a 'wounded butterfly' when he rose in slow motion from his chair to acknowledge the adulation by blowing a kiss. Still, some of the old magic was there when he walked to the stage where Mayor John Jenkins handed him the gift of a gold pen.

Leaning slowly over the podium to get as near as possible to the microphone, Ali, with a smile on his face, mumbled, 'I came all the way to Maine, and this is all I get!'

* * *

Muhammad Ali was the featured guest at the Disabilities Awareness Luncheon at the Century Centre in South Bend, Indiana on 8 November. Among the 1,200 people who turned up to see him receive the local Rotary Club's 'Humanitarian of the Century' award was a crew from CBS' *60 Minutes* led by journalist Ed Bradley, filming him for a future feature. As a huge line formed to meet him, many grew anxious they might never get to the top. An announcement was made that Ali would stay in the cavernous room as long as it took to shake every hand.

Although the rules for the day clearly stated he wouldn't be signing autographs, many businessmen and women present came bearing items for his signature. One enterprising character arrived at Ali's table bearing six photographs, one of him as a teenage Cassius Clay at the Louisville Golden Gloves. He asked Ali to sign it 'in your old name'. And he did. As was the norm, he stayed two hours over time to make sure nobody went home without spending a few moments in his presence. 'He is truly a great person, a magnificent human being,' said 51-year-old Tom Grimes. 'That's why I'm here standing in line for an hour and a half.'

* * *

As Muhammad Ali sat at his table in the Hall of Fame Card Show in the ballroom of the Holiday Inn West in Middleton, Wisconsin, a teenager started to mock-taunt him. 'Hey Muhammad, there's Joe Frazier,' shouted the youngster. 'There's Frazier. He's around the corner.'

Always up for a jape, Ali made to get out of his chair as if to engage. Except that simple act of rising to his feet took so long that it drained all the humour out of one of his standard party pieces during public appearances. It was 15 October and Ali was being paid $35,000 plus expenses to sign a maximum of 500 autographs over the course of an event to which only 325 fans turned up. 'His left hand shook badly as he tried to hold a boxing glove steady enough to autograph it with his right,' wrote Rob Schultz in the *Capital-Times*. 'It took him seven seconds just to scribble Muhammad on that bright red glove as his smiling personal assistant sat closely next to him to make sure he didn't drop the pen. It was painful to watch.'

The atmosphere in the ballroom was curious. Ken Norton was present too and, apart from the few times he shouted friendly taunts across at his old adversary, the place was eerily quiet for an autograph show.

Still, there were plenty of satisfied customers. 'Best 60 dollars I ever spent,' said Anthony Brown, executive director of Madison's Equal Opportunities Commission. 'He's an inspiration. He was then and he is now. And even though in these latter years his health has limited his travel, he still carries the same message he did in the 60s. That's the reason you see all the people here to see him today.'

Marlon and Judy Weisensel had come from Waterloo with their son-in-law Mark Jungbluth and their grand-daughter Jade. They brought a poster for Ali to sign. It was to be framed and hung in the room of their late daughter Patt. She died of leukaemia three years earlier and was buried in an Ali T-shirt.

* * *

Rich Ledbetter was a five-year-old boy in Missouri when his mother dragged him along to a Teddy Pendergrass concert. Too young to appreciate the music, he was bored out of his mind for most of the evening. At least until he clapped eyes on Muhammad Ali. The large man turned and smiled at the curious boy suddenly staring at him. Then, he hugged him and called him 'little man'.

On Thanksgiving Day 20 years later, Ledbetter, by then a student teacher, drove 360 miles from St Louis to Berrien Springs to meet the man who'd been his hero since that meeting. He didn't have Ali's address, just the name of the town and a willingness to ask for directions. At the second gas station where he made enquiries, he met a woman whose boyfriend had done some work at the Ali property. Minutes later, he found himself outside the gate but decided that a stranger calling in the dark of night might not be welcome. So, he booked into a hotel.

Next morning, Ledbetter returned to the farm at noon, and figured to write a letter explaining what Ali meant to him before he tried to gain an audience. He even tried to compose poetry in the style of Ali's doggerel and was on his fourth page when a limo pulled up to the gate just after 1.30pm. 'The driver wore a camel hair coat and looked like Joe Pesci,' said Ledbetter. 'I asked if I could see Ali. He said, "No way!" I said I drove all the way from St Louis and just wanted to say "hi". He shut the gate and drove on. The limo came back about 2.30[pm]. The window opened. Ali was looking at me.'

Like thousands before him, Ledbetter blurted out the first thing that came to mind. 'You're the greatest!' he said, handing Ali his manuscript. 'You're my hero!'

'Is your number on here?' asked Ali. 'I'll call you. Goodbye and God bless.'

The limo started to pull away before suddenly reversing. Ali and the driver got out, went to the trunk and got out the signed pamphlets he liked to distribute everywhere he went. He handed the visitor 15 of them and, newly emboldened, Ledbetter asked for permission to get his camera for the photo he would need to prove the veracity of the encounter to his friends and family. 'He put his right fist up to my jaw,' said Ledbetter. 'He shadow-boxed with me. His hands are massive and powerful. It took two of mine to grab one of his hands. He motioned for me to give him a jab but I couldn't do it. He gave me this little smack to the cheek.'

After the driver had clicked enough photographs, Ali climbed back into the limo and they drove away.

* * *

On 21 December, Muhammad Ali Rotisserie Chicken announced it had signed a contract to open two new restaurants in Egypt in 1996. The first location in Cairo was scheduled to start serving as early as June. Talib Rashada said the deal with American Egyptian for International Trading Co. would lead to a further eight restaurants bearing the Ali name across the African nation over the following decade. He also claimed deals were in the works for similar operations in Malaysia, Singapore and Saudi Arabia. 'Just as Muhammad Ali was more than just a boxer,' said Rashada, 'we want Muhammad Ali Rotisserie Chicken to be more than just a restaurant.'

ROUND FIFTEEN

1996

Muhammad has started to cut back on his travel because
he adores Asaad. He's planning to spend half his time
on the farm. But there are so many worthy causes and
Muhammad wants to help all of them. He's booked so far
in advance it'll be a while before he can truly cut back.

Thomas Hauser, *New York Daily News*, 8 March

SHORTLY AFTER 9pm on 22 January, having kept his audience waiting for nearly an hour, Fidel Castro swept into a reception room at the Palace of the Revolution wearing combat fatigues and sporting the most famous straggly grey beard in the world. 'Buenas noches!' said the 70-year-old to the assembled crowd. 'Buenas noches!'

Then he walked directly towards Muhammad Ali and embraced him. 'I am glad to see you,' said Castro through an interpreter. 'I am very glad to see you and I am thankful for your visit.'

The Cuban leader stared into his eyes but Ali didn't respond, even as the cameras flashed to capture the moment.

He had arrived in Havana four days earlier as part of a charitable mission delivering $500,000 in medical supplies to the

Cuban people. Among his travelling party was his wife Lonnie, Howard Bingham, a CBS *60 Minutes* television crew led by Ed Bradley, a scriptwriter named Greg Howard, then researching an Ali movie, and the famed American magazine writer and author Gay Talese. Also by his side for much of the week-long trip was Teofilo Stevenson.

A three-time Olympic champion from Cuba, Stevenson is regarded as the greatest amateur heavyweight of all time. Throughout the 1970s, there had been serious and persistent talk about him meeting Ali in the ring if he chose to accept any of several lucrative offers to turn professional. He didn't, so the fight never happened. But, having visited Ali in Michigan the previous year, the 6ft 5in superannuated boxer became the official chaperone for Ali's visit, as well as the man who filled in the gaps when Ali, instead of speaking to Castro, playfully raised his right fist towards the chin of the leader.

Stevenson spun a yarn about how the two fighters had put on an exhibition a couple of days earlier in the Balado gym, watched by some of the new generation of Cuban contenders. Perhaps for the benefit of his leader's ego, he made the encounter sound more like the contest the sporting world had once wished for between the pair. 'Stevenson did not actually explain that it had been merely another photo opportunity,' wrote Talese in his subsequent article about the visit for *Esquire*, 'one in which they sparred open-handed in the ring, wearing their street clothes and barely touching each other's bodies and faces; but then Stevenson had climbed out of the ring, leaving Ali to the more taxing test of withstanding two abbreviated rounds against one and then another young bully of grade-school age who clearly had not come to participate in a kiddie show. They had come to floor the champ. Their bellicose little bodies and hot-gloved hands and helmeted hell-bent heads were consumed with fury and ambition;

and as they charged ahead, swinging wildly and swaggering to the roars of their teenage friends and relatives at ringside, one could imagine their future boastings to their grandchildren: On one fine day back in the winter of '96, I whacked Muhammad Ali! Except, in truth, on this particular day, Ali was still too fast for them. He backpedaled and shifted and swayed, stood on the toes of his black woven-leather pointed shoes, and showed that his body was made for motion – his Parkinson's problems were lost in his shuffle, in the thrusts of his butterfly sting that whistled two feet above the heads of his aspiring assailants.'

Earlier in the visit, there had been a press conference where the two would-be heavyweight rivals posed for photographs and one reporter asked Ali how the fight between him and Stevenson might have gone. With a smile on his face, he whispered his answer to his wife on the dais, and she said, 'It would have been a tie.'

The perfect diplomat's response – and Ali was playing that part perfectly. He had visited Havana's Neurological Institute, a destination for Parkinson's sufferers from around the world, delivering a shipment of Carbidopa/Levodopa drugs for the patients. He did not, as some had rumoured, seek any treatment there himself. 'We are here on a humanitarian mission,' said Lonnie Ali. 'We're hoping we can do something to relieve some suffering. Muhammad has always been willing to transgress political boundaries to do what is important. Muhammad has always been an ambassador to the world. He's not a political animal.'

For the meeting with Castro, the Ali camp had come bearing gifts. Bingham handed over an enlarged, framed version of one of his photographs, in which the 21-year-old fighter still known as Cassius Clay is walking along a sidewalk in Harlem with Malcom X. 'TO PRESIDENT FIDEL CASTRO, FROM MUHAMMAD ALI', read the inscription under which Ali had also added a little heart. Castro lifted it up closer to his eyes, surveyed the work and announced, 'Que bien!' before showing it to his interpreter.

At one point in the encounter, Bradley got a microphone in front of Castro and started asking questions. That interaction was cut short by Ali starting to do magic tricks to entertain the crowd, a distraction that caught Fidel's eye. If those who travelled with Ali had seen him make a handkerchief disappear a thousand times before, the First Secretary of the Central Committee of the Communist Party of Cuba appeared taken aback by such a wondrous feat. 'Where is it?' cried Castro, who approached Ali and started to examine his hands. 'Where is it? Where have you put it?'

Castro was so impressed by what he had just witnessed that Ali, through an interpreter, had to explain it to him, outlining the crucial role played in the ruse by a fake rubber thumb. Even then, he insisted on attempting it himself so Bingham, who as Ali's oldest friend had perhaps witnessed this particular trick more times than any man alive, gave him a brief lesson. Castro made the handkerchief disappear, the crowd duly applauded and Ali insisted he could keep the rubber thumb as a memento.

* * *

HBO held the premiere for its documentary *The Journey of the African-American Athlete* at the New York City library on 8 February. The moment Muhammad Ali arrived, he was corralled into a roped-off area to pose for photographs with his old friend, the NFL icon and fellow activist Jim Brown. With his left hand shaking and the lightbulbs flashing, he stood beside the man with whom he'd soldiered in the struggle for athlete and civil rights in the 1960s. Brown eloquently captured what Ali stood for after all those years. 'Ali was probably the most popular athlete of all time and also the most unpopular athlete at one time,' said Brown. 'He stuck his neck out on the line like nobody else did and that eventually made him as popular as he has become. He's a great person and he proved it by never getting a big head. Ali always loved people, especially children, and he always stayed in the streets with the people, shopped with the people and ate with the people.'

Thirty minutes before the film in which he featured prominently began, Ali was led to his seat in the auditorium and a steady stream of visitors, some famous, others not, came to pay homage to him there. Eventually, a ten-year-old boy was brought to him and he perked up immediately, clenching one of his shaking fists and throwing a phantom punch in the child's direction. For regulars in Ali's world, the sight of him shaking off physical travails to make a memory for a child was nothing new. 'At something like this, a great number of people know it will be their only chance to ever see Muhammad Ali, to ever hug Muhammad Ali or to ever shake hands with Muhammad Ali,' said Thomas Hauser. 'Muhammad understands that and takes great pleasure in it. With Muhammad Ali, you're not just talking about the most famous man in the world but also the most loved man in the world. I've gotten used to events like this, with people's reaction to Muhammad, but I've never taken them for granted.'

* * *

Ninety-four young men and women were honoured at The Chestnut Street YMCA Black Achievers' 17th annual awards banquet at the Commonwealth Convention Centre in Louisville, Kentucky on 17 February. When Muhammad Ali was presented with the 'Adult Achiever of the Year' prize, he did not speak but responded to one of the many standing ovations afforded the mere mention of his name by blowing a kiss to the audience. Lonnie Ali spoke on his behalf about how his hometown was his foundation and reminded the crowd of nearly 200 how he never forgot his roots there. 'That is why this award means so much to him,' she said before counselling the prize-winning youth about what they could learn from Ali. 'He got to be who he is by visualising his dream every day.'

* * *

A total of 35,000 runners, cyclists and wheelchair athletes lined up for the 11th running of the Los Angeles Marathon on Sunday, 3 March, treated to the traditional soundtrack of Randy Newman's 'I love LA!' blasting out on repeat. Some of them got a little bit more than they bargained for on the way to begin the race. They met Muhammad Ali, flanked by six LAPD officers as he ambled down Flower Street, shaking hands and prompting outbreaks of 'Ali! Ali! Ali!'

'Oh my god, it's Muhammad Ali,' said 43-year-old Beatrice Pacheco from Lake Forest when she bumped into his entourage. 'I'm so choked up. I can barely breathe. He's a living legend!'

* * *

Governor Paul Patton declared 6 March to be Muhammad Ali Day in Kentucky. To mark the occasion, Ali visited Patton and his Lieutenant-Governor Steve Henry in Lexington. There, he received a framed proclamation outlining the honour being afforded to him by Patton, who announced himself awed just by being in his presence. Ali smiled for the cameras, signed a pair of boxing gloves for one fan and kissed another's child on the cheek. Wearing a black shirt under a grey suit, when his sleeves rode up the words 'The Greatest' could be seen embroidered into his cuffs. 'You are the most famous person in the world,' said Patton. 'You are an inspiration to young people around the world. We're just so proud of you.'

* * *

On 16 March, Mike Tyson fought Frank Bruno for the WBC version of the world heavyweight title at the MGM Grand in Las Vegas. Three thousand miles away, at the Official All-Star Café in Times Square, Sylvester Stallone hosted a private party to mark the 20th anniversary of the release of the first *Rocky* movie. Among the attendance were Riddick Bowe and Lennox Lewis from boxing's present, Sugar Ray Leonard and Willie Pep from its past and various other luminaries from New York's fistic community. On this night, they were all taken aback by the sight of one former champion, wearing a dark red, long-sleeved shirt, sitting at a table with his wife Lonnie and his son Asaad. 'Everybody tried to avoid looking at Muhammad Ali,' wrote Pete Hamill, the veteran New York journalist and author. 'His head was bowed and he was trying to eat. But his right hand was shaking so hard that he could not get the piece of chicken to move two inches to his mouth. His wife, Lonnie, put her hand over his to quell the shaking and gently guided the chicken to its destination. Ali chewed diligently but did not raise his head.

'Across the evening, people came over to the table to lean down and speak to the ruined 54-year-old man. Sometimes he smiled. Sometimes he whispered a reply. Sometimes he rose to pose for pictures. But then he would be back in the chair, the once-lithe and powerful body sagging, the eyes wide and wary, a plastic straw clenched in his mouth, all of him shaking with the Parkinson's disease, with the damage caused by the fierce trade he once honoured.'

Hamill spent the evening closely watching Ali, whose condition reminded him of his then 85-year-old mother after she'd suffered brain damage in a mugging. By his reckoning, the only time Ali seemed to focus properly was when Mike Tyson appeared on the big screen to begin his walk to the ring in Las Vegas. After Tyson had subsequently disposed of Bruno, Ali rose from his chair, hugged Stallone goodbye and then, arm in arm with Lonnie, departed the room.

Having chronicled Ali's career through the decades of glory, exile and glory renewed, Hamill made the encounter in New York the centrepiece of an essay he wrote for *Esquire* magazine two months later. In 'Blood on their Hands', he eviscerated the boxing authorities for allowing a sport he loved to become too corrupt and too barbaric, and called for the game to be cleaned up. 'No more kids should be reduced to zombies for the entertainment of people who lead safe, well-defended lives,' wrote Hamill. 'People who still hear the roar of *Ah-lee, Ah-lee, Ah-lee!* People like me. People like us.'

* * *

The St Patrick's Day edition of CBS' *60 Minutes* broadcast Ed Bradley's feature about Muhammad Ali that included the trip to Cuba filmed earlier in the year. All week long, the network played trailers for the show during regular programming and so sad and disturbing were the images of a frail, reduced Ali that, on the Sunday night it aired, the *New York Daily News* gathered three boxers to watch it live in the company of a reporter. They saw Ali speak a dozen words in a 14-minute segment and get up and walk out of a sit-down interview with Bradley. 'He looks sick,' said Carlos Ortiz, a 59-year-old former junior welterweight and lightweight champion. 'But look at his eyes. He still has his humour. That's what made him. He'll never lose that.'

'Yes,' agreed Emile Griffith, the then 58-year-old whose punches ended up killing Benny 'The Kid' Paret in a welterweight clash at Madison Square Garden in 1962. 'But he's moving around. God bless him!'

If the three men didn't quite deliver the chorus of regret the newspaper must have envisaged, both the retired fighters, who knew Ali in his pomp, agreed he took too much punishment during his illustrious career. Orlando Canizales, a 30-year-old super-bantamweight champion, was of a different mindset. 'I have good reflexes so I don't get hit as much as other guys,' said Canizales. 'So, when I see what happened to Muhammad Ali I don't get so afraid. I don't think what happened to him is because of boxing.'

Mike Lupica, the marquee columnist in the paper, thought differently. In a sobering piece, he wrote, 'Everybody on *60 Minutes* kept saying we should not feel sorry for Ali, that he does not feel sorry for himself, that he is a happy man. Then there is another blank stare on the television screen. Perhaps the saddest picture of all has him seated at a table, signing autographs. A man slides a photograph under his pen and Ali painstakingly signs. When he is finished the man pulls the photograph back, Ali barely seems to notice. He boxed too long. He took too many shots to the head.'

In that Sunday night-time slot, *60 Minutes* drew a 26 per cent share of the audience in America's 33 largest television markets, easily beating its current affairs rival *Dateline: NBC*. The show also resulted in a surge of charitable contributions to the Parkinson's Disease Foundation.

* * *

An 18-year-old art student at Benton Harbor High School, Eric Bradford was charged with making a piece to enter for a scholarship competition at the Kendall College of Art and Design in Grand Rapids, Michigan. He decided to produce a 6ft by 7ft-high painting of the famous *Sports Illustrated* photograph of Muhammad Ali standing over Sonny Liston at the conclusion of their second fight. On 19 March, Kim Forburger, Ali's assistant, drove him up from Berrien Springs to see the work for himself.

When the car pulled up outside the home of Paul Kussy, Bradford's art teacher, a crowd had gathered by the window, still scarcely believing he was coming to visit. 'It's him,' whispered one of the onlookers.

Moments later, he was in the living room, shaking hands, posing for photographs and doing magic tricks. Somebody produced a chocolate cake and he devoured a slice. He also took in the larger-than-life painting, not saying anything but smiling before signing the canvas with a magic marker. Then Kussy asked him if he'd mind dipping his knuckles in black acrylic paint before pressing them on to the piece. Ali did as he was asked. 'It's an honour for my painting to attract a celebrity,' said Bradford. 'You can't do better than Ali! Just meeting Muhammad Ali has been an astronomical boost to my ego!'

* * *

Lawyers acting for Muhammad Ali filed a $500,000 lawsuit in Los Angeles against Forever Films on 23 May. The suit alleged that the film production company had been granted the right to use Ali's name and likeness to promote its 1989 film *Champions Forever* but, in 1994, the company had allowed Amerivox, a Nevada-based outfit, to use his photograph on a phone card. 'Those rights were limited to the movie,' said Kevin Gaut, one of Ali's attorneys. 'We didn't say they could do whatever they wanted.'

* * *

On the way through to the back of the Warner Bros Studio Store at Lenox Square Mall in Atlanta, Georgia on 13 June, Muhammad Ali caught the eye of an old sports columnist of his acquaintance. He stopped abruptly, pulled the mean face once reserved for pre-fight pantomiming and then winked, letting his target know they were good. He was en route to a room hung with eight new portraits of him in his 1960 Olympic-winning pomp. They were painted by Steve Kaufman, one-time protégé of Andy Warhol, somebody who knew something about the nature of fame. 'Seeing Muhammad Ali in person is like seeing the pope,' said Kaufman. 'He's like a giant rainbow. To paint Muhammad Ali, I had to use the most brilliant colours I could think of.'

He autographed the paintings twice, once as Cassius Clay and then as Muhammad Ali. He sat behind a table in the store and never spoke aloud for two hours. He did mug for each camera thrust in his direction, handed every visitor three pamphlets about Islam and doled out individual memories to all who crossed his path. 'A middle-aged woman kissed Ali on the lips then danced away like a giddy schoolgirl,' wrote Terence Moore in the *Atlanta Journal-Constitution*. 'A guy had his friend snap a picture of Ali and himself trading jabs and then the guy said, emotionally, "This means a lot to my mother". There also were the kids, some wide-eyed while shaking Ali's hand and others wild-eyed while staring from a distance. Then Ali was gone, moving into the night to deliver more Islamic pamphlets to those rushing his way. Mostly, he was delivering something more intriguing. Himself.'

* * *

On 20 June, Muhammad Ali was the official host for a breakfast featuring 150 adults and children at the United Cerebral Palsy Nassau in Roosevelt, Long Island. Many present paid tribute to him through poetry and songs, sometimes accompanied by hugs and kisses. Three local high school students had won the right to be there by finishing first, second and third in a competition where they were charged with writing essays in his honour. 'When he was coming in, he was still kidding around and everybody was laughing at his antics,' said Eunico Charles, a 12th grader whose essay had also earned her a $500 savings bond. 'He just seemed so full of life, even though he does have a disease now. That's what I really admire about him. He doesn't want anybody to feel sorry for him.'

After breakfast, Ali spent three and a half hours walking around the facility and watching on as staff and those who visited daily participated in an annual wheelchair cleaning event. That he barely spoke didn't seem to matter. 'Muhammad Ali was at it again yesterday,' wrote Rob Parker in *Newsday*. 'He was making people laugh. He was making some cry. Joking with others and putting up his dukes to anyone who looked at him funny. In other words, Muhammad Ali was being Muhammad Ali. Sure, he doesn't move the way he used to before being diagnosed with a neurological condition probably caused by poundings in the ring. And he doesn't articulate or rhyme in the same fashion that made him famous, not to mention Howard Cosell. Still, one thing Ali hasn't lost is the ability to electrify a room. It's an incredible spectacle to watch. Ali, speaking or not, moving or not, takes over a room when he's in it.'

The room for the evening portion of his visit to Long Island was Leonard's of Great Neck, which hosted an awards dinner and an auction. The promise of a night breathing the same air as Ali attracted 1,000 people. The crowd included big names from the NFL and NHL, and boxing personalities like Arthur Mercante (referee for Ali-Frazier I), former heavyweight champion and one-time Ali opponent Floyd Patterson and LeRoy Neiman, the artist who had painted the most famous face in the sport more than once. Many spoke eloquently of Ali. 'He was the first man I could tell "I love you!" to,' said Dick Schaap, the ESPN and ABC announcer who served as MC and traced his friendship with Ali all the way back to 1960. 'Truly, it is a love affair for many with Ali.'

Those who had witnessed Ali's energy with children in the morning and the manner in which his subdued public persona still awed grown-ups that night waxed lyrical about what they witnessed. A man rising above his own reduced circumstances to help others similarly afflicted. 'He's turned it inward and that inward glow is what everybody perceives,' said Dr Joseph Carozza, the event's general chairman. 'You watch him work a crowd, watch him with the kids, he's purely selfless. His being here puts Nassau County's cerebral palsy association on the map. The recognition that we've gotten as a result of this man being here has really meant nothing but further success.'

* * *

Everybody knew Muhammad Ali was in town for start of the XXVI Olympiad at Atlanta's Centennial Olympic Stadium. Very few realised that he was there to light the flame at the opening ceremony on Friday night, 19 July. Secrecy surrounding his contribution was such that, at one point, Don Mischer, the director of the event, Dick Ebersol, head of NBC Sports (the host broadcaster), and Howard Bingham held a meeting about Ali's specific role in a garbage room at the stadium. Anywhere away from prying eyes.

Ali's own rehearsal and walk-through actually took place in the empty venue at 3am and all of those clandestine efforts meant his emergence at the top of the ramp near the end of a four-and-a-half-hour extravaganza sent the 83,000 people in the stands into a frenzy. Wearing the white T-shirt and white trousers, the official uniform of the relay, he held his torch out to be lit by Janet Evans, one of America's greatest swimmers. Then he held it aloft in his right hand while his left shook uncontrollably by his side. His facial expression was glazed.

Those in the arena and the tens of millions watching on television around the world had not seen him in this condition live before. They were shocked, horrified and moved in equal measure. Some feared as he stood for a few seconds that he would be unable to complete his task. Indeed, when he held the blazing torch over the carrier in the cauldron that was the final step in the process, it didn't catch fire for a few excruciating seconds. It was long enough for the flames to start licking back down and appearing to graze his arms. He never flinched and eventually the fire struck. Some spectators were in tears. Others broke into 'Ali! Ali! Ali!' And then, as quickly as he had come, he disappeared from view again. 'For all his world title bouts, this was Ali's finest moment,' wrote Patrick Smith in the *Sydney Morning Herald*. 'His most courageous [act]. Muhammad Ali let the world see what has become of him. His face is bloated from drugs that wrestle with his illness. He needs help to walk and can barely speak. He had to hold his hands together to stop the shaking from causing him to lose balance. This is courage at its most courageous. To hide nothing and not fear being stripped of dignity.'

That was the predominant reaction to his cameo around the world. Aside from providing the most memorable moment in the history of Olympic opening ceremonies, by putting himself on the biggest stage in such a diminished state, he demonstrated how greatness can change and still endure. In the 15 years since losing to Trevor Berbick, Ali had wandered the world, a man on a quest that often lured him off the beaten track. Now, everybody glimpsed the true nature of the fight he waged and the indomitability of spirit on view reminded the global audience here was somebody truly, more than ever, worthy of the title of icon.

In Atlanta, he came, they saw, he conquered. Anew.

EPILOGUE

MUHAMMAD ALI passed away on 4 June 2016, his death prompting a global outpouring of affection that confirmed, how, over the two decades since that hot and humid night in Georgia, he had become the most beloved sports figure in the world. Among the speakers at his funeral were a comedian, an imam, two rabbis, a former Democratic president, a Republican senator, a pair of Native American Chiefs, a Protestant preacher and Malcolm X's daughter Attallah. An eclectic line-up that demonstrated how he transcended sport and fame, broke down barriers between race and religion, and forged so many friendships that defied easy characterisation.

Some of his fast friends from the wilderness years departed in different circumstances.

In 2005, Richard Hirschfeld hanged himself using plastic wrap in the laundry room of a federal detention centre in Miami. He was awaiting transfer to Virginia to face charges of obstruction and perjury. His relationship with his most famous client ended acrimoniously in the 1990s when he was accused of signing away the rights to Ali's life story without permission. Having spent years on the run from the US government in the Canary Islands and Cuba, he regularly claimed to have been a covert operative for Washington throughout much of his professional life.

Dr Rajko Medenica died of a heart attack at his home in New York in 1997. The 58-year old's licence to practise medicine had been revoked in Colorado due to what a judge called 'substandard and grossly negligent medical care'. He had served a year in prison in Switzerland for fraud and been successfully sued for $13m by a patient for unorthodox treatment of her breast cancer that cost her vision and kidney function. Every obituary mentioned his lengthy association with Muhammad Ali and one writer described him as the kind of doctor who 'created devoted patients and determined enemies'.

Sheikh Mohammed Al-Fassi died of complications from an infected hernia in Cairo, Egypt on Christmas Eve 2002. At the time of his death, the 50-year-old was living in the Hilton Hotel and was being pursued for $223m by one of his ex-wives, money owed from their divorce settlement. Ten years earlier, he'd been imprisoned and flogged by the Saudi Arabian government for his support of Saddam Hussein in the first Iraq War and was only freed after a prominent list of supporters, including Noam Chomsky and Muhammad Ali, took out a full-page ad in the *New York Times* calling for his release.

Arthur Morrison died in May 2010. In 1997, he was sentenced to 25 years in prison for a litany of offences, including wire fraud, extortion, threats to blow up a police station, harassment of ex-girlfriends, promises to inflict physical violence upon them, and several counts of transmitting in interstate commerce threats to injure certain persons. During a three-week trial by jury in the New York District Court, he was described as president of Champion World Brands, and his assertion that he enjoyed a long-standing relationship with Muhammad Ali was one of the few instances where his testimony was regarded by the judge as wholly truthful.

SOURCES
SELECT BIBLIOGRAPHY

Allison, Dean and Henderson, Bruce B: *Empire of Deceit: Inside the Biggest Sports and Bank Scandal in History*, Doubleday, New York, 1985

Berger, Phil: *Blood Season*, Queen Anne Press, London, 1989

Berger, Phil: *Punchlines, Four Walls Eight Windows*, New York, 1993

Conrad, Harold: *Dear Muffo*, Stein and Day, New York, 1982

Cushman, Tom: *Muhammad Ali and the Greatest Heavyweight Generation*, South East Missouri State University Press, Cape Girardeau, 2009

Doust, Dudley: *Sports Beat – Headline-Makers Then and Now*, Hodder and Stoughton, London, 1992

Dundee, Angelo: *I Only Talk Winning*, Contemporary Books, Chicago, 1985

Early, Gerard: *I'm a Little Bit Special*, Yellow Jersey Press, London, 1999

Early, Gerard: *The Culture of Bruising*, Ecco Press, New Jersey, 1994

Eig, Johnathan: *Ali*, Houghton Mifflin, New York, 2017

Gorn, Elliot J: *Ali: The People's Champ*, University of Illinois Press, Chicago, 1995

Hannigan, Dave: *Drama in the Bahamas*, Sports Publishing, New York, 2016

Hauser, Thomas: *Muhammad Ali & Company,* Hastings House, Norwalk, 1998

Hauser, Thomas: *Muhammad Ali: His Life and Times*, Pan Books, London, 1992

Hauser, Thomas: *Muhammad Ali: In Perspective*, Collins Publishers, San Francisco, 1996

Izenberg, Jerry: *Once There Were Giants*, Skyhorse Publishing, New York, 2017

Kindred, Dave: *Heroes, Fools & Other Dreamers*, Longstreet Press, Atlanta, 1988

Kindred, Dave: *Sound and Fury*, Simon and Schuster, New York, 2006

Kolb, Larry J: *Overworld – The Life and Times of a Reluctant Spy*, Riverhead Books, New York, 2004

Lyons, Thomas and Saltman: *Shelly: Fear No Evel*, We Publish Books, Rancho Mirage, 2007

Mahdi, Dr Abuwi: *Muhammad Ali – The Untold Story*, Affinity International Publishing, USA, 2019

McIlvanney, Hugh: *McIlvanney on Boxing*, Beaufort Books, New York, 1982

Miller, Davis: *The Tao of Muhammad Ali*, Vintage Books, London, 1997

Monaghan, Paddy: *Street Fighting Man*, John Blake
   Publishing, London, 2008

Newfield, Jack: *Only in America – The Life and Crimes of Don
   King*, William Morrow, New York, 1995

Pacheco, Ferdie: *Tales from the Fifth Street Gym*, University Press
   of Florida, Gainesville, 2010

Pacheco, Ferdie: *The Fight Doctor*, Birch Lane Press,
   New York, 1992

Reed, Ishmael: *The Complete Muhammad Ali*, Baraka Books,
   Montreal, 2015

Smith, Gary: *Going Deep*, Sports Illustrated Books,
   New York, 2000

Snyder, Todd D: *Bundini*, Hamilcar, Boston, 2020

Strathmore, William: *Muhammad Ali – The Unseen Archives*,
   Paragon, Bath, 2001

Stravinsky, John: *Muhammad Ali*, Park Lane Press,
   New York, 1997

Tanner, Michael: *Ali in Britain*, Mainstream, Edinburgh, 1995

Taylor, Jim: *Forgive Me My Press Passes*, Horsdal and Schubart,
   Victoria, 1993

West, David: *The Mammoth Book of Muhammad Ali*, Constable
   and Robinson, London, 2012

Newspapers and Periodicals

*The Age, Akron Beacon Journal, Alabama Journal, The Alliance
Times Herald, The Anniston Star, Argus Sun, Arizona Republic,*

Asbury Park Press, Atlanta Journal-Constitution, Austin American Statesman, Baltimore Sun, Bangor Daily News, Battle Creek Enquirer, Billings Gazette, Birmingham Evening Mail, Boston Globe, Boston Herald, Catholic Courier, Cedar Rapids Gazette, Charlotte Observer, Chicago Sun-Times, Chicago Tribune, Clarion Ledger, Corvallis Gazette-Times, Daily Citizen, Daily Mirror, Daily Oklahoman, Daily Star, Dayton Daily News, Democrat and Chronicle, Des Moines Journal, Detroit Free Press, Edmonton Journal, El Paso Times, Esquire, Estherville Daily News, Eugene Register-Guard, Evening Standard, Fayetteville Observer, Five Cities Times-Press Recorder, Florida Journal, Fort Lauderdale News, Fort Worth Star-Telegram, Fresno Bee, Galveston Daily News, Green Bay Press Gazette, Greenville News, Greenwich Time, Greenwood Commonwealth, The Guardian, Gulf News, The Hanford Sentinel, The Hartford Courant, The Herald-Palladium, Honolulu Advertiser, Indianapolis Star, The Irish Times, The Ithaca Journal, Jamaica Gleaner, Jamaica Observer, Johnson City Press-Chronicle, Journal of the American Medical Association, Kansas City Star, Lancaster New Era, Lakeland Ledger, Las Vegas Sun, The Leader-Telegram, Lexington Herald, Liverpool Echo, Longview Daily News, Los Angeles Times, Louisville Courier-Journal, Miami Herald, Milwaukee Journal, The Missoulian, Montreal Gazette, Morning Call, Muncie Evening Press, Nassau Guardian, National Post, Newark Advocate, Newark Star-Ledger, Newsday, New Straits Times, New York magazine, New York Daily News, New York Times, The Observer, Ocala Star-Banner, Ottawa Citizen, Pacific Daily News, Paducah Sun, Palm Beach Post, Pasadena Star, Philadelphia Daily News, Pittsburgh Press, Playboy, Poughkeepsie Journal, Quad City Times, Rapid-City Journal, Reading Eagle,

Reno Gazette-Journal, Rocky Mountain Telegram, Rolling Stone, Sacramento Bee, Salam, San Bernadino County Sun, Santa Maria Times, Sapulpa Daily Herald, Sarasota Journal, Sault Star, South Bend Tribune, South Florida Sun-Sentinel, Spartanburg Herald-Journal, Spokesman Review, Sport, Sports Illustrated, St Cloud Times, St Louis Post-Dispatch, St Petersburg Independent, Sumter Daily Item, Sunday Correspondent, Sydney Morning Herald, The Tennessean, The Times, Toronto Globe and Mail, The Town Talk, Tyler Courier-Times, Vancouver Sun, Victoria Advocate, Vidette Messenger of Porter County, Virginian-Pilot, Washington Post, Wausau Daily Herald, Wisconsin State Journal, York Daily Record.

Websites

https://www.youtube.com/watch?v=GMCp1hHyVqk (Ali fights in Iran)

https://www.youtube.com/watch?v=qrd3V9ZWOmQ (Ali on Letterman, 1984)

https://www.youtube.com/watch?v=qDLuO8eis3o (Ali on Wogan, 1989)

https://www.youtube.com/watch?v=2yW2ahrGFF8 (Ali on Arsenio Hall, 1990)

https://www.youtube.com/watch?v=PF9kK27BFk8 (Ali lights the flame in Atlanta, 1996)

https://boxrec.com/en/proboxer/180 (Ali's professional record)

Also available at all good book stores

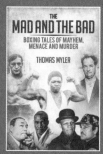

9781785313950

9781785313196

9781785312960

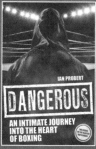

9781785311994

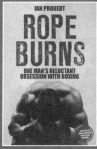

9781785312007

9781785311956

9781785317859

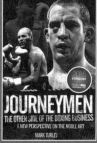

9781785311444

9781785311437